MW00807982

OUR NATION BETRAYED

Mutually Assured Destruction for America

By
Garland Favorito

BLACK FOREST PRESS
San Diego, California
May 2000
First Edition

OUR NATION BETRAYED

Mutually Assured Destruction for America

By
Garland Favorito

PUBLISHED IN THE UNITED STATES OF AMERICA
BY
BLACK FOREST PRESS
P.O.Box 6342
Chula Vista, CA 91909-6342
1-800-451-9404

DEDICATION

For Linda Ives, who has valiantly fought the mutually assured destruction political policy, in hopes that she will one day attain justice for those who murdered her son, Kevin, and his friend, Don Henry;

For the family of Larry McDonald (D, 7th-GA), my former Congressman, who gave his life on KAL 007 for our freedom before I even understood what it meant to be free;

And, for the many American patriots who spent their personal time and money attempting to ensure that equal justice applies to all Americans, including the President of the United States.

Printed in the United States of America
Library of Congress
Cataloging-in-Publication

ISBN:1-58275-016-5
Copyright © May 2000 by Garland Favorito

CONTENTS

FORWORD

It has been my privilege to know Garland Favorito for nearly six years and I have found him to be an American patriot in the purest sense. He has worked timelessly at his own expense researching and studying to decipher essential facts often overlooked or excluded by the establishment media.

Garland is a citizen activist, that is, he works as a computer analyst or programmer during the day and in his spare time organizes rallies, networks with other patriots and writes articles. He is also a frequent guest on talk shows; lobbies for righteous causes and gives his time and personal funds to those causes he believes are worthy.

Garland cares not about political correctness. His sole purpose in writing this book is not to please the political bosses, but instead hold them accountable for their numerous criminal and treasonous acts.

Garland provides a fresh and insightful look (much from first hand experience) at how a relatively small group of dedicated Americans fighting for truth impeached the most powerful leader in the world all the while their real motives were withheld from the American public.

We must never forget that the freedoms, we as Americans take for granted, were bought with the sacrifice, blood and courage of our forefathers.

This book hopefully will inspire you to continue the noble fight to keep America free.

Pat Matrisciana

ACKNOWLEDGMENTS

The following are a few of the resources that I used who deserve special thanks for their ongoing work:

- Pat Matrisciana and Citizens for Honest Government, who had the courage to videotape corruption in government of a magnitude never before seen by the American people;

- Bill Triplett, Ed Timperlake and other Congressional investigators who refused to remain silent while the politicians sold our country to the Communist Chinese military;

- Jerry Seper and the dedicated columnists at the *Washington Times*, who were proven factually correct time and time again, one Congressional investigation after another;

- John McManus and all the wonderful people at the John Birch Society, who endure constant character assassination for exposing the traitors in our government who threaten the freedom of American citizens;

- Will Grigg and all the intriguing journalists at *The New American* magazine, who exposed fascinating information not available to the general American public;

- Chris Ruddy, Reed Irvine and Accuracy in Media who made dedicated efforts to give American people the truth about the evidence that indicated Vince Foster was murdered;

- Paul Weyrich, the founder of so many valuable organizations, who demonstrated real investigative reporting by producing "American Investigator" for the America's Voice TV channel;

- Col. Bo Gritz, whose dedication to the Prisoner of War recovery effort led him to discover one of America's darkest and best kept secrets: CIA drug trafficking;

- Michael Ruppert, From the Wilderness publisher and former LAPD narcotics officer who confronted CIA Director Deutch during an L.A. town hall meeting about agency involvement in drug trafficking;

- Sara Flounders, Brian Becker and the International Action Center authors, who reported from around the world, the evidence of NATO atrocities committed against Yugoslavia;

- Ramsey Clark, who persisted in attempting to hold accountable those within the American government responsible for the slaughters in Waco and Yugoslavia;

- Elizabeth and Joe Farah, who opened a gateway of previously unavailable information through the World Net Daily web site of the Western Journalism Center;

- Dr Gene Shroder and his associates, whose research work into the origin and history of unconstitutional executive orders has helped prevent tyranny on America;

- Jim Robinson and the many Free Republic members, who research and exchange vital government related information through their web site;

- Larry Klayman and Judicial Watch, who exposed Chinese Communist infiltration of Clinton / Gore campaigns and the DNC;

- Willis Carto, Andy Arnold and all those at Liberty Lobby, who survived attacks by the CIA, FBI, IRS and BATF to continue publishing books and Spotlight articles that most other media outlets would not dare to print.

- Jim Agresti of *JustFacts.com* and all the talented people of *Black Forest Press* who helped turn my pipe dream into a reality.

- My mother, Dorothy Hudson, whose wealth of historical information gave me the initial incentive to write this book.

PREFACE

During the decade of the 90s I underwent a transformation from complete political naïveté to a state of learning things that sometimes I wish I did not know. As the depth and breadth of corruption in the Clinton administration became evident, I decided to join the impeachment movement.

However, I was surprised when opposing House Republican leaders kept serious evidence of the crimes that originated the impeachment movement out of the Articles of Impeachment. I was further stunned when Senate Republican leaders set up trial procedures to ensure that hostile witnesses and damaging evidence against the President would not be heard at his trial.

At that time, I knew something was rotten in the American government and I decided to find out what it was. It didn't take long before I had uncovered plenty of existing research for what had corrupted and compromised the Republican leaders. This détente of mutually assured destruction that paralyzes the American form of government is so threatening to our future that I knew I had to write this book to tell the story.

The intent of the book is:

- To document the astounding evidence of Clinton administration corruption collected in many Congressional investigations and other sources but not readily available to the public;

- To explain how major media organizations distorted political news to protect Bill Clinton and manipulate public opinion to implement their own agenda;

- To detail the incredible cover-up that the Republican leadership established to keep Bill Clinton in office and explain the real reasons behind it.

- To illustrate how citizens like me can awaken, get involved and make a real difference in protecting their freedom and preserving the American form of government that made us the most powerful nation on the face of the earth.

As a citizen author, I have assembled evidence from many different researchers who, I believe, provide accurate factual assessments. If you find the level of current government corruption too hard to fathom, I simply ask that you consider the evidence, verify it for accuracy and then reach your own conclusion.

INTRODUCTION

This book presents overwhelming evidence that President Bill Clinton and his circle of power were involved in criminal activity in Arkansas, treason and bribery with the Communist Chinese government, and abuse of government agencies like the IRS and FBI, which were used to persecute political adversaries. Much of the evidence presented was actually collected in Congressional investigations but not used in the Articles of Impeachment.

Many people made personal sacrifices in an attempt to hold Bill Clinton accountable to the same standards of justice that apply to other American citizens, including:

- Pat Matrisciana, who produced unprecedented videos that documented government corruption and awoke the American citizens;

- Howard Phillips, who assembled the Coalition for a Congressional Impeachment Inquiry and remained determined to fight for our Constitutional principles during five long years;

- Bill Dannemeyer, the former Congressman who used his experience, contacts and knowledge to pursue impeachment doggedly on his own time and at his own expense;

- Bob Barr (R, 7th-GA), who mustered enough courage to confront the Washington, D.C. power structure by introducing H. Res. 304, the Presidential Impeachment Inquiry;

- Larry Klayman, the Judicial Watch founder, who took on the U.S. Department of Justice and became the only real independent counsel in Washington;

- Jim Robinson, the Free Republic founder, who circumvented a corrupted national media by proving he could rally thousands of people to a critical cause through the Internet.

Despite sincere, dedicated efforts of these individuals and thousands of others, the Republican Congressional leaders decided to protect Bill Clinton. Instead of presenting the serious evidence and conducting a standard impeachment trial, which would have surely resulted in conviction, House Republican leaders suppressed that evidence, and Senate Republican leaders sabotaged the trial so that most of the facts would never be heard by the American public.

Immediately after the trial, Yugoslavia became the fourth country to fall victim to impeccably timed bombs ordered by Bill Clinton during the peak of one his scandals. The bombing killed 2000 innocent Yugoslavian civilians and displaced hundreds of thousands of Kosovars who we were allegedly trying to help. It completely diverted national attention from the release of the Cox Report, which documented devastating treasonous administration policies. The report detailed how the administration allowed the Communist Chinese military access to prohibited dual use military technology and precious nuclear secrets. Previous congressional investigations determined that the Communist Chinese military paid for that access by funneling millions of dollars in illegal campaign contributions to the Clinton / Gore campaigns and the Democrat National Committee.

Despite these offenses, the Republican leadership was ultimately paralyzed during the impeachment by the need to conceal several worldwide CIA drug trafficking operations controlled by former President George Bush. Bill Clinton took beginning steps to reveal this dark secret immediately after the House Judiciary Committee voted to begin the impeachment inquiry. Had Republicans seriously attempted to remove him, President Bill Clinton was capable of revealing as much of this secret as necessary to devastate the year 2000 Republican presidential candidacy of the former President's son, George W. Bush. This book tells the incredible story. Buckle your seat belt and dig in.

I
The Real Impeachment Movement

CHAPTER ONE
MY AWAKENING

AN AWAKENING

It was the summer of 1988 and the Democrats had come to my hometown of Atlanta to hold their national convention and select nominees for the upcoming Presidential elections. Their eventual candidate, Massachusetts Governor, Michael Dukakis, would take on then Vice President George Bush, who was completing two terms under President Ronald Reagan, the most popular president in my lifetime.

Dukakis selected as his running mate for Vice President, Texan Lloyd Bentsen, who was head of the Treasury Department and would later oversee a Treasury investigation into the Bureau of Alcohol, Tobacco and Firearms (ATF) attack on the Branch Davidian church at Waco, Texas. There, six Davidians and four ATF agents were killed on February 28, 1993. The investigation was conducted by three of the officials who were responsible for the 1985 firebombing of a Philadelphia MOVE house, which resulted in the destruction of nearly a full city block.

One historically significant occurrence of the convention was a stirring speech by John F. Kennedy Jr., son of President John F. Kennedy, who was assassinated on Nov. 22, 1963, in an event still cloaked in the secrecy of sealed government files. John Kennedy JR's life would also conclude in an unusual death 36 years after his father's when his plane crashed neared Martha's Vineyard with his wife, Carolyn, and sister-in-law, Lauren Bisset, aboard.

The national news media would repeatedly imply that Kennedy was a somewhat reckless, inexperienced pilot, who was flying in a dark haze without an instrument rating certification. In reality, good visibility allowed visual flight rules to be in effect, Kennedy was within sight of the island, he had sterling references from his flight instructors and he had flown over 300 hours when only 40 were needed for an instrumentation license. By the time of his death, I would realize that this reporting was just one more example in a stream of false and distorted politically related information generated by the national news media.

At the convention, the individual who gave the nominating speech was a governor from Arkansas named Bill Clinton. He possessed some of the charisma of John Kennedy, Jr., however, it waned somewhat when his speech, which was supposed to be about 15 minutes, lasted approximately 52 minutes. Some of the crowd waved white handkerchiefs of surrender while he was talking, and many cheered when he said "In conclusion...". That was the first time most of America got to see Bill Clinton. Little did I or anyone else outside of Arkansas know the about the evidence trail of money laundering, drug trafficking, embezzlement, extortion and illicit sex that Bill Clinton had already left in his state.

Like most Americans, I had little or no interest in politics or the inner workings of the American government. When I moved to Georgia, I entered the Marietta district of Larry McDonald, a Democrat whom I quickly grew to admire because he kept in touch with the citizens. I remember receiving a flyer from him explaining how he had voted on ten key issues. Since I agreed with most of his positions, it gave me a level of comfort that my interests were being taken care of in Washington without my being involved.

We lost Larry on the ill-fated flight, KAL 007, that was supposedly shot down by the Soviet Union in September of 1983. Almost 15 years later, I began to learn the unusual details behind the downing of that plane described in *Incident at Sakhalin* and other books. I started to realize how valuable Larry McDonald had been to us as citizens, and I invited his widow, Cathy McDonald, to be a co-host of the first National Town Hall on Impeachment in Marietta, Georgia, on March 17, 1998. By then, I discovered that all Congressmen are not like Larry McDonald and that citizens must become involved in their government to protect their own freedom.

Before the KAL 007 plane crash, I got married and moved to Stone Mountain, Georgia. During this time my civic involvement was basically limited to occasional editorials that I would send to the *Atlanta Journal Constitution*. I usually refuted statements from a previous editorial since I had little motivation to originate my own viewpoint. I kept my letters concise and logical while trying to make a good counterpoint. I achieved about an 80 percent success rate at getting my letters published. I was even invited to several *Atlanta Journal* editorial dinners for letter writers and met the editor, Durwood McCallister, whom I admired. However, much later after he retired, my editorials turned to issues of honest government, and my success ratio dropped to about 20 percent.

At Stone Mountain we were represented by another Democrat named Elliot Levitas. I met him and my future Congressman at my first *Atlanta Journal* editorial dinner. I attended several annual editorial dinners, but this one was particularly interesting because the other Congressman in attendance was Newt Gingrich, who had been recently elected to represent a western area of Georgia. A few years later we moved into what is now the 6th District of Georgia, and Newt Gingrich became my Congressman when he also moved into my district and won the seat. Gingrich moved after his original district was gerrymandered under the leadership of the nation's longest running State House Speaker, Tom Murphy, who apparently did not relish the thought of Newt as his Congressman. Gingrich would go on to be elected Speaker of the U.S. House and hold that position when the House impeached President Bill Clinton.

Before we moved from Stone Mountain, Elliott Levitas was defeated by Republican, Pat Swindall. Ironically, Pat Swindall was indicted three weeks before the 1988 elections on charges of perjury, the same charge passed in the Articles of Impeachment against Bill Clinton by the House of Representatives. He was later convicted after being forced to resign from Congress. The case centered around an IRS sting operation that could have easily been considered entrapment. The perjury charge resulted from his statements involving his lack of knowledge about the source of a mortgage loan for his home. Compared with the standards subsequently set by President Bill Clinton, it was relatively trivial, but it proved to be historically significant. The prosecutor was a U.S. attorney who later won the Congressional district represented by my former Congressman, Larry McDonald. I would come to know him as Bob Barr, the Congressman who filed the H. Res. 304

Presidential Impeachment Inquiry and went on to be a House manager in the Senate impeachment trial of President Bill Clinton.

THE 1992 ELECTION

Bill Clinton left Atlanta in 1988 with many believing he was the buffoon of the Democrat National Convention. He redeemed himself somewhat with an appearance on *The Johnny Carson Show,* where he seemed to be a likable guy who may simply be a little long winded. I did not expect him to play a major role in politics again, but much to my amazement, he was nominated for President in 1992 by my own governor, Zell Miller. Miller was a successful governor of Georgia who also mentored his successor, current governor, Roy Barnes. I would later find out that Barnes, while in the Georgia House in 1996, actually opposed an exact duplicate of his own amendment to pass a Georgia fingerprint law. The law supported a national ID scheme to standardize all state drivers' licenses biometrically. The scheme was apparently based on a clause inserted by Senator Dianne Feinstein into the 1996 Illegal Immigration and Reform Act, a part of the overall Defense bill.

Zell Miller was able to make the successful nomination after Bill Clinton received some unusual help, unbeknownst to me and the rest of America. His public perception was improved by a *60 Minutes* broadcast designed to doctor his negative image from an affair with Gennifer Flowers. His financial saving grace came in the form of a $3,000,000 loan from the Worthen Bank. Worthen Bank was co-owned by a heavy financial supporter of both political parties named Jackson Stephens and the soon to be famous, LIPPO GROUP. It would be years before intelligence reports revealed that the LIPPO GROUP also had a banking partnership with China Resources, "an agent of political, military and economic espionage" for the Communist Chinese government according to DIA and Senate Governmental Affairs investigators.

Although a presidential nominee usually tries to balance the ticket, geographically and politically, Bill Clinton chose former Tennessee Senator, Al Gore, as his Vice Presidential running mate. It was a strange choice since they were from adjoining southern states. Six years later congressional investigation evidence would show that both independently received significant illegal financing from the Communist Chinese Government.

After he was nominated, Bill Clinton was speaking on television once as I watched with some good friends from Vietnam who did not have the privilege of being raised here. They mentioned how deceptive Bill Clinton acted when he spoke. I had noticed how everything he said was carefully planned and rehearsed, even as he was saying it. He never spoke from the heart. I wondered why my friends could see that clearly, and other people who were born and raised in America could not. Perhaps his biggest deception of all came during his candidacy when Bill Clinton promised "the most ethical administration in the history of the Republic".

Former Vice President Bush won the Presidency in 1988 and became popular, even with opposition party leaders, after the Gulf War, which started when Iraqi troops moved into Kuwait. An alliance of nations using a plan named Desert Storm, drove the Iraqi army out of Kuwait with a minimum loss of life, despite severe threats of chemical and biological warfare.

Years later, after meeting Capt. Joyce Riley and Dr. Len Horowitz, I would learn that the war against Iraq was not as successful as we were led to believe. The death toll continued to climb after the war was over while the Defense Department denied the existence of Gulf War Syndrome. The United Nations started chemical and biological weapons inspections in Iraq after the war, and they continued for years. These inspections would eventually play a surprising part in the impeachment process.

By 1992, the economy was tight, and President Bush's popularity was slipping because he lacked no clear domestic economic policy. Democrats were complaining that unemployment was around seven percent even though inflation and interest rates were around five percent or less. I remembered when Reagan and Bush took office inflation peaked around 13 percent, interest rates had zoomed to 19 percent and unemployment was over 10 percent. The unemployment, inflation and interest rates combined into what was called the "financial misery index", which was at an all time high.

Despite these facts, Bush only mentioned their success in reducing the financial misery index once in the very last debate. In fact, he totally distanced himself from former President Ronald Reagan and rarely mentioned his name throughout the campaign. I found this unbelievably strange since Reagan was immensely popular. I would not understand until years later of the conflict and potential reasons for their distance and the unpopularity of George Bush even within his own party.

During this time, former IBM salesman and EDS founder, Ross Perot, formed a group named United We Stand. He developed a specific agenda, communicated the precise problems that America was facing and entered the Presidential race, making it a three-way contest. Perot inspired citizens and attracted my interest and attention since we were both in the computer business. He actually captured the lead in the polls before resigning while citing Republican dirty tricks planned to ruin his daughter's reputation. In another strange twist, he then decided to re-enter the race after his poll numbers had shrunk. I realized much later that Ross Perot never wanted to be President.

During the campaign, I noticed that Ross Perot constantly attacked George Bush while barely mentioning Bill Clinton. At first, I assumed that it was because Bush was the incumbent, but he strangely continued the trend even when it appeared that Bill Clinton had forged ahead in the polls. It would take years for me to learn the underlying reasons, involving drug trafficking and POW recovery, as to why Ross Perot despised George Bush.

Perot's entry into the 1992 race may well have cost Bush the election. The final numbers were Clinton 43 percent, Bush 38 percent and Perot 19 percent. Bill Clinton was elected President with the lowest percentage of popular votes since the Civil War. As a perfect example of media distortion, the *USA Today* newspaper headlined his victory as a "landslide". Six years later, when Bill Clinton became the first elected President to be impeached, the *USA Today* headline instead touted his "poll ratings surge". These are only a few of the minor media distortions that those in the impeachment movement would face for over four years.

MEDIA DISTORTIONS OF THE
JOHN KENNEDY ASSASSINATION

During 1993, my curiosity and interest in government activity began to grow because of the movie JFK. I was one of
the majority of Americans who believed that there had been
more than one gunman in the assassination, but I had no real
details of it. I decided to attend the 30th anniversary of the assassination of John F. Kennedy in Dallas, and I began to learn
how major media organizations could completely and consistently distort facts. The major media organizations had always
told Americans that Lee Harvey Oswald, a lone crazed assassin, fired three shots from the sixth floor of the Texas
School Book Depository in Dallas and killed JFK.

A simple review of the film from Abraham Zapruder clearly
shows that the shot which killed JFK struck him in the right
front temple and had to come from the grassy knoll. No one
ever claimed that Lee Harvey Oswald was on the grassy knoll;
therefore, he could not have possibly killed JFK. In addition,
the famous Altgens photo shows Lee Harvey Oswald standing
in the door of the school book depository as the motorcade is
passing. The identification is unmistakable, despite FBI attempts to convince the public that the individual in the photo
was another person named Billy Lovelady.

The Zapruder film showed that after JFK was hit in the
throat, Gov. Connolly turned to see what was wrong and was
also hit, then JFK was struck in the right front temple by the
third bullet. Gov. Connolly confirmed this sequence of events
in testimony before the Warren Commission and House Select
Committee. Since the time span of five seconds was too short
for one person to have fired all three shots from a manual
reload rifle, the Warren Commission concluded that two bullets
created all of the wounds to both Connolly and Kennedy. This
conclusion required that a single "magic bullet" entered
Kennedy's back, turned upward and exited his throat, turned
right to enter Gov. Connolly, paused in mid-air for two seconds
to account for the time difference between when Kennedy and
Connolly were hit, made five more entrance and exit wounds in
Gov. Connolly and then appeared in pristine condition on a cot
in Parkland Memorial Hospital. The counsel who proposed this

magic bullet theory was Arlen Specter, who would eventually become a controversial Senator in the impeachment trial of President Bill Clinton.

MEDIA DISTORTIONS OF THE KING ASSASSINATION

Some light research into the Kennedy assassination at the Georgia Tech and Atlanta libraries led me to the House Select Committee investigation into the assassination of Dr. Martin Luther King. Since he was also from Atlanta, I decided to spend some time researching the general circumstances of his death. Immediately I found a similar distortion of facts by the media. The media claimed that James Earl Ray shot Dr. King in the neck with a single bullet fired from a boarding house a block away and overlooking the Lorraine Motel where Dr. King was staying.

My analysis of investigation evidence matched conclusions that were eventually reached in 1998 expert testimony during the request by James Earl Ray for a new trial. The ballistics expert testimony revealed that the bullet which killed Dr. King "was not of the same lot as the bullets in the five unfired cartridges found associated with the alleged murder weapon". In addition, a spent cartridge found near the crime scene was determined to have been fired from the weapon. The testimony went along way to show that the gun James Earl Ray brought to the scene was not the murder weapon and it confirmed his 30-year contention that he was not the assassin.

Ray was an escaped convict with no known marksmanship expertise. Before the assassination, Ray was funded for over a year to do various types of gun running and other projects for a man he knew only as Raoul. The funds included money to buy a two-year old Mustang and expenses for travel all over the country and to Canada. After the assassination, he traveled back to Canada and received money and passports to London and Portugal. He was caught in London going from Portugal to Belgium. He used as an alias, Eric S. Galt, a Canadian based-intelligence operative who had a top secret security clearance.

In 1977, the House Select Committee on King's assassination resisted nearly all significant efforts to determine who had helped Ray. Ray tried to withdraw his guilty plea three days after being sentenced to life in prison. Eventually Loyd Jowers, who ran Big Ed's Grill beneath the boarding house which was the alleged site used by the assassin, offered to come forward with testimony admitting that he hired a hit man. His involvement was based on orders from reputed mobster Frank Liberto, who, he believed, got his orders out of New Orleans from Carlos Marcello.

Judge Joe Brown was on the verge of granting James Earl Ray a new trial when he was removed from the case after extensive maneuvering by federal officials in Tennessee. Brown, no longer involved in the criminal action request, was eventually rewarded with his own television show. Ray died after his attorney, William Pepper reportedly traced the likely trigger man to a deceased Memphis police officer named Earl Clark.

Janet Reno, in a phony quest for "accountability" denied the King family the right to waive all criminal prosecution of Jowers in exchange for his testimony. The King family was forced to file a wrongful death civil suit against Jowers to get his testimony on record. In late 1999, more than 30 years after King's death, the King family obtained a small measure of justice when the civil trial jury ruled that Dr. King was killed as a result of a conspiracy, which according to jurors, involved numerous government officials.

MEDIA DISTORTIONS OF THE ROBERT KENNEDY ASSASSINATION

Since I had researched two of the three major political assassinations of the 60s and was stunned with what I had found, I decided to review the third, which involved Robert F. Kennedy. Even though his assassination was never investigated by the federal government, I was able to locate books and other information which I expected simply to confirm the original media reports. The media reports had claimed that a lone crazed assassin, Sirhan Sirhan, shot and killed RFK at the Ambassador Hotel in Los Angeles.

The autopsy report and physical evidence showed that RFK was killed by a bullet fired an inch or two away from the back of his head. All witnesses, including the maitre d' who wrestled the gun away from Sirhan, stated that Sirhan was never behind RFK or that close to him. Sirhan fired all eight of his bullets, yet there were at least 10 and possibly as many as 13 bullets fired, based on several independent crime scene analysis conclusions confirmed by one of the investigating FBI agents. Witnesses stated that a man in a security guard uniform also had a gun drawn.

The two heads of the special task force that investigated the assassination were CIA operatives on loan to conduct the investigation for the LAPD. In all three assassinations there appeared to be a federal government cover-up facilitated by the major news media organizations. Therefore, I came to an undeniable conclusion that I could not trust major media organizations to tell me the truth about anything political in nature. However, I was about to get some firsthand, close-up, current experience to validate my conclusion.

MEDIA DISTORTIONS OF THE REPUBLICAN REVOLUTION

In 1994, Newt Gingrich, the House Minority Whip, adopted many United We Stand platform planks, promised a vote on each issue, put them into a Contract with America and got fellow House Republicans to sign them. For perhaps the first time, voters knew what they were getting ahead of time and could cast their ballots accordingly. The contract was a huge success, sweeping the country with over 70 House seat changes and creating Republican majorities in both the House and Senate.

Since Bob Michael, the previous Republican Minority Leader, was retiring, my Congressman became Speaker of the House while Bob Dole moved from Senate Minority Leader to Senate Majority Leader. In the first 100 days of the new session, the House not only voted on all 10 of the Contract with America planks, but actually passed nine of them. Although some were eventually derailed in the Senate or by a Presidential veto, Newt Gingrich became a hero to many, both locally and nationally.

Since my Congressman was now the Speaker of the House, my interest in government began to peak. One of the first things that I learned was how politicians can lie without conscience.

Since America was awash in a trillion doller debt and billion doller budget deficits, my pet issue, as with so many other Americans, was the balanced budget amendment, which passed the House with a two-thirds majority. I had seen on the Rush Limbaugh show, advertisements from Senate Minority Leader Tom Daschel, stating how he was fighting for a balanced budget amendment. Yet Daschel voted against the amendment, along with other Democrats who had supported a similar amendment when they were still in power. Newly elected Democrat Senator Robert Torricelli, who campaigned for a balanced budget amendment while he was in the House, essentially cast the deciding vote against it.

After the 1996 elections two years later, when Republicans gained the Senate seats needed to pass the amendment, Trent Lott replaced Bob Dole as Majority Leader and never reintroduced the bill even though he had been an advocate of the amendment. I had expected Trent Lott to be a better Senate leader than Bob Dole, but this was only a clue of what was to come. In an additional two years, I would learn how far my expectations were from the truth.

After the first 100 days of the new Congress, Newt Gingrich was on a television special to report that the newly managed, Republican-led House had kept its promise. Dick Gephardt, who went from Majority to Minority Leader after the change in power, followed Newt Gingrich and claimed that the school from where he was speaking was losing its lunch program because of the new leadership commitment to balance the budget. Calls to the school and federal program administrators indecated these charges were false; however, no one in the media ever corrected the facts for the public. I was beginning to learn that it wasn't just Congressmen who were deceptive, but that media organizations could professionally distort political news without anyone's knowing unless they had firsthand knowledge of the circumstances.

One such media distortion occurred when Newt Gingrich appointed Christina Jeffrey as House Historian. I got to meet Christina years later when she ran for Newt's Congressional seat. Christina had suggested that those who are teaching about World War II should also include the Nazi perspective. This was obvious to me because in order to prevent wars you must understand how they start. However, Representative Chuck

Schumer, with significant help from the media, falsely portrayed her comments as being anti-Semitic. Gingrich was eventually forced to withdraw her nomination, much to her dismay. Schumer, a Judiciary Committee member who I believe falsely portrayed several other key issues during the impeachment and Waco investigations, eventually became a Senator from New York.

I had expected my Congressman to become a hero for implementing common sense issues like balancing the budget but was stunned to watch the media consistently portray him as a villain. News articles and reports would appear that implied poor people were going to die if we balanced the budget, even though the budget would still be growing at a rate of one percent per year (instead of five percent). Then, news reports indicated that Medicare and Medicaid would be cut by $270 billion between 1995 and the projected balance year of 2002. In reality, per capita spending was actually increasing from $4,800 to $6,700 per person per year, and this was later negotiated up to $7,200 per year. The "cut" was actually not a cut at all, but an increase of over five percent, yet major news organizations led the American people to believe that the budget was being cut.

Not only did the media attempt to deceive the American people about the balanced budget issue, it began to attack my Congressman simply for mentioning this and other issues. The media used magazine cover stories such as "The Grinch who Stole Christmas" to portray him falsely as some sort of cold, heartless, uncaring individual. In reality, he was almost always promoting local and national charity efforts like Habitat for Humanity, Make a Wish Foundation and an Earning by Learning school reading program.

I was amazed at how the major news media organizations consistently provided false information to the American people. I could understand how a few might be off base because of a liberal bias, but I was witnessing a concerted effort to deceive the American people into supporting a more socialistic agenda. I realized that this was not bias, it was a deliberate, coordinated agenda of deceit that included personal attacks on individuals not conforming to the agenda. I considered the national media organizations as a threat to American freedom and decided that I had to get involved.

I stopped by my Congressman's nearby campaign office and picked up some literature. I also occasionally volunteered to help pass out information, put up yard signs and perform other support functions. I eventually started going to town halls and other meetings that I found helpful in determining what was actually going on in Washington. Things I used to think were boring became essential to protect my freedom.

In 1996, not long after getting involved, I unknowingly received my first clue that my efforts for more honest government may have been misdirected. At a stop on a local campaign bus trip, I saw two guys in a truck that had a sign saying "Ask Newt, who is Callista Bisek?" It would still be two years before a friend I met, who had also become disillusioned with Newt Gingrich, told me that Newt had gotten involved with the Wisconsin Congressional aide. Another year later, after Newt Gingrich resigned as speaker, the American public would know about "Newtie's Cutie" and his subsequent divorce.

It would still be two years before I found out about the socialist history, origins and ownership of major media organizations and how tightly controlled the news information is that flows to and within them. As it turned out, the national news media suppressed the Newt Gingrich affair for about four years while he was the House Speaker, even though it was widely known inside Washington.

I realized just before the affair was publicly exposed that the media uses those situations to control all sides of the political spectrum and implement its agenda. When the impeachment movement caught fire, Newt Gingrich personally delayed the process for over a year and helped withhold devastating evidence from the Articles of Impeachment, all for his supposed adversary, Bill Clinton.

REFERENCES

Michael Brun, *Incident at Sakalin,* Four Walls and Eight Windows.
Kirby Ferris, *A Mountain of Lies,* Rapid Lightning.
Jim Garrison, *On the Trail of Assassins,* Warner Books.
Col. James "Bo" Gritz, *Called to Serve,* Lazarus Publishing.
Dr. Len Horowitz, *Emerging Viruses,* Tetrahedron.

William Pepper, *Orders to Kill,* Carroll & Graf.

Ross Perot, *United We Stand,* Hyperion.

Michael Collins Piper, *Final Judgment,* The Center for Historical Review.

Capt. Joyce Riley, *Gulf War Illness Fact or Fiction?* (video), Alpha-Bet Pictures.

Capt. Joyce Riley, *Gulf War Syndrome* (video), Alpha-Bet Pictures.

Bill Turner & John Christian, *The Assassination of Robert F. Kennedy,* Random House.

JFK Assassination: The Jim Garrison Tapes (video), Westron.

Who Killed Martin Luther King? (video), White Star.

CHAPTER TWO

THE '90s: DECADE OF
GOVERNMENT CORRUPTION

THE CLINTON PRESIDENCY

One of Bill Clinton's first and most important tasks when he began his Presidency in 1993 was to appoint an Attorney General. On the third attempt, after nominations of Zoe Baird and Kimba Wood failed, he was able to confirm Janet Reno. I remember watching Janet Reno on Larry King Live shortly after she was appointed and hearing her state that her major objective was to make the Justice Department more accountable. I was pleased to hear that after the recent fiascoes at Ruby Ridge and Waco. I would eventually realize that her statement on the *Larry King Show* rivaled the biggest lie ever told by Bill Clinton.

During 1993, I had not learned yet where to go for accurate political news and was totally misinformed by major media organizations, which seemed willing to cover up superbly for the Clinton administration. Like most Americans I was totally unaware that Reno quickly fired all 94 U.S. attorneys without a peep as the media focused on events such as a $200 haircut Bill Clinton received while holding up air traffic at L. A. International Airport. In another unprecedented move, Reno fired FBI Director William Sessions on trumped up misappropriation chargers the day before Vince Foster's body was found and quickly pronounced a "suicide" by the media. When questioned, she replied that the firings were a joint decision with Bill Clinton, herself and Webster Hubbell, the Associate Attorney General, who would eventually be indicted for multiple scandals.

Hubbell was perhaps most knowledgeable about the Whitewater scandals, which were plaguing the President. The media had completely concealed the fact that Clinton had helped his Whitewater business partner, James McDougal, bilk what eventually cost taxpayers $60,000,000 from the Madison

Guaranty Savings and Loan that McDougal owned. In addition, there was growing concern about the Travel Office scandal where the Clinton administration fired the entire staff, filed what proved to be false charges against Billy Dale and audited his UltrAir air service. While most of this was concealed from the general public, it was not going unnoticed by the knowledgeable leaders of many different civic organizations.

IMPEACHMENT BEGINNINGS

It was the fall of 1993, when Pat Matrisciana, a Christian film producer, received a phone call from John Hillyer, an NBC cameraman who lived near me in Marietta, Georgia. Hillyer was frustrated over the unwillingness of NBC to report on the evidence of drug trafficking and money laundering in the Clinton administration while Bill Clinton had been Governor of Arkansas. He believed that as President, Bill Clinton posed a serious threat to the security of the American citizens and asked Pat to use his talents to document facts that were being withheld from the American people.

Pat had never done that type of a film before and thought it would be too much of a stretch, so he declined. But John was persistent and contacted Pat several more times before the year was out. Although Pat was living in California, he had once lived in Arkansas and had family there. He was aware of some of the Arkansas corruption and the implications concerning President Bill Clinton. Finally, in January of 1994, he relented and hired John as a cameraman who could also do investigative research for a new film to be entitled *Circle of Power*. It was a monumental decision. For the first time, American citizens would have a television and motion picture film producer who could circumvent the government-related reporting distortions of the television news industry with accurate and reasonably current information.

The video was completed in February of 1994. It was the forerunner to the famous *Clinton Chronicles*, which was completed in June of 1994. That video spurred many other incredible videos such as *Obstruction of Justice, Mena Cover-up*, and *The Death of Vince Foster*. These videos started a whole new cottage industry of factual documentaries containing governmental information that is suppressed by major media organizations. However, John Hillyer never got to see the results of his efforts. Hillyer, a very healthy individual, suddenly died of a heart attack while investigating the Arkansas Development Finance Authority. He became one of many victims on the mysterious Clinton death trail.

COALITION FOR A CONGRESSIONAL IMPEACHMENT INQUIRY

During this time, Floyd Brown of Citizens United and David Bossie had reported numerous articles of information involving Clinton corruption in Arkansas. Most of the evidence so far had focused on Whitewater, along with the money laundering and drug trafficking activity while Bill Clinton was Governor of Arkansas. However, new scandals were beginning to break during the Clinton Presidency, including the FBI file and travel office scandals and the mysterious death of Vince Foster.

The Whitewater, travel office and FBI file scandals were more than enough to warrant a serious Congressional response. So on February 8, 1994, the impeachment movement officially began when Howard Phillips, the Conservative Caucus chairman assembled an organization of over 80 civic leaders, called the Coalition for a Congressional Impeachment Inquiry. Phillips eventually became a Presidential candidate in 1996 for the U.S. Taxpayers and again in 2000 after they were renamed as the Constitution Party.

Both Brown and Bossie joined the coalition. Brown eventually went on to host a talk show, and Bossie became an investigator for the House Government Reform and Oversight Committee under Dan Burton. As his committee got close to uncovering serious wrongdoing, Bossie was fired by Burton who was under political pressure from Democrats and the media.

The coalition recommended that the House Judiciary Committee open an impeachment inquiry and produced a list of 20 questions that required answers. The announcement was made at the National Press Club but received a near total blackout from the major news organizations. It would be three years before I found out that the event had occurred.

Likewise, Congress also elected to ignore the quest for an inquiry. Pat Matrisciana and Lt. Col. Tom McKenney delivered a copy of *The Clinton Chronicles* to every single member of Congress during the 1994 session, the last one with a Democrat Party House majority. The video outlined a clear case of remarkable corruption in Arkansas, but perhaps to nobody's surprise, no one in Congress had the guts to do anything about it.

The change in power to Republican leadership in 1995 resulted in a one-year transitional power struggle with Democrats attempting to sabotage proceedings while they adjusted to their newly found minority status after a 40-year reign as the majority party. However, thanks in part to Howard Phillips and the coalition as well as *The Clinton Chronicles* video, Republicans were obligated to conduct several House and Senate investigations into the serious charges.

CONGRESSIONAL INVESTIGATIONS

Some examples of the investigations and the amazing evidence collected are:

- The Senate Whitewater Investigation collected evidence of embezzlement from Madison Guaranty, extortion of the Small Business Administration and witness tampering at the Resolution Trust Company.
- House Banking Committee investigations corroborated the witness tampering and collected evidence of Mena, Arkansas drug trafficking and money laundering through the Arkansas Development Finance Authority.
- A Senate Judiciary Committee hearing collected evidence that White House Counsel, Bernard Nussbaum and Security head, Craig Livingstone, illegally obtained over 1,000 FBI files on political adversaries.
- A Senate Governmental Affairs Committee determined that the Secret Service agents who contradicted Craig Livingstone's testimony were then investigated by the Treasury Department, which concealed the investigation and lied to Congress twice, stating that the agents were not under investigation.

- A House Appropriations Committee collected evidence that Bill Clinton and Al Gore were aware of and encouraged an INS voter fraud scheme that tripled the normal number of yearly immigrants registered and resulted in 70,000 criminals and 180,000 illegal immigrants' being registered in time for the 1996 election.
- The House Travel Office investigation collected evidence that the Clinton administration filed false charges against Billy Dale, illegally obtained his FBI file and had the IRS audit his air charter service.
- The House Waco investigation collected evidence that Janet Reno approved the CS military gas attack on the Davidians, allowed the FBI to destroy a Davidian building with tanks while people were still inside, and circumvented the Posse Comitatus Act, that prohibits using military equipment and personnel against American citizens.
- The Senate Ruby Ridge investigation collected evidence regarding Janet Reno's refusal to support the conclusion of a Justice Department investigation that found an FBI sniper shot which killed Vicki Weaver was unconstitutional.
- A House Resource Committee and Judiciary Oversight Committee collected evidence that Bill Clinton prevented the State of Utah from mining the same type of clean burning coal as Indonesia, a source of illegal campaign contributions. He did this by declaring 1.7 million acres in southern Utah as a national monument against the will of the people in Utah and the opinions of directors in the Council on Environmental Quality.
- A Senate Campaign Finance Investigation and House Government Reform and Oversight Committee investigation collected evidence that the Clinton / Gore campaigns, the DNC and other Democrat Party candidates had at least seven separate sources of illegal revenue through 11 revenue streams, all traceable to individuals and organizations connected to Communist Chinese military. They also identified numerous instances where the Clinton administration had given the Communist Chinese government sophisticated American military technology over the objections of the our own government agencies, such as the National Security Administration and the Departments of Defense, State and Justice.

Former astronaut John Glenn, the ranking minority member of the Senate Campaign Finance Investigation, chaired by Senator Fred Thompson, appeared to do as much as he could during committee hearings to sabotage the investigation and prevent the Communist Chinese infiltration into the Clinton / Gore campaigns and the DNC from becoming public. Afterwards, Glenn, a man I once admired, was rewarded by the Clinton administration with another trip into space and then portrayed by the media as a hero to the public. I can think of no greater example of how the media has duped the American people than its acclaim for John Glenn, a man I believe is clearly guilty of high treason against America.

Through most of 1995 and parts of 1996, I watched many of the hearings in these investigations, some of which were not completed until 1998. Perhaps the most stunning occurrence of all in the impeachment movement for me, would happen in 1998 when the Republicans were unwilling to use a single iota of this Congressional investigation evidence when they drafted the Articles of Impeachment.

THE DEATH OF VINCE FOSTER

In 1994, Robert Fiske produced a report stating that the death of Vince Foster was a suicide. Fiske, who was appointed by Janet Reno as Whitewater counsel, turned out to be a lawyer for International Paper, Inc., the company that sold Whitewater land to the Clinton / McDougal partnership. Unbeknownst to me because of media distortions, he had reached a conclusion that could not be supported by any of the evidence. In fact, the evidence clearly indicated that Vince Foster was murdered. For example:

- Foster's prints were not on the gun;
- The gun was not Foster's and he had no ammunition for that type of gun;
- The autopsy report showed a rear skull exit wound, but no skull fragments were ever found;
- No bullet was ever found in the park although others dating to the Civil War were found;

- No powder burns were on Foster's mouth, where he allegedly shot himself;
- Powder burns on both forefingers indicate that he tried to push a gun away as he was shot;
- No dirt or grass was on Foster's shoes although his body was found 200 yards into the park;
- Foster's suit, shirt, tie and underwear were covered with carpet fibers (Fort Marcy is definitely not carpeted).

There were so many discrepancies between the conclusion and the FBI lab analysis evidence that the impartiality of Robert Fiske was called publicly into question. Subsequently, a three judge panel decided to appoint Ken Starr as the Whitewater counsel, despite the fact that he had been on Janet Reno's short list when she appointed Fiske. Much investigative work on the death of Vince Foster was contributed by Christopher Ruddy, who had described the discrepancies in many of his news articles for the *New York Post* and *Pittsburgh Tribune Review*. Ruddy left the *Post* for the *Tribune Review* because the *Post* stopped printing his stories. *The New Times* would not cover the story accurately and completely either, even after Reed Irvine, chairman of Accuracy in Media, met with the publisher and took out ads in the magazine. It was an Accuracy in Media ad about the death of Vince Foster in the *Washington Times* that initially triggered my interest in seeking the truth about the Clinton administration.

OKLAHOMA CITY BOMBING

On April 19, 1995, exactly two years after the fatal attack on the Branch Davidians at Waco, I was stunned, like the rest of America, by the Oklahoma City bombing, America's most severe terrorist act. It was very disturbing that such an act where hundreds of people were killed could take place in America. I felt particularly sorry for the victims and the people of Oklahoma, who rose to the occasion and epitomized my idea of Americans. It would be almost two years until I realized that the bombing could not possibly have happened the way it was reported.

Eventually I would find disturbing details from Brigadier General Partin, a 25-year weapons expert with two engineering degrees, and other highly qualified sources. Partin proved that a truckload of fertilizer and ammonium nitrate delivered to the Murrah Building in Oklahoma City by Timothy McVeigh could not possibly have blown out concrete posts in the building. Two concrete posts were still standing directly between the truck bomb pit and one of the posts in the back that had been blown out. The truck bomb, which was already too weak to blow out an adjoining concrete post would have had to circumvent the two posts and travel 25 feet through thin air without dissipating in force. Although I knew nothing about weapons, I had enough common sense to know that this was impossible. An aerial view of the damage shown on the cover of an issue of *The New American* magazine, as well as supporting diagrams and articles, illustrated the implausibility of what we had been told. When this became obvious, I noticed that the *USA Today* newspaper curiously cropped the picture of the building so that it did not show its readers the post in question.

Seismic evidence from Oklahoma City and the University of Oklahoma confirmed two unmatched sound waves indicating two explosions. In addition, local television stations in constant contact with federal agencies such as the ATF, reported that there were multiple bombs in the building and not all of them were detonated. In fact, the rescue operation was delayed while the bombs were diffused and removed. Witnesses such as Jane Graham also stated that there were several seconds between the two bomb blasts.

Dozens of witnesses saw another man, who was not Terry Nichols, deliver the bomb with Timothy McVeigh, but the FBI seemed to have no interest in finding him. ATF informant, Carol Howe, other witnesses and a credit card phone bill with a charge made by Timothy McVeigh, implicated three additional individuals of a Neo-Nazi group from Elohim City in the bombing. One of those present in the group at that time, Andreas Streissmeir, is the nephew of a former head of the German Christian Democrat Party who reported to Helmut Kohl.

Even more astounding was the evidence of pre-bomb knowledge the ATF had, as printed later in both *The New*

American magazine and *The Secret Life of Bill Clinton* by Ambrose Evans Pritchard. Carol Howe had penetrated the Neo-Nazi group, found out that it was plotting a bombing, gathered bomb assembly evidence and took ATF agent Angela Finley to targeted bomb sites in Oklahoma City. Her reward for risking her life to give the ATF the information was that the FBI exposed her undercover identification and decided to prosecute her for possessing the evidence that she was under contract to the ATF to collect! Naturally, the charges were dismissed, but the questions of why the FBI refused to investigate the other bombing suspects and why they prosecuted the ATF's own informant have never been answered.

RON BROWN PLANE CRASH

In April of 1996, almost a year later, another tragedy befell America when Ron Brown, Secretary of the Commerce Department, and about 60 other government officials and corporate executives were killed on a trade mission when their plane crashed in Bosnia. The funeral of Ron Brown showed the artificial nature of Bill Clinton perhaps more than any other event. As Bill Clinton left the funeral of his close friend, he was laughing and chatting with Rev. Compolo, who would later become one of his spiritual advisers. When he saw a camera filming them, he stopped laughing, pretended to cry and wiped a fake tear from his eye, all in less than three seconds. The NBC clip was picked up by Rush Limbaugh and played over and over again. Although it showed how phony Bill Clinton was, I would not understand the real relationship between Ron Brown and Bill Clinton for another year.

That understanding occurred after meeting Pat Matrisciana and receiving a phone call from Pat. He said Christopher Ruddy found that Ron Brown had what seemed to be a bullet hole in the top of his head, based on statements of military forensic experts who examined him after the plane crash. Brown was under investigation by seven different government agencies as well as a potential target in a lawsuit by Judicial Watch, which exposed John Huang and the Communist Chinese infiltration of the Clinton / Gore campaigns and the DNC. I did not want to believe this finding because it sounded too incredible. The implications were stunning. Someone would have had to bring down a plane full of people to kill one or two key officials. But the evidence was mounting on this event, too.

The three pathologists who examined Ron Brown confirmed the existence of a perfectly round .45 caliber hole in the top of his head and *The New American* magazine even printed the picture of it. I had read a *Wall Street Underground* intelligence report and knew that the air traffic controller had died of a gunshot wound to the chest, and it was ruled a suicide. That sounded familiar. The report also pointed out that a stewardess, Shelly Kelly, survived the crash but was then found dead on arrival at the hospital.

The intelligence report indicated that a ground crew used a separate beacon to divert the plane into the mountain where the plane crashed after being unable to gain enough height to clear the mountain. This sounded implausible to me because it would require a team of a several people and besides, where would they get a beacon and learn how to use it? Another year would go by before I learned that beacons were used in Operation Watchtower by an American special action team to route drug trafficking planes from Colombia into Panama.

Under normal procedures, many questions could have been cleared up by an investigation, but once again we would find a total cover-up. There was only a partial Air Force safety investigation, no FAA investigation, no NTSB investigation, no airplane manufacturer investigation, and no black box transcripts were ever made public. As in the case of Vince Foster, Ron Brown's X-rays were either lost or destroyed. Comedian Dick Gregory summed it up best when he went to Washington and placed crime scene tape around the U.S. Justice Department.

THE TWA 800 PLANE CRASH

On July 17, 1996, just days before the Atlanta Olympics, another plane crash and cover-up occurred. TWA 800 crashed into the ocean off Long Island, killing everyone aboard, after taking off from JFK airport. At this time I was so focused on the Olympics that I was not even aware of the cover-up that was taking place. Officials eventually stated that the crash was caused by a center fuel tank explosion. It would be three years after the tragedy before I learned that the fuel tank explosion was not the originating event that caused the plane to crash.

Over 130 witnesses stated that they had seen a reddish orange missile streak coming up from the ocean, moving towards the plane or crashing into it. The FBI interviewed 34 of these people, including pilots and military personnel, and found the witnesses to be certifiably credible. Several pictures of the missile streak and the streak of its target missile were taken. One is shown in the background of a photo taken by Linda Kabot, as illustrated in the book by James Sanders, entitled, *The Downing of TWA 800*.

The FAA radar tapes showed another blip converging on TWA 800. The FAA radar technician who analyzed the radar concluded that there were "conflicting radar tracks that indicated a missile". The NTSB reconstruction of the plane, as seen in Sanders' book, clearly showed a large hole on the right side where the missile entered the plane near a galley just in front the right wing. Reconstruction also showed a corresponding hole on the left side where the missile apparently exited the plane. Reddish orange residue containing traces of elements determined to be consistent with rocket fuel were found as early as August 3, 1996, only on seats in rows 17 through 19, which just happen to align with the entry and exit holes in the plane. The cockpit voice recorder and flight data recorder also respectively contained sounds and data consistent with a missile explosion.

So if a missile downed TWA 800, the question remains as to whose missile was it? Some individuals have recognized that TWA 800 was downed by a missile and even provided additional evidence, but they contend that it was a terrorist missile fired by individuals from a rogue nation. However, facts of the crash dispute these assertions.

The altitude of TWA 800, at over 13,700 feet, made it outside the range of any shoulder-based missile system that could have been available to terrorists. The photos and witnesses indicate that the missile was launched from sea, not from land. No other foreign ships with missile launching capability were known to be in the area where the missile was launched. The debris pattern indicated that missile was inert since its entry and exit did not cause an initial explosion. It is not likely that terrorists would use a dummy missile to down a plane.

Several U.S. naval vessels, including the USS Normandy, and P-3 Orion planes were in zone W105 near Long Island on a classified mission to test the Aegis missile system by firing drones to intercept hostile missiles. James Sanders illustrates in his book, priority message R015060, dated 11:07 pm 7/16/96, advising the FAA of phone conversation from a Ms. Cosby of Naval Air Base, Oceana, Virginia, to Mr. Dombrowski of FAA Ron Konkoma, Long Island, (15 miles north of the crash site) that reserved a zone south of Long Island for military use as of 8:00 pm on July 17, 1996. Missile testing activity at the time of the crash has been confirmed by many independent sources, and the evidence points to a target adjustment failure that resulted in a Navy missile's hitting TWA 800. If a terrorist organization or rogue country had brought down TWA 800, there would be no need for a massive cover-up to hide the missile evidence from the American public.

THE 1996 ATLANTA OLYMPIC GAMES

While I took note of the tragedies and watched some of the investigations during 1995 and 1996, I was still focused on the Olympics coming to Atlanta, the events I would attend and my duties as a badminton line judge, which required some weekend training sessions. The rest of the Olympic experience was also a once in a lifetime opportunity that I wanted to live to its fullest advantage. Therefore, I had tuned out many other activities.

When the Olympic Games arrived, they proved to be an incredible experience exceeding my expectations. I attended the ceremonies, judged on certain days and went to other events each day. At the opening ceremony when Bill Clinton was introduced, I came within an eyelash of screaming at the top of my lungs "Who killed Vince Foster?" Somehow I refrained out of respect for Billy Payne, who had put his heart and soul into getting Atlanta the Olympics. Had I seen the video that I was about to purchase a few months later, I could not have held back.

During the Olympics, I got another taste of media reporting and government cover-up. On Friday night, July 26, my wife and I were returning from a downtown event and walked through the crowded Centennial Olympic Park to enjoy some of the festivities. We left before midnight because I had tickets for a beach volleyball semi-finals the next morning. A little over an hour after we left, a bomb exploded in the park and killed a Georgia woman. A security guard named Richard Jewell was proclaimed a hero for his work both before and after the bomb detonation.

Later the hero became a suspect. The FBI invited him to film a training video where they asked him questions, supposedly for future training of FBI agents. In the middle of the friendly session, Jewell was surprised to find that he was a suspect when the FBI suddenly read him his Miranda rights. Local Atlanta agents testified before Congress that the order to read Jewell his rights came straight from FBI Director, Louis Freeh. Consequently, the local and national media attempted to convict Jewell without a trial, producing numerous false and misleading reports for which Jewell is still collecting damages through court suits and settlements.

I realized immediately that Jewell was innocent, based on the evidence of a phone call from an individual who had alerted authorities about the bomb. The caller had an accent that was in no way similar to Richard's southern drawl. Also, the call was placed from a location that was so heavily crowded that it would be impossible for Jewell to return to his post in the five-minute window of time allotted by the FBI. The FBI and the media both knew this but continued to use Jewell as a scapegoat for the bombing.

The bombing was the only bitter pill in an otherwise up-lifting Olympic experience. The Atlanta Committee for the Olympic Games eventually closed its doors as a financial success and with a tremendous local, national and international respect. Ironically, three years later, after the Atlanta Committee for the Olympic Games had shut down, it became the target of a Congressional investigation. After Dennis Hastert replaced Newt Gingrich as Speaker, the House of Representatives decided to spend taxpayer money to investigate the International Olympic Committee bid process, an activity for which it had no jurisdiction. A Commerce subcommittee performed the investigation at the same time it was ignoring the role of the Commerce Department in setting up the 11 illegal revenue streams from the Clinton / Gore campaigns and the DNC to the Communist Chinese government. It would prove to be one of many Republican led diversions to take the focus away from illegal Democrat activity and lead me to the inevitable conclusion that new House Speaker Dennis Hastert was equally as big a traitor as Bill Clinton or Al Gore.

MY AWAKENING

One day in 1996, I heard two co-workers talking about the death of Vince Foster. They mentioned remarkable evidence I described earlier that would lead any rational person to conclude that Vince Foster was murdered, and yet we had been told by the media that he committed suicide. I could not correlate these facts with what the media told me. I immediately reflected back to the Kennedy assassination and the discrepancies there and knew that something was wrong. I went on about my work and kept this information in the back of my mind. Later I found an ad in the *Washington Times* and ordered a report about Vince Foster's death from Accuracy in Media. The report confirmed what I had been told, and I decided to join Accuracy in Media and subscribe to the *Washington Times*. The subscription opened my eyes to a whole new world of factual political information.

A few months later, I was visiting a co-worker in his office, and he had a computer screen saver that showed a picture of Bill Clinton. His screen saver would make Bill Clinton's lips move and his nose grow at the same time. I started laughing, and we talked a little about the President. He told me that Bill Clinton was involved in a drug trafficking operation in Arkansas. I assumed that he was a little biased because if that were true, surely we would have heard about it from the media by now, and Bill Clinton would have never been elected President of the United States.

Shortly after the Olympics, I saw an ad in the *Washington Times* for videos. It was placed by a citizen from Charleston, South Carolina, named Jerry, who was acting as a volunteer distributor, paying for ads out of his own pocket and barely recovering the expense of the ads in video sales. He had previously placed ads at his own expense to encourage Congress to balance the budget. I admired his sacrifice and dedication. However, despite all that I was learning, I was still skeptical of the credibility of the videos and ordered only one about the death of Vince Foster.

When I saw the video I was stunned with lab analysis and other facts that it documented, as well as the dramatic fashion in which it was produced. It confirmed what I had read earlier, and the facts presented could not be disputed. I was stunned that I had been taken for an incredible ignorant ride by major news media organizations. I called Jerry back and ordered the remaining set of videos, including *The Clinton Chronicles*, *Obstruction of Justice* and the *Mena Cover-up*.

I was surprised to find that they factually confirmed what my co-worker told me about Bill Clinton's involvement in drug trafficking operations in Arkansas. What bothered me the most was a dramatic documentary of the murders of Kevin Ives and Don Henry entitled *Obstruction of Justice*. They were killed after they stumbled across a drug drop point, and their murders were apparently covered up by the Arkansas medical examiner, who had approximately 20 phony suicide and accidental death rulings documented by the *L.A. Times*. When the people of Arkansas wanted him removed, he was given a raise by Jocelyn Elders and moved to a different department by then Governor Clinton. Seven others with knowledge of the deaths were murdered, and all were still unsolved.

The videos, particularly *Obstruction of Justice*, moved me more than anything ever had before. I HAD to get involved. I could not stand back and let the American government be destroyed by corruption. I called Jerry back and ordered more videos for my friends. I also contacted Citizens for Honest Government (CHG), the organization founded by video producer Pat Matrisciana, and volunteered my services as a co-ordinator for Georgia along with a meager financial donation..

I thought that I could help make an impact since both Speaker of the House Newt Gingrich and Congressman Bob Barr were in my state. I had met Bob Barr once before at a town hall meeting shortly after he went to Washington, and I knew he had a background as a prosecutor. I had watched him in the Waco investigation and thought he was doing a good job trying to get at the truth. I realized from the investigation that ATF agents never even attempted to serve the warrant on the Davidians peacefully and just started shooting. Evidence that would prove those allegations, like the Mt. Carmel complex front door and ATF videos of the raid, were "lost" by the FBI and ATF. The investigation appeared to be uncovering the truth, so I went to the town hall meeting to express my support and raise the concern that this investigation would not turn into cover-ups like those of the assassinations of John Kennedy and Dr. King. I would later find that although the investigation exposed much of the truth, it did nothing to admit actual wrongdoing on the part of the ATF and FBI or to prevent such a grotesque violation of the Fourth Amendment from occurring again.

THE 1996 ELECTION

As the 1996 election approached, there was a chance that Bill Clinton may not be re-elected. In fact, had the media told the American people the truth about the evidence of criminal activity, bribery and abuse of power that had been collected to date, Bill Clinton could not have even received a double digit voting percentage. However, some interesting factors helped him.

During Bill Clinton's first term, Rush Limbaugh started a half-hour daily TV show. He became popular because he provided a unique, conservative commentary, exposing some of the softer Clinton wrongdoings with information that still could not be found anywhere else on TV. Although he achieved good ratings, his show was always placed in extreme late night or early morning time slots where viewers would be scarce. In spite of this, the show was successful, and he developed a loyal following. He had even received some of the credit for the Republican revolution. However, months before the 1996 election, he surprisingly refused to renew his television show and went off the air.

Ross Perot also entered the Presidential campaign again after United We Stand was converted into the Reform Party.

But this time he had lost too much credibility, mostly because of his 1992 election withdrawal. Perot even bought his own election eve television time to expose newly discovered information about illegal donations made to Clinton / Gore campaigns and the DNC from the Chinese Communist government through fundraising schemes established by John Huang. He welcomed the President to defend himself against the allegations on television at Perot's expense, but Clinton naturally declined. It was still one of the finest political speeches that I ever heard, but it went to no avail. Later I would find out that Perot's information had come from Judicial Watch.

Bill Clinton eventually won re-election over Republican Bob Dole, who may have lost even if he were unopposed. Dole, known as the "hatchet man" while he was Vice President under Gerald Ford, never attacked Bill Clinton on a single scandal and even stated in one debate how much he liked the President. He never mentioned the Contract with America or never apparently understood what it meant to the citizens. The final results were Clinton 49 percent, Dole 41 percent and Perot eight percent. I am convinced that Bob Dole never actually tried to win the 1996 Presidential election.

The remaining two percent of the 1996 election vote was split between four other candidates who also had a mathematical chance of winning the electoral college. The Federal Elections Commission, which is controlled by Democrats and Republicans, would not allow any third parties in the Presidential debates, even though most were on the ballot in all 50 states.

Three other candidates, Howard Phillips of the U.S. Taxpayers Party (now the Constitution Party), Harry Browne of the Libertarian Party and John Hagelin of the Natural Law Party participated in an independent debate televised by C-Span, the only source of unfiltered political information on television. Former consumer advocate, Ralph Nader of the Green Party did not participate even though he, too, was on the ballot in enough states to win the election mathematically.

There were no media representatives who controlled the questions, so the debate focused on real issues. There were one-minute time limits for responses to questions, so the scope of the issues covered was tremendous. The candidates also offered creative, pro-American solutions not even mentioned by Democrats and Republicans for many issues. It was the finest debate that I had ever seen.

By the time of the election, I was familiar with the mounting evidence of corruption that was building against the President. I concluded that someone could have placed the picture of each of the six Clinton opponents on one side of a die, cast the die, moved the winning individual into the White House and America would have likely had a better President. Once Bill Clinton was re-elected, I knew that I would have to devote personal time and money to help seek his impeachment.

REFERENCES

What Really Happened in Oklahoma City? (video), American Opinion Book Services.

Mena Cover-up (video), Citizens for Honest Government.

TheClinton Chronicles (video), Citizens for Honest Government.

The Death of Vince Foster (video), Citizens for Honest Government.

Investigation into the Activities of Federal Law Enforcement Agencies toward the Branch Davidians, House Government Reform & Oversight Committee & House Judiciary Committee.

Obstruction of Justice (video), Integrity Films.

Martin Gross, *The Great Whitewater Fiasco*, Ballantine Books.

Jerry Longspaugh, *Cover-up in Oklahoma* (video), American Opinion Book Services.

Waco: The Big Lie (video), American Justice Federation.

Ambrose Evans-Pritchard, *The Secret Life of Bill Clinton*, Regnery Publishing.

Christopher Ruddy, *The Strange Death of Vince Foster*, Free Press of Simon & Schuster.

James Sanders, *The Downing of TWA Flight 800*, Zebra.

The Federal Raid on Ruby Ridge, Idaho, U.S. Senate Judiciary Committee.

The New American magazine, Vol. 11 - No. 16, Vol. 11 - No. 95, Vol. 12 - No. 10.

CHAPTER THREE
THE VIEW FROM INSIDE

PERSONAL MEDIA BLACKOUT EXPERIENCES

During the 1996 campaign, I got my first real life taste of media blackout. I was invited by Reform Party members who I met when I gave them videos, to a special *Larry King Live* pre-election show on the Talk Back Live show set at CNN in Atlanta. It featured Presidential candidates, Ross Perot, Howard Phillips, Harry Browne and John Hagelin. Ross Perot was on first by himself because of his friendship with Larry King. I sat directly behind him, in camera view for much of the show.

I decided to ask his opinion of the charges raised by Citizens for Honest Government regarding Bill Clinton's involvement in the Mena drug trafficking operation. I had made friends with one of the hostesses who had decided to start the questioning with me. However, after she relayed the question through her mike and headphones to her producer, she was not allowed to come to me for my question at any time during the entire show.

I then found out that all *Talk Back Live* questions are pre-screened through a producer prior to the show or during commercials without the knowledge of the audience. I returned to the show several other times but was never allowed to ask a question and now realize that the spontaneous appearance of audience participation is totally contrived by the producers.

Afterwards, I decided to bite the bullet and place newspaper ads for the videos like my friend Jerry. I thought I would use the *Atlanta Journal/Constitution* since I had contributed numerous editorials over the years and was viewed favorably by *Journal* editors. I had some experience with ad creation and created my own tactful, local ads for the videos to help spur national sales. I took them to the advertising department, and after a few days the advertising director, Joe Winter, who seemed to be a nice guy in a bad position, called me to tell me the ads were rejected.

I asked who rejected them, and he told me that there was some review board that looks at political ads, but he did not know much about it. I asked why they were rejected, and he said that the board does not explain why, but that I could change them and resubmit them. I asked how would I know what to change if I did not know what was wrong with them. Needless to say, he could not answer that question either.

I realized that Mrs. Cox of the parent Cox Newspapers was a close friend of Bill Clinton, so I tried once again with a different combination of videos that mentioned only the death of Vince Foster and the drug trafficking-related Ives / Henry murders. The ads were rejected again, and I concluded that it was a useless waste of time.

I knew about media blackout of news stories, but I did not know media organizations would even black out paid ads. I was finally beginning to realize that we would have to circumvent the entire national news media to impeach the President of the United States.

PERSONAL EXPERIENCE WITH
"SCORCHED EARTH" POLICY

Soon after becoming involved with Citizens For Honest Government, I got to meet Pat Matrisciana, Lt. Col. Tom McKenney and future CHG director John Wheeler on one of their visits to Atlanta. It was then I began to realize the costs Pat was paying to achieve his desire of honest government. I was interested in discussing many things with him, but I spent much of the time getting a taste of what was to be called the Clinton "scorched earth" policy. It seems that two of the people that I knew Pat had hired to help manage the organization appeared to be trying to disable it. Pat said that when they visited his office, one or both apparently broke into Pat's files during the night to get background information. Pat and Tom decided to release them since funding was short anyway. Afterwards, these individuals ordered computers for themselves and tried to bill it to CHG. They also attempted to claim ownership of the web site. CHG eventually was forced to file a civil suit and as a result of the suit, found out that they were under the protection of the FBI. Later, a somewhat distorted version of financial information from the CHG files was leaked to the *Salon* magazine web site, an apparent leader in Clinton "scorched earth" policy. That information was picked up again on CNBC by Geraldo, who became a Clinton "scorched earth" facilitator. The news stories just happened to break right after we had sent out the press releases for our "National Town Hall on Impeachment." We would find out later from a Judicial Watch lawsuit that CHG was on the Clinton enemy hit list.

During this time, two Arkansas police officers sued Pat Matrisciana and CHG for $14,000,000 in damages over the *Obstruction of Justice* video. The suit was based on the word "eyewitnesses" used once in the video in regards to implicating the officers and other named federal officials for further questioning in the investigation of the deaths of Kevin Ives and Don Henry. No other facts presented in the video were challenged. Linda Ives, the mother of Kevin Ives, and Jean Duffey, a former drug task force investigator, eventually explained to me about two police reports that implicated the officers and told me about their discussions with one of the witnesses. However, the judge did not allow the police reports to be entered into evidence. He ruled the reports "prejudicial".

Pat was convinced that the officers filed suit against their will and were funded by someone else. He knew that the officers did not want anymore publicity because Linda Ives, the mother of Kevin Ives, and Jean Duffey, a former drug task force investigator, both strongly believed that they killed her son. In fact, they later stated on local television news that they were "convinced that the officers were the hands on killers of the boys". Despite their pleas the officers were never investigated for the murders. As a result of suit depositions, Pat said that he discovered the officers were deputized by the FBI and trial testimony eventually revealed that a FBI agent suggested to the officers that they sue Pat. The Janet Reno "Department of Injustice" had apparently struck again.

THE "DEPARTMENT OF INJUSTICE"

By now it had become obvious that CHG was not the only victim of the Janet Reno Justice Department. She had already fired all of the U.S. attorneys and the FBI director. The replacement director, Louis Freeh, "mishandled" cases involving the FBI files, FBI lab work, Waco, Ruby Ridge, Richard Jewell, Gary Aldrich, illegal immigration checks and the Oklahoma City bombing. Reno even oversaw the INS while it registered 70,000 criminals and 180,000 illegal immigrants after it tripled the number of immigrants normally registered each year in time for the 1996 election.

Reno had also blatantly protected Bill Clinton. She appointed Robert Fiske as Whitewater prosecutor even though he was a lawyer for International Paper, the company that sold Whitewater land to the Clinton / McDougal partnership. She prevented the expansion of the Espy probe to protect Don Tyson, a major Clinton campaign contributor from Arkansas. She stalled investigations into the Clinton administration by making privilege claims for the Clintons that were unanimously rejected by the Supreme Court. She refused immunity for Buddhist nuns to testify about the illegal campaign contributions received at the Hsi Lai temple where Vice President Al Gore held his "community outreach" meeting. She refused repeated requests by the House to appoint a special prosecutor to investigate illegal contributions from the Communist Chinese government despite evidence that the Clinton / Gore campaigns, the DNC and the Democrat Party had seven sources of illegal revenue traceable to the Communists.

Even more disturbing were obstruction of justice allegations involving cases of drug trafficking and organized crime. A drug task force investigation found evidence linking Arkansas drug trafficking to local and state officials. One prosecutor, Dan Harmon, was convicted in 1997 on drug trafficking charges, thanks in part to the persistence of Jean Duffey and CHG. The investigation implicated other officials in drug trafficking and even could have helped solve the murders of Kevin Ives and Don Henry, but Arkansas U.S. attorney, Chuck Banks, shut the investigation down. The FBI then decided that he should be charged with obstruction of justice, but the Justice Department under Janet Reno never charged him.

Another astounding case involved Arthur Coia, a union boss who was a top ten DNC fundraiser, collecting almost $17,000,000 from 1995 through 1996 for the DNC. The Justice Department determined in a complaint that he was "associated with influence from and controlled by" organized crime.

Reports from the National Legal and Policy Center and *Reader's Digest* indicated that Coia was under investigation for extortion, embezzlement, racketeering and death by fire-bombing. The Justice Department planned to take over the union, but after Coia raised the first $4,500,000 with Hillary Clinton at the Fountainbleau Hotel in Miami, the Justice Department signed a consent decree, allowed him to clean up the union and never brought charges against him.

THE FIRST STARR COVER-UP

After the first finding from Ken Starr, concerning the death of Vince Foster, we quickly realized that Janet Reno was apparently not the only one protecting Bill Clinton. In July of 1997, Starr simply confirmed the Fiske ruling that Vince Foster committed suicide in Fort Marcy Park. It was almost beyond belief the two supposedly independent counsels would rule that Foster committed suicide, despite the overwhelming evidence of murder, such as the lack of his fingerprints on the gun that was used to kill him.

Citizens for Honest Government immediately countered with two page ads in the *Washington Times*, explaining the evidence and exposing the fact that Ken Starr may have been compromised since he was retained by a Communist Chinese company named Citisteel. In addition, his employer, Kirkland & Ellis, gave 86 percent of its PAC money to Democrat candidates during the time of the Foster murder investigation. Christopher Ruddy followed with his book, *The Strange Death of Vince Foster*, which outlined hundreds of pieces of corroborating evidence that, I believe, prove beyond reasonable doubt that Vince Foster did not commit suicide in Fort Marcy Park.

The Clinton administration had to be directly involved in the murder of Vince Foster because individuals in the administration produced the briefcase, which was seen in the park by three witnesses, and the suicide note, that hand writing experts determined to be a forgery. The suicide note which turned up all of a sudden in the briefcase on the third time that it was searched was such an obvious forgery that any individual could see the pen dots where the letters had been drawn instead of written. This would not be the last time that Ken Starr appeared to cover up crimes that involved the Clinton administration.

DISCOVERING WHY THE MEDIA LIES

By now the media had begun portraying Ken Starr as a biased, overzealous counsel, who was out to get the President. In reality, I knew that he had probably covered up the murder of Vince Foster, and I feared that his team would likely do the same in the future for other serious Clinton offenses. I reflected on all the false reporting of the balanced budget, the new Republican revolution House members who were falsely portrayed as "extremists" and the vicious distorted attacks on Newt Gingrich for ethics charges resulting from two incorrect statements made by his lawyers in regards to his knowledge of the GOPAC political action committee. In contrast, there was a complete media blackout of the activities of a man who would likely become the most corrupt President in American history, assuming that history book authors were more honest than news editors. Finally I thought back to the political assassinations of the '60s and realized that this had been going on for years.

I could not understand it. Obviously one or two TV networks or several newspapers could be biased. But this was not bias. The news was deliberately being distorted and falsely portrayed to Americans consistently by major networks and newspapers. It was a complete distortion of political news dating back to the beginning of my lifetime. How could this possibly be? It began to bother me. My desire to help the impeachment effort and clean up government corruption had been diverted to determining why the media lies so consistently. I had no explanation, was not even close to determining the reason and knew of no way to find out why this was happening.

One day I mentioned this to the co-worker who had told me about the Mena, Arkansas drug trafficking operation. He began explaining how media organizations were generally controlled by the same people. He mentioned that he was a member of the John Birch Society and that they had done a lot of research on this topic. He seemed a little shy to talk about the society because it had been falsely portrayed in the media as some type of "right wing extremist" group. That did not bother me in the least because the media said the same about the new Republican Congress. America needed more of these "extremists" who were willing to balance the budget and restore fiscal integrity to our nation. By this time, I had decades of evidence that the media lied consistently about anything political, and I was more apt to believe the opposite of whatever the media organizations said. After reviewing the society literature, meeting some members and reading a book authored by one of them, I realized that the media had performed a character assassination on this group that was second to none. Nowhere had I seen more caring, astute individuals who were truly concerned for America.

The society had already produced a special issue of *The New American* magazine that documented amazing links between many media moguls and the Council on Foreign Relations. The issue traced the positions of leadership that the members of the CFR had attained. It included wire service chairmen, network news presidents, managing editors, editorial page editors, TV news anchors, magazine editors, political columnists and many other key positions of power in the media world. The issue also traced the socialist and even fascist roots of the CFR and quoted the Congressional record from 1917 where Congressman Oscar Callaway explained how J.P. Morgan interests had bought two dozen of the largest national newspapers in March of 1915 and installed their own editors. It outlined a one world government strategy of the council and its sister organization, the Tri-Lateral Commission, and explained how the plan would be implemented at the expense of American sovereignty. Finally I had the answer I had been seeking. It was the only logical explanation for why the media organizations could lie so consistently.

But *The New American* magazine issue went further. It also showed how CFR members dominated many government agencies, monetary institutions such as the Federal Reserve and public policy foundations such as the Rockefeller Foundation. All Presidents since Richard Nixon, with the exception of Ronald Reagan, were CFR members, and many of their cabinet members were as well. It also explained how the Federal Reserve was neither federal nor did it have adequate reserves. Essentially, the members of a single organization dedicated to global socialism helped set American political agendas, controlled American monetary policy and manipulated public opinion to implement their agenda. For the first time, I now knew what George Bush meant when he talked about the "new world order."

The issue also listed many Democrat Party Congressional members that belonged to the CFR as well as key Republicans like Newt Gingrich, Jim Leach and Henry Hyde. My society friends tried to enlighten me that Newt and Bill Clinton were actually on the same team. I had just been fed an overload of information and could not even begin to digest such a strange concept. Newt and Bill Clinton were diametrically opposed in almost every way. It would be another year before I could finally conclude that the person most responsible for protecting Bill Clinton was Newt Gingrich.

PROMISE KEEPERS

The scope of what I learned was depressing because it forced me to realize the obstacle that we faced in impeaching Bill Clinton. We would have to circumvent the entire national news media and there may even be politicians and others who pretend to be on our side but end up deceiving us. The battle was only just getting started, and I was losing hope that anything could be done to rectify the corruption in Washington.

Then along came an event that restored my faith. On October 4, 1997, one million men, organized by a former Colorado coach, Bill McCartney, convened on the mall in Washington to pray for America. It was an incredible spectacle. I stayed with my mother in Richmond, Virginia, took the train to Washington and met lots of great people. I looked forward to going because I believe that America is a blessing from God, the Constitution was divinely inspired and that we have a duty to maintain the American form of government so as to preserve the freedom and power that we have been given.

I went to support a rally by the Coalition of Politically Active Christians, organized by the founder, Charles Phillips. It took place in a park between Union Station and the Capitol. It had many great speakers anchored by Alan Keyes and included a fabulous Ohio-based gospel choir. Since it was a separate event from the Promise Keepers rally, I felt somewhat guilty afterwards that I did not get to participate in the full Promise Keeper event and pray with them. Shortly thereafter, I returned to D.C. with Pat Matrisciana and stopped by Congressman Barr's office for a few minutes to discuss plans for filming an event with him. Inspired by Promise Keepers, we then prayed in the House chambers, Senate chambers and on the Capitol steps. I believe the Promise Keepers concept of a million citizens praying for our government may be the only hope Americans have left.

GETTING INVOLVED

My experiences with media blackouts and the Clinton "scorched earth" policy had left me frustrated but only made me more determined to help expose the truth. I did not really know how to proceed, and then suddenly an interesting coincidence occurred. I was at a party with many of my Vietnamese friends, where I was introduced to Jimmy, who knew Congressman Bob Barr. Jimmy also became one of my friends, and he told me that he would invite me to a future meeting with the Congressman. It wasn't long before I got to see Bob Barr again at breakfast and once more at a meeting in Chinatown. This time I brought him *The Clinton Chronicles* and *Death of Vince Foster* videos. I was generally uncomfortable with politicians and did not expect anything ever to come of it. Little did I know, that his response would exceed my wildest expectations.

A few months later, Congressman Barr wrote a letter to the House Judiciary Chairman, Henry Hyde, requesting a formal impeachment inquiry. Then he followed that up with a letter to Hillary Clinton which was published in the *Wall Street Journal*. That letter complimented the work she had done on the Nixon impeachment inquiry and stated that it was excellent groundwork for the Clinton impeachment inquiry. Based on the Nixon impeachment inquiry investigation, which was co-authored by Hillary Rodham, Bernard Nussbaum and other lawyers, the grounds for impeachment of Bill Clinton had already been exceeded.

Henry Hyde responded that a Presidential impeachment inquiry was "premature". By now it was 1997, and I was familiar with evidence in many of the 11 Congressional investigations into the President. I knew full well what a ridiculous position Henry Hyde had taken, but I did not know why. I decided that if the House Judiciary Committee would not began an inquiry and establish the Articles of Impeachment, that we the citizens would have to produce our own indictment of the President to get the facts out. Unbeknownst to me, former Congressman Bill Dannemeyer had already drafted four Articles of Impeachment based primarily on the FBI file case and the Travel Office firing scandal. He had apparently already circulated them to some friends in Congress, including Henry Hyde. Bill Dannemeyer told me later that his concern had peaked after receiving videos about the Waco massacre produced by the American Justice Federation in Indiana. Like myself and many other Americans, he was deeply disturbed by the abuse he saw and decided to get involved.

I concluded that I had a golden opportunity to go over Henry Hyde's head since my Congressman was Speaker of the House. I produced signs, bumper stickers and a 25 count Citizens' Presidential Impeachment Indictment of major allegations. I described evidence to support each allegation and referenced it to the appropriate source. The indictment covered criminal activity in Arkansas, abuses of power in Washington, treason and bribery with the Communist Chinese government and a whole host of obstructions of justice that the President apparently committed with Attorney General Janet Reno to cover up the other crimes. I then began to pepper the constituents of the Speaker of the House, Newt Gingrich, with these indictments at every town hall or other meeting, in hopes that they would pressure him to move on impeachment.

The response was great. Over half of the people that received a copy of the indictment burst out in a joyous smile and seemed so relieved that someone was actually doing something about Clinton administration corruption. Some people ignored me, but no one ever seriously even challenged me or the evidence I had compiled.

I received wonderful encouragement, and even people who disagreed me were frequently fun to have met. One little old lady saw my "Impeach Clinton" sign at a tax reform town hall and said, "You must be a very sick man." Another lady saw my "Honk for Impeachment" bumper sticker at a traffic light and waved her finger in a circular motion around her ear to give me the "crazy" sign. I wanted to pass an indictment to her through the window, but I could not stop laughing.

Many others honked and waved their approval as they passed by. The district obviously supported impeachment. A friend named Bill, whom I had met recently told me prophetically that "it doesn't take a whole lot of effort to accomplish something significant." I hope that all American citizens now know that he is right and realize what they can help accomplish.

PAULA JONES SUES BILL CLINTON

During this time Paula Jones filed what would prove to be a historically significant sexual harassment civil suit against Bill Clinton because it forced him to testify. We were familiar with her suit because Pat had already videotaped her telling her story for *The Clinton Chronicles*. In fact, Pat was placed under a gag order by a judge, at the request of Clinton attorney Bill Bennett, in response to the suit. Anyone who saw *The Clinton Chronicles* knew she was credible, but the media organizations which could not black out this story, chose to portray her as a floozy.

One apparent example was the actions of the *Washington Post*, which obtained an exclusive on her story and sent Michael Isikoff to cover it. After Isikoff interviewed her, he realized that she was credible and returned to Washington with the facts. When the *Post* editors found out that Isikoff articles were not going to destroy her, they refused to print them. Isikoff and the editors got into an argument which resulted in Isikoff's leaving the *Post* for *Newsweek* magazine, another Clinton apologist. It was clear to us from this event that the *Washington Post* was also on the Clinton "scorched earth" team.

After Jones filed her suit she was audited by the IRS, despite the fact that her husband made only $30,000 a year. Bill Clinton also had Janet Reno file a privilege claim to seek a ruling that he could not stand trial while he was in office because he was commander in chief of the military. Finally on May 27, 1997, the U.S. Supreme Court issued a unanimous decision that allowed the case to go forward. Over a year later, her case would be thrown out of court by Judge Susan Webber

Wright, a former student of Bill Clinton. Judge Wright ruled that even if everything that Paula Jones claimed were true, she still did not prove any damages. We would later learn that Bill Clinton had perjured himself several times during the testimony, and Judge Webber Wright, by holding him in contempt of court, was forced to make the same conclusion.

THE TAX REFORM DIVERSION

During 1997, I was temporarily set back by a hernia operation as the Republicans diverted attention from Clinton corruption to tax reform legislation. National tax reform debates sponsored by Citizens for a Sound Economy and Citizens for an Alternative Tax System started around the country. The debates typically featured Billy Tauzin, a national sales tax proponent, and Dick Armey, a flat income tax proponent, extolling the virtues of their proposals and taking questions from the audience. By now I had become addicted to C-Span, and I watched the tax reform testimony of witnesses who had been persecuted by the IRS for taxes that they legally did not owe. I was excited about the possibly of a national sales tax to eliminate this and many other tax problems. I found out that the Tauzin / Armey debate was coming to Atlanta. I thought I could let myself have a diversion for a day or two and that I might even be able to work an impeachment-related question into debate if I attended. Then I found out that the debate would occur on the evening of the day that I was to be hospitalized for a hernia operation.

Fortunately for me, hernia operation techniques had improved over the previous two decades to the point where doctors could simply add a supporting mesh screen to cover the tissue tear rather than attempt to sew it back up. Therefore, although it takes a day or two for recovery and two weeks to get back to normal, I decided to attend the event after I got out of the hospital. Needless to say, my wife, who was already not too pleased about the time I was spending on the impeachment effort, was irate about my desire. Somehow, I was able to get her to agree to attend and help get me there.

Their debate was advertised on two radio stations, and thousands of people were there. It was hosted by Neal Boortz, who had replaced Sean Hannity as Atlanta's top talk show host after Sean's move to the *Hannity and Colmes* show on Fox News television in New York. Newt Gingrich and Bob Barr also attended, and the questions that were asked were, for the most part, extremely intelligent. It was the most successful of all of the debates, and yet C-Span did not televise it. It was the first inkling of a revelation I would receive next year when I found that C-Span may not be quite the non-partisan network I thought it was.

My wife let me out at the Galleria. I limped up the escalator, slipped into the main room that held only about 250 attendees, saved her a seat, found her and led her back into the main room where the debate would be held. When it was time for questions, I limped into the line. When my turn came, I held up my wrist with the hospital band still attached, thanked the sponsors, host and Congressmen and told them how much I wanted to attend because of the historic nature of the event. Even Billy Tauzin started to clap. I had already realized that this was not the appropriate time for an impeachment question, so I mentioned that I saw in the hearings how the IRS had persecuted citizens over disagreements about income owed and asked Dick Armey how a flat income tax would solve that problem. Naturally, he could not effectively answer that question or many others. He was outgunned by his opponent, Billy Tauzin, the content of their proposals and the audience that was about 95 percent in favor of a national sales tax to replace the income tax.

Republican Congressman throughout the country began scheduling tax reform town halls, including Newt Gingrich, who had two on consecutive weekends. The time had come to pressure Newt publicly for impeachment, but I was not sure how best to do it since the town halls were supposed to be limited to tax questions. In addition, Newt was somewhat intimidating because he was brilliant, articulate and extremely knowledgeable. I went to the first town hall just to listen and pass out indictments and decided to wait for the second town hall, which ironically would occur at Centennial High, a newly built school named after the Olympics, a previous two-week passion of mine.

Newt mentioned at the previous town hall that he would like to send out a survey to the citizens asking them about their preferences for tax reform. However, he was reluctant to do that because it would cost about $60 million. When it was my turn for a question, I first recognized the fact that he had endured more false press attacks than anyone I had ever known and thanked him and his wife, Marianne, for having the determination to withstand them and continue to represent us. The crowd cheered.

I then mentioned that my concern with the IRS was that Bill Clinton had used it to persecute political adversaries, and I reeled off the names of a few organizations that have been audited. I then suggested that the $60 million he needed for the survey was the exact amount of money that it cost us to shut down Madison Guaranty. I said that we should make James McDougal pay the money back and that if he could not, Bill Clinton should pay it back because he was warned five years in advance of Madison's insolvency by two government agencies.

Before I could even finish my sentence the crowd was cheering again. Finally I mentioned that other evidence indicated Bill Clinton had committed treason and bribery with the Communist Chinese government. I concluded urging Newt to "unite the Republican Party, impeach the most corrupt President in the history of our nation and save this country for our children and our grandchildren."

The crowed cheered again and Newt, who unbeknown to most of us, had held up the impeachment inquiry for months, was in a minor predicament. He could not confront me because his supporters were on my side. Therefore, Newt, who always gave us straight answers, did not respond, became somewhat red-faced and simply went to the next person. Despite all of his antagonistic confrontations with an unfairly hostile press, it was the only time I had ever seen Newt seemingly a little embarrassed.

BOB BARR'S H. RES. 304

I also began attending town halls and functions for Bob Barr and found that his constituents were already pressuring him to move forward on the impeachment issue. This personal firsthand experience flew in the face of another media lie that claimed Bob Barr was driven simply his own partisan motive. His former background as a U.S. attorney made him the perfect person to carry the impeachment banner in Congress, and his constituents wanted him to take the lead.

Several national civic leaders were encouraging him to have a press conference, and he actually went to the point of calling one and then canceling it, apparently after pressure from Newt. We, as citizens, began calling conservative talk show hosts like Rush Limbaugh and got no support whatsoever. Barr was careful and even somewhat reluctant to proceed. He would have to take on the entire Washington power structure with little support from the people allegedly claiming to be on his side, and he would risk becoming a victim of "scorched earth" policy. Yet, if he didn't, he would lose respect from his constituents. It appeared to be a no win situation. Then more developments occurred to help push him over the top.

The John Birch Society decided to join the effort and form the Impeach Clinton ACTION Committee. ACTION stands for Activate Congress to Improve Our Nation. I was ecstatic. The society was loaded with the most knowledgeable, caring people that I had met, and they were organized in every Congressional district in America. They could help apply significant pressure in support of the impeachment effort.

In addition, Howard Phillips rallied the organizations in the Coalition for a Congressional Impeachment Inquiry via some conference calls to obtain a pledge from them to support an impeachment resolution. Finally, on November 5, 1997, three and a half years after the coalition was formed, Bob Barr introduced House Resolution 304, Presidential Impeachment Inquiry, with 17 brave co-sponsors. Despite the historic nature of the event and a press conference with a multitude of civic organizations supporting the resolution, the introduction of the impeachment inquiry received a complete national TV blackout with the exception of Fox News network.

The President shrugged off the entire event with the comment, "Bob Barr carries the water buckets for the NRA." We decided that Bob Barr deserved something better. Pat, Tom and John came to Atlanta for another meeting that happened to be on the same day as one of Bob Barr's town hall meetings.

We decided to attend the town hall, and in recognition of his courage, to present him with an engraved glass flame award that he eventually placed on the credenza in his local office. On the marble base of the award was a gold plaque inscribed with the sentence: "Thank you for carrying the water buckets of the American citizens."

FORCING THE MEDIA TO CHANGE TACTICS

The introduction of H. Res. 304 was a watershed event because now the Republicans were threatening to expose some of the evidence that they had collected of criminal activity in Arkansas, using government agencies to persecute political adversaries and the millions of dollars that had likely been funneled into the Clinton / Gore campaigns and Democrat Party candidates by the Communist Chinese military. If the Republicans included this evidence in the Articles of Impeachment, the media would be forced to report it to the American people, and the public would finally figure out what Bill Clinton had done to them.

The major media organizations had covered up the criminal activity in Arkansas to get Bill Clinton elected, covered up his abuses of power to get him re-elected and were covering up the Communist Chinese infiltration of the Clinton / Gore campaigns and Democrat Party to avoid his impeachment. H. Res. 304 threatened to expose the media organizations, and they were now in a dilemma.

Within a month, the same media organizations that had blacked out every attempt to expose Clinton corruption and even participated in the "scorched earth" policy, began attacking Bill Clinton on issues related to sexual morality, which they had covered up all along. At the same time, Attorney General Janet Reno suddenly authorized Ken Starr to look into sexually related allegations with White House intern, Monica Lewinsky, whose affair with Clinton had almost nothing to do with the scope of his investigation. In addition, Judge Susan Weber Wright ruled that witnesses like Lewinsky could be called in the Paula Jones suit.

The media could have broken the story five months earlier in July, when Monica had an incident at the White House gate where she was refused entry while Elanor Mondale was visiting Bill Clinton. In fact, Michael Isikoff was apparently prepared to break a sex-related Clinton scandal at that time for *Newsweek* when all of a sudden former White House intern and Clinton campaign worker, Mary Caity Mahoney, was murdered at the Georgetown Starbucks, where she was a manager.

Reports indicated that Mary Caity Mahoney was shot five times in the head by two men who apparently used silencers on their guns, left $4000 in the store and locked the doors when they left. Two co-workers were shot once in the head and also killed. Only the *Washington Weekly* followed up on the murders after the initial reports. The *Newsweek* story was canceled, and the murders received a national media blackout. Several reports quoted Monica Lewinsky as saying that she "did not want to end up like Mary Mahoney."

The media accomplished three things with the focus on the Lewinsky sexual matter. First, it diverted attention from the real crimes and redefined the impeachment movement as a matter about sex. Second, it made the media appear more un-biased since it was finally attacking Bill Clinton on one of his shortcomings after covering up all of the criminal, treasonous and tyrannical activity that gone on during his Presidency. Third, it fooled most Americans into thinking that Bill Clinton simply had a personal problem and was no threat to their freedom or the American form of government. It was a brilliant strategy that would surely deceive the majority of American citizens into opposing impeachment. We had to find ways to strike back, circumvent the media with the truth and counter the "immaculate deception."

REFERENCES

House Appropriations Subcommittee Meeting, 4/4/97.
What Really Happened in Oklahoma City? (video), American Opinion Book Services.
The Clinton Chronicles (video), Citizens for Honest Government.
Investigation into the Activities of Federal Law Enforcement Agencies toward the Branch Davidians, House Government Reform & Oversight Committee, House Judiciary Committee.

Obstruction of Justice (video), Integrity Films.
Jerry Longspaugh, *Cover-up in Oklahoma* (video), American
    Opinion Book Services.
Ethics Watch (various issues), National Legal and Policy Center
Reader's Digest, 4/96.
Chris Ruddy,*The Strange Death of Vince Foster*, The Free
    Press of Simon & Schuster.
Year of the Rat, Ed Timperlake & Bill Triplett, Regnery
    Publishing.
The Federal Raid on Ruby Ridge, Idaho, U.S. Senate Judiciary
    Committee.

CHAPTER FOUR
THE IMMACULATE DECEPTION

NATIONAL TOWN HALL ON IMPEACHMENT

To combat the sexual diversion and maintain focus on the real corruption that generated the impeachment movement we needed a national event. Now that the H.R. 304 had been introduced, national support had been confirmed and the media had begun to turn, Bob Barr seemed more open to do an impeachment-related event with us. We knew that the major media organizations would attempt to distort the event, so we settled on the concept of a town hall to keep everything as refined as possible.

We rented the Cobb Civic Center theater, which was in Bob Barr's district but was also near Newt's adjoining district, We wanted to put pressure on Newt since Barr had mentioned that Newt was holding up at least a hundred more co-sponsors for the resolution. We had a very limited budget for advertising, but the event still drew about 400 people in all. The town hall was free, and we scheduled a reception afterwards for a small fee at a nearby hotel. We divided the event into three phases, a background on impeachment, the allegations and an audience question and answer period.

I did the logistical support and local marketing while John Wheeler did the agenda and press releases. John's contacts and experience were the key to success. He even knew local contacts that became invaluable in their assistance. Our three primary coordinators were Sherry for on-site support, Monica for press contacts and Gene for the stage. My wife and our friends, Jerry and Judy, handled the entrance and product table, along with John Wheeler's son, John Christopher. All were godsends that I would like to acknowledge more fully, but given the now proven Clinton "scorched earth" policy, I feel I must withhold their last names for their protection.

Our only significant problem, aside from countering the Clinton "scorched earth" policy, was that we could not find a host. Most local and national talk show hosts were petrified at the thought of hosting such an event. Because of the complete media blackout of Clinton corruption there was little public understanding or support for impeachment. The hosts were obviously aware of the corruption, but appeared afraid that we would be crazed lunatics ranting and raving at the President.

Therefore, John and I decided to host it ourselves, with his introducing of the speakers and my conducting the town hall. This was a superb idea because it meant we had no major media organization representatives on the stage. We had put our hearts and souls into the event and knew how we wanted to conduct it. We minimized our roles to keep things moving and to the point. Cathy McDonald, the widow of Larry McDonald, knew many of the speakers and was very articulate in helping co-host with John. The audience was well aware that the media would attempt to distort its reaction and was very refined, despite numerous outbreaks of applause.

The event started with Pastor Robert Rutherford's giving a stirring opening prayer that moved the audience to applause. Steve Fitchen of the National Legal Foundation then outlined some remarkable historical facts and precedents of impeachment. Herb Titus followed by contrasting the Nixon and Clinton administrations brilliantly. Howard Phillips then added his fascinating perspective while challenging Congress and Newt Gingrich to do their jobs. Bob Barr, our keynote speaker, then closed out the segment to several standing ovations.

Congressman Helen Chenoweth called in to explain why she co-sponsored H. Res. 304 and Larry Klayman, who was in the middle of preparing depositions in the FBI file case, also called in to report his progress. Pat Matrisciana covered some fascinating experiences in Arkansas and also received a standing ovation. Former Congressman Bill Dannemeyer used his vast experience to detail the abuses of power in Washington, and John McManus closed the second segment with a stunning presentation on the Clinton global agenda.

We decided to circumvent the expected poor TV media coverage by hiring our own filming crew, renting a satellite truck to beam the program up and buying satellite time to send the program to all networks and affiliates. Despite all this, we received only brief, but relatively positive media coverage on each local Atlanta station and national TV network, including *ABC World News Tonight.* We got good coverage from the local *Marietta Daily Journal,* but the *Atlanta Constitution* distorted the event, using a reporter who works directly for Cox Newspapers. He employed a frequently used technique that gave us broad coverage but focused on irrelevant peripheral issues and completely avoided all substantive content in the town hall.

In terms of total coverage, the media blackout continued. NET decided not to cover the event after being bought out just before the town hall by new owners who eventually changed the channel to America's Voice and canceled all Free Congress programming. However, C-Span, the only vehicle for unfiltered political news on TV, was even more disappointing. Despite the historic nature of the first event of its kind in history and the fact that we paid for all filming expense, bought the satellite time to send it to them, hired the same contract video firm that they used in Atlanta and offered them full operational control, C-Span refused to carry the town hall live or taped even though they had no other significant programming scheduled. C-Span would later carry two town halls organized by anti-impeachment Congressmen, Chris Shays (CT) and Bobby Scott (VA).

INCREASING INVOLVEMENT
AND KNOWLEDGE

The National Town Hall on Impeachment led me to a number of new friends who helped stimulate involvement within several metropolitan communities. We began having regular monthly meetings to show videos and disseminate information. I compiled visuals all of the Clinton scandals, computerized them and began giving presentations throughout the metro area. I also began doing presentations for the Impeach Clinton ACTION committee in other states.

I became good friends with Chuck, who agreed to host many of the video showings at his antique mall. He also sent me several informative books and numerous articles to help keep me abreast of the many events that were happening at once. Another person named Victoria, that I met at the town hall, organized an impeachment meeting all by herself. She did the flyers, got some local press coverage and turned out 30 people single-handedly without spending any money on advertising. It was a perfect example of what can be done by a committed citizen.

Eventually I cut a video for a public access channel, was a guest several times on a public access TV show, was a guest on several radio talk shows and even guest hosted a couple of talk shows for John Bennett, the Citizens for Honest Government radio show host, on the American Freedom Network. Don Weideman, founder of American Freedom Network, was one of the first individuals to arrange for radio shows to be broadcast through the Internet. It was a fabulous technology that meant anyone with a computer could get the truth.

I quickly became paranoid when I first started my activities. During my first guest appearance on John Bennett's show, I gave a no holds barred account of the evidence that I had assembled against Bill Clinton and placed into our 25 count Citizens' Presidential Impeachment Indictment. The very next evening the studio burned down. A day after that I returned to an airport to get in my car, only to find the door ajar and the battery run down because the interior light had been on for a couple of days. It took me about a month before I convinced myself that the fire was an accident and that I did not shut the door tightly when I got out of the car.

CLINTON RULE BY EXECUTIVE ORDER

When I was a guest on the John Bennett show, we received a call from Randy Yarborough, another talk show host who was nice enough to send me some research work on executive orders by Dr. Gene Schroder. I had a growing concern that Bill Clinton was systematically dismantling the American form of government with unconstitutional executive orders.

In 1994, Bill Clinton had already implemented Executive Order 12919, which allows the federal government to take over private property under any emergency that he defined, no matter how bogus. Specifically listed are food, water, energy, transportation, health resources, materials and supplies. In 1996, he implemented Executive Order 12986, which appeared to grant immunity to international agencies which take the property of American citizens for conservation purposes. In 1998, he implemented Executive Order 13083, which allowed the federal government to take over specific state government functions for uniformity, cost effectiveness or other regulatory purposes defined by the federal government.

He had also previously issued Presidential Decision Directive 25, which required American troops to serve under foreign United Nations commanders. This resulted in the suit by Michael New, a decorated soldier who refused the unconstitutional order. In the first week of 1999, he would follow this up with Executive Order 13107, which basically subordinated the Bill of Rights to the United Nations.

Paul Begala of the Clinton administration summed up the presidential perspective best when he said; "Stroke of the pen, law of the land, kinda cool". His unconstitutional, anti-American attitude was no problem for MSNBC, which hired Begala as a talk show co-host.

This Executive Order threat was so serious that it forced me to deviate from the impeachment shortly to see if I could get the Republican Congress to deal with them. I thought that this may not be hard since the first sentence of the Constitution states that "All legislative power granted herein is vested in the Congress of the United States..." Congressman Barr introduced legislation on the steps of the Georgia Capitol to stop Executive Order 13083, and many local activists went there to support him. Still, I was bothered by the frustrating prospect of introducing legislation to stop orders that were unconstitutional in the first place, particularly since the legislation could be vetoed.

I then asked Newt Gingrich about it, and he told me Tom Delay's office was checking into it. I called Delay's office only to find that it was such a low priority that no one was working on it. Finally I found a concurrent resolution that was introduced by Congressman Metcalf to void all orders that exceeded the authority of the Executive branch but discovered that it specified no procedure by which to accomplish voiding the orders. In addition, since the bill was only a resolution, it had no basis in law. Thus, the Republicans had proposed three separate solutions to address one threatening issue, and none of the solutions actually solved the problem. I was finally beginning to wonder if Republicans were a true opposition party to Democrats. Before long I would have my answer.

PREPAREDNESS COMES TO ATLANTA

During one of my presentations in a different state, one of the attendees showed me a brochure indicating that Preparedness '98 was coming to Atlanta. It was an excellent exposition and seminar about getting ready for the year 2000. It covered psychological, physical and political aspects. Preparedness gave me the opportunity to meet some interesting people including Steve Vaus, Terry Reed and Bo Gritz. Steve would later put together the Dear Mr. President campaign, using the voices of young children to ask the President to get them out of trouble when they commit the same acts that he did, such as lying. He would also experience media blackout of his paid advertising campaign. But Terry Reed and Bo Gritz provided new revelations for me.

Chuck had given me a copy of the book *Compromised* by Terry Reed. Reed claimed to be a pilot in the Contra operation when Barry Seal, a DEA drug informant and CIA pilot, was assassinated. Reed had implicated both Ollie North and former President, George Bush, in the Mena, Arkansas drug trafficking operation, which he claimed for some period of time was tied to the Contra re-supply effort. I was aware of George Bush's strange background, including his sealed financial records, his membership in the secretive Skull and Bones group at Yale and his mysterious involvement in anti-Castro Cuban activities around the time of the Kennedy assassination. Some researchers already believed that he had knowledge of the Kennedy assassination, and now he was implicated in drug trafficking.

I knew about the involvement of Bill Clinton because CHG videos explained that he was the only authorized payer for the Arkansas Development Finance Authority, which was established by Webster Hubbell and used as a money laundering agency for the Mena drug operation according to ADFA director, Larry Nichols. I was also aware that the money appeared to be laundered through Lasater and Co., owned by Dan Lasater, the President's friend, campaign contributor and apparent cocaine supplier. Lasater, a former employer and apparent supplier of Roger Clinton, was convicted of drug distribution in a case that involved giving cocaine to teenage girls. He was later pardoned by Bill Clinton after serving five months in jail.

I had met Ollie North briefly once and found the charges that Terry Reed raised were hard to believe. I had heard the allegations before when they were raised by talk show host Joe Maddison at a live radio debate with Ollie North at a Washington, D.C. restaurant. Maddison was supported during the debate by a professor who I found to be quite credible with his research in the Kennedy assassination. Terry and his wife, Janis, were quite convincing. Terry graciously answered any question that I had, and Janis talked with me several times over the course of the event. Their sincerity and the debate began to raise serious doubts in my mind about Ollie North.

I also got to meet Bo Gritz, one of America's most decorated Vietnam veteran, whose book, *Called to Serve*, implicated the CIA and DOD in Southeast Asian drug trafficking. This was just a little too much of a stretch for me to think that both our current and former Presidents, who are members of opposing political parties, could be involved in illegal drug trafficking operations. One could possibly be involved, but two from opposite parties? I was reminded by John Birch Society friends that both were members of the Council on Foreign Relations and the Tri-Lateral Commission; however, the concept was still just too difficult from me to perceive at the time.

BILL CLINTON COMES TO ATLANTA

As publicity of Clinton wrongdoing grew, protesters were appearing most everywhere he traveled. My stomach turned when I found that he decided to come to Atlanta to attend a fundraiser for Democrat Michael Coles, a cookie company founder who ran against Republican Senator Paul Coverdell. I had met Michael Coles two years earlier in a park when he was challenging Speaker Newt Gingrich for his 6th District Congressional seat. I explained to him at that time about

Clinton corruption in Arkansas and sent him the *Obstruction of Justice* and *Mena Cover-up* videos. He promised me that he would view them and get back to me. I called his office a half a dozen times, extending to months after the elections. Neither he nor anyone in his office ever responded.

I determined from this experience that Michael Coles would simply be part of the corruption if he ever were elected to public office. I concluded that we could not let Bill Clinton come to town without showing him we cared about what he had done to America. I decided to try to help organize my first protest ever on that day, August 9. My friends, Jerry, Bill and Victoria and many others, including the "Chicken Men", turned out with impeachment signs.

The heavily pro-Clinton Atlanta police tried to move us to areas where the cameras could not record us and literally ordered us off a public sidewalk at one time, falsely claiming that it was the property of the hotel that Clinton was visiting. In one case they ordered another man who was not with us to cross the street and then arrested him for jaywalking while he crossed.

Despite their efforts and the interesting way in which most local news stations avoided covering us, one local station decided to balance its coverage by including one of the "Chicken Men" and me. They asked me what I thought about Michael Coles' having Bill Clinton do a fundraiser for him. My response was "I am amazed that Michael Coles would tie his campaign to what I believe is the most corrupt President in U.S. history." To my astonishment, I made the first five minutes of the six o'clock news.

As Bill Clinton left downtown, I was the last person with an impeachment sign just as he entered the interstate. He looked at me, saw the sign, smiled and waved as though he appreciated the publicity, even if it was negative. I marveled at his confidence, but it would only be just over another week before his attitude began to change.

Perhaps the most interesting part of Bill Clinton's visit for me was making contact with General Barry McCaffrey, his appointed drug czar, who was appearing with him at a drug prevention rally. He was also scheduled to appear at *Talk Back Live* in the afternoon, so I went there again, this time to raise the issue of government involvement in drug trafficking. I had raised that issue with one of his staff members months earlier at a meeting. Just seconds after the staff member told me that he had plenty of time to discuss any issue, the staffer said that he had to leave.

At *Talk Back Live*, I tried to get a watered down question past the host and producer while we were live, but I could not. I eventually was forced to ask the general a question while they were cleverly prescreening during the commercial breaks. I asked him to address it live, but naturally he would not. However, after the show I caught him off line. Three times I raised the issue of drug trafficking in Mena, Arkansas and asked for help in resolving the murders of Kevin Ives and Don Henry. All three times the general turned and walked away from me without saying a word. I decided that my suspicions had been confirmed and that the war on drugs and its drug czar were frauds.

BILL CLINTON IS TRAPPED

By now the media attacks on Bill Clinton's sexual morality were reaching a frenzy while the evidence of his other crimes were completely blacked out. Clinton had testified in the Paula Jones suit that he did not have sex with Monica Lewinsky and repeatedly denied having an affair with her to the press. In one pressure situation, he pointed his finger and sternly uttered his famous quote, "I want you to listen to me. I am going to say this again. I did not have sexual relations with that woman,... Miss Lewinsky."

Linda Tripp, who was an assistant in Bernard Nussbaum's office and one of the last people to see Vince Foster alive, approached Starr's office, telling him she had taped some of her conversations with Lewinsky and proved that Bill Clinton was lying about their affair. Lewinsky, then in a bind, decided to switch lawyers and eventually cooperated with Starr's team by giving them truthful testimony in exchange for immunity which was agreed to on July 28, 1998.

Her testimony created another major problem for the President. It seems that during one of his trysts with Lewinsky he left a deposit on her dress. Lewinsky did not have the dress cleaned, based on advice from Tripp, and the Starr team sent it out for DNA testing. The mess on the dress caused Clinton to confess. On August 17, 1998, after Tripp and Lewinsky testified before the Starr grand jury, Bill Clinton testified in a special deal with Ken Starr via closed circuit television from the White House.

It was a now famous disaster, which had him redefining the word "is" regarding the state of his relationship with Lewinsky. He also redefined the word "alone" regarding his time together with her when they met in the Oval office. That night Bill Clinton went on national television to admit his "inappropriate relationship". Clinton had committed perjury in the Paula Jones civil suit trial and likely in the Starr grand jury trial as well. Three days later, on August 20, Clinton bombed an asprin factory in Sudan that was allegedly making chemical weapons and bombed targets in Afghanistan to retaliate for bombed African embassies. The Afghanistan government had nothing to do with the bombings and the allegations against the asprin factory were proven to be unfounded. We would soon learn that he planned the bombing without consulting a single one of his Joint Chiefs of Staff.

Paula Jones appealed Judge Wright's ruling and eventually settled her suit out of court for $850,000. She was the victim of an IRS tax audit immediately after filing her suit, despite the fact that her husband made only $30,000 a year. Tripp, along with another White House aide, Kathleen Willey, were victims of many harassing incidents.

Willey went public with information that Clinton had made sexual advances to her in the White House when she asked to move from volunteer status to paid staff. The Willey incident occurred on the day her husband was found shot to death in a northern Virginia park. His death was also ruled a suicide, much like the death of Vince Foster. Ed Willey was one of eight people involved in Clinton-related campaign financing who mysteriously died. These people were part of a bigger list containing around 70 names of people related to Bill Clinton who mysteriously died of suicide, unsolved murder, plane and car crashes or heart attacks.

THE STARR REPORT

During this time, anticipation was growing because the Starr team had announced that they would produce a report to Congress, which may identify impeachable offenses. Starr had jurisdiction over the FBI file scandal, the Travel Office scandal and Whitewater-related activity. Yet the major media organizations suggested that his report would likely include only the sexual scandal. It was almost inconceivable that Starr would leave out impeachable offenses from all of the investigations he had conducted into the Clinton administration during the last four years. The Starr team had only begun the sex scandal investigation during the previous year, so it would be very unusual if that were completed before the other investigations had finished.

Sure enough though, the Starr report was released on September 9, 1998, and the media organizations were found to be correct. The report built a credible case for impeachment based on six counts of perjury and essentially five counts involving obstruction of justice, but all exclusively involved the sexual activity of Bill Clinton, primarily in regards to Monica Lewinsky. It was apparent that someone on the Starr team was leaking information to the media.

The Starr report still created a frenzy when it was placed on the Internet. It was also produced in book form, which generated significant public interest, despite the fact that none of the more serious evidence and crimes were included in it. Despite its limitation, the report did attract attention to the topic of impeachment. All of a sudden, conservative and even non-conservative talk show hosts, all who thought impeachment was crazy a year earlier, were beginning to use the dreaded "I" word.

Starr had spent four years and $40 million investigating the other scandals. His team had reportedly recovered about $30 million in various fines and obtained nearly 20 convictions, making it the second most successful investigation in history. However, every time the trail led to Bill Clinton or his close associates the investigation would go nowhere in spite of the evidence.

We were somewhat suspicious of Starr because we believed he had already covered up the murder of Vince Foster; however, for him to ignore four years of investigative research and evidence was still a surprise. We had known for over a year that the media organizations would deliberately focus on sexual-related problems to protect Bill Clinton, but we did not know that Ken Starr would become an accomplice to the scheme.

REFERENCES

Col. James "Bo" Gritz, *Called to Serve*, Lazarus Publishing.

The National Town Hall on Impeachment (video)- March 14, 1998, Citizens for Honest Government.

New American magazine special report, Conspiracy for Global Control.

Terry Reed & John Cummings, *Compromised*, Shapolsky Publishers.

Obstruction of Justice (video), Integrity Films.

Dr. Gene Schroder, *War and Emergency Powers*, American Agriculture Movement.

CHAPTER FIVE
THE MILLENIUM BETRAYAL

THE IMPEACHMENT INQUIRY BEGINS

This lack of evidence and limited scope of the Starr report were cause for serious concern, but there was still the primary avenue that would rectify even a compromised independent counsel. The opposition party, called Republicans, controlled both sides of Congress and had the authority to include whatever it felt was appropriate in Articles of Impeachment.

Since the success or failure of the impeachment conviction hinged on the evidence included in the articles, I decided to ask Newt about this. He had always given his constituents straight answers even if it meant disagreeing with them. I caught Newt after a special event at his campaign headquarters one Saturday just before the House inquiry vote and simply asked him if Articles of Impeachment are created would they include evidence of other impeachable offenses collected in some of the 10 or so Congressional investigations. I was somewhat relieved when he replied, "That's exactly what would happen."

On October 8, 1998, the House of Representatives voted 258-176 to open an impeachment inquiry. Unbeknown to me, an hour or so later, a report from the CIA Inspector General regarding CIA drug trafficking allegations was also publicly released and would eventually prove that I had acquired a false sense of relief.

THE MARCH FOR JUSTICE

In October, just before one of my impeachment presentations, my friend, Victoria, told me about something called March for Justice in Washington, D.C. It was a rally organized by members of Free Republic, a non-profit web site founded by Jim Robinson, a software developer, who had created the web site in his spare time. He was attempting to gather concerned citizens together by announcing the March for Justice exclusively through the web site. I was skeptical and told her I did not really want to go, especially since it was on Halloween. In a couple more weeks, I had a dramatic change of mind.

A few days before Halloween, I received a call from someone named Roger, who would also eventually become a good friend. Roger, who was an attendee of our National Town Hall on Impeachment, called to say he had a discount air ticket that was not being used and that I could have it for a paltry sum of about 50 bucks. He also convinced me, without hardly trying, of the importance of the event. I decided to go. Victoria also went, and Roger met us there.

It was an incredible event at the Washington Monument attended by about 5,000 people. The speakers included Alan Keyes, Bob Barr, Larry Klayman, Gary Aldrich and many others. There was every kind of custom sign and costume imaginable. One guy posed in a full PLA uniform carrying a model of a nuclear missile, while his friend had a Bill Clinton mask and a suit with dollar bills sticking out of it. Another was dressed as a cigar, in reference to what Monica did with a cigar during one of her trysts with Bill Clinton. C-Span reluctantly decided to cover the event after some significant pressure. The event was particularly historic since it was probably the first major Washington rally held to impeach an American President, and it had been arranged and promoted almost exclusively over the Internet by volunteers.

THE 1998 ELECTION

The March for Justice took place the weekend before the election. The Clinton corruption was expected to be a boon for Republicans in the 1998 elections. However, the Republicans never made Clinton corruption an issue in the election, except for a few last ditch commercials that briefly mentioned soft points such as "What do we tell the children?" In fact, Republicans had no real agenda at all. As a result, the Republicans broke even with Democrats in the Senate and lost five seats of their majority in the House since most of the American public believed that the impeachment movement was merely about sex.

One of the Republican leaders behind the election strategy was House Speaker Newt Gingrich. That was particularly interesting since Newt had promised earlier that he would mention real Clinton corruption in every one of his speeches. Many House Republicans were already upset with him because they felt he had compromised the conservative agenda. After the election, a handful of them reportedly went to Newt saying that they would vote for Minority Leader Dick Gephardt as Speaker. That would be enough to offset a new razor-thin Republican majority and cause the Speaker position to change hands back to Democrats.

Newt decided to resign the position to heal the division in the party. Since he would no longer be Speaker, he also decided to resign his House seat after winning his district by a 70 percent to 30 percent margin. Bob Livingston, the Appropriations Committee chairman who had already solicited House Republicans to be the next Speaker after Newt left, was selected to succeed Newt. It was a stunning turn of events. The Clinton administration was riddled with corruption, but the Speaker of the House resigned.

JUDICIAL WATCH INTERIM IMPEACHMENT REPORT

A significant portion of the Clinton administration corruption had been expertly assembled via documents and testimony compiled into a newly released Interim Impeachment Report to Congress from the lawyers at Judicial Watch. The report outlined impeachable offenses in the Travel Office and FBI file cases and the China scandal, which had been originally uncovered when Judicial Watch founder, Larry Klayman, deposed John Huang.

In the Travel Office case, the Clintons had fired Billy Dale and the Travel Office staff to bring in their own friends. This was actually an acceptable practice for the President, but the Clintons went much further. They filed frivolous charges against Billy Dale, which were dismissed in two hours by a grand jury. After he was fired, the IRS suddenly showed up to audit Billy Dale's Altair air charter service, and his FBI file was believed to be illegally obtained when Craig Livingstone told the FBI that Dale was being "considered for access".

In the FBI file case, White House Counsel Bernard Nussbaum signed for and Security Chief, Craig Livingstone appeared to illegally obtain over 1,000 FBI files, mostly on Clinton adversaries. Nussbaum had access to both Clintons, and two FBI agents were told by White House Counsel William Kennedy that Hillary Clinton hired Livingstone. The FBI agent statments were later corroborated in a documnet uncovered by Judicial Watch. Two Secret Service agents contradicted Livingstone's testimony that his list of individuals was left over from the Bush administration. The agents were later illegally investigated by the Treasury Department. There was also a six-month gap of file access records that were either lost or destroyed.

In addition, the Judicial Watch Interim Impeachment Report laid out against the President a serious case of jeopardizing national security. The report showed how the President had forced the hiring of John Huang at the DNC and Commerce Department and how Huang had received a top secret clearance and made many phone calls back to LIPPO GROUP subsidiaries. He also helped arranged seats on trade missions in exchange for donations. The report was impressive and similar to what we had expected from Ken Starr. Larry Klayman gave it to House Judiciary Chairman Henry Hyde, who said the House Judiciary Committee would consider it in the Articles for Impeachment. It turned out to be another broken Republican promise.

STARR TESTIFIES

The majority Republican Judiciary Committee conformed to the Republican election strategy by delaying any movement on the Starr report until after the 1998 elections. When they did, they decided to call special counsel, Ken Starr, for testimony instead of the fact-based witnesses. For over a year, Starr had been badgered by major media organizations, which portrayed him as a conservative Republican out to get the President. We knew that this was one of the biggest lies of all.

Christopher Ruddy had done some interesting reporting in regards to the Starr appointment and ongoing investigation. He found that Starr, who had been on Janet Reno's short list when she appointed Robert Fiske, had staffed the team with many liberal Democrats, including Mark Tuohey, who had thrown a party for Janet Reno in his house. Starr hired Sam Dash, who later tried to claim that Starr had ethically overstepped his bounds. Starr also hired Miguel Rodriguez, a liberal Democrat who was sincerely trying to solve the Vince Foster murder. Rodriguez complained to Starr that Tuohey was interfering with the investigation, and when Starr did nothing, Rodriguez resigned, citing ethics problems. Starr even failed to conclude that the White House had produced talking points that someone had apparently given to Monica Lewinsky.

During the hearing, Starr handled himself almost flawlessly. He showed that his case had merit and that he was far from having any bias. He even received a standing ovation from many of the people in the hearing room when he concluded. But during the testimony, he casually dropped a couple of bombshells. He told Clinton defense lawyer, David Kendall, that he did not find impeachable offenses in the Travel Office investigation or the FBI file investigation, and he stated that he had not made a determination in Whitewater. Perhaps the most incredulous statement in his testimony was when he testified, "The controversy surrounding the death of Vince Foster has dissipated because of our thorough and accurate reporting."

During the testimony, Congressman Barr asked Starr point-blank if he had interviewed Mack McLarty, the chief of staff, in regards to the FBI file case. Starr answered that he believed that his staff had done so. In reality, the Starr team had not interviewed McLarty, and I believe Starr had to know it.

Larry Klayman of Judicial Watch had been making a point on talk shows for several weeks that the depositions he had taken in the Judicial Watch lawsuits indicated that Starr had not interviewed chief of staff McLarty or records manager, Terry Good. This was significant because evidence uncovered by Judicial Watch indicated that McLarty was the individual who changed the FBI file acquisition procedure to bypass the FBI resident White House liaison, Dennis Sculimbrene. Even if that were not true, it was virtually impossible to determine that no impeachable offenses existed without interviewing both of them.

I found it fascinating that Starr had been portrayed as a strong Christian with high moral values when in reality, it seemed that he had repeatedly done everything within his power to protect Bill Clinton. I concluded that Starr had, in all likelihood, lied multiple times under oath, protected Bill Clinton's illegal use of FBI files and persecution of Travel Office staff members, and worst of all, covered up the murder of Vince Foster.

It was already clear that the Starr report would not be adequate for an impeachment conviction. Former Congressman Dannemeyer and I, along with many other concerned citizens, exerted as much pressure as possible on the House Republican leadership and House Judiciary Committee members to include in the Articles of Impeachment, more serious Congressional evidence before sending the articles to the House floor for a vote. It would prove to be a fruitless effort for all of us.

THE DEPARTMENT OF INJUSTICE

The China scandal had just been fully detailed in the new book, *Year of the Rat*, co-authored by Ed Timperlake and Bill Triplett, investigators in the Burton and Thompson committees. The information from the investigations had been accessible for almost two years, but now the American public had a simple, readily available document that they could read to find out the severity of the problem. The book showed that the Clinton / Gore campaigns and the DNC had seven sources of illegal revenue traceable through 11 revenue streams to the Communist Chinese government. Several of the sources were known Communist Chinese agents and/or members of Asian organized crime. The book also illustrated some of the very sophisticated military technology that the Clinton administration gave the Communist Chinese government over the objections of the Department of Defense, Department of State, Department of Justice and the National Security Administration.

However, no amount of information seemed to make a difference. Janet Reno had already refused three separate 1997 House requests for an independent counsel to investigate DNC fundraising. In addition, FBI Director Louis Freeh recommended an independent counsel, but Reno ignored him. Justice Department investigator, Charles Labella, was hired and after a preliminary study also recommended an independent counsel, but Reno refused again, and Labella returned to San Diego as acting U.S. attorney, a position that he was later denied.

The House Government Reform and Oversight Committee, chaired by Dan Burton, requested the memos, and Janet Reno refused to comply, so they voted to hold her in contempt. Finally she allowed the House Judiciary Committee counsels to review the memos at the Justice Department but not to take any notes about the content. Both the minority counsel and majority counsel, David Schippers, who had been recently hired by Henry Hyde, were Democrats. The House Judiciary Committee members were not allowed to see the unredacted memos.

Schippers wanted to pursue the more serious charges and eventually proved to be another Democrat who seemed sincere in wanting to do the right thing. However, House Republican leaders eventually shut down his efforts and refused even to vote on the contempt recommendation by the House Judiciary Committee.

RESIGNATION AND IMPEACHMENT ENDORSEMENTS

By now endorsements for resignation and impeachment were growing. We had already gotten long-term informal support from the U.S. Taxpayers Party, which was eventually and appropriately renamed to the Constitution Party. The California Republican Party became the first political organization to pass an impeachment resolution, which was co-authored by Ray Morton, whom I met at Promise Keepers. It called for the impeachment of both Bill Clinton and Al Gore. Soon after, a few other state Republican Parties followed suit.

In June of 1998, the Libertarians became the first national party to pass an impeachment resolution. Then Paul McHale from Pennsylvania became the first Democrat to call for resignation. He was immediately attacked by Geraldo Rivera, a Clinton "scorched earth" facilitator, who appeared to distort McHale's military record, but eventually backed off. It took tremendous courage for McHale to speak out against Clinton. My own representative, Newt Gingrich, who was supposed to be the leader of the opposition party, had gone stunningly silent and would remain so, despite the fact that months earlier he said he would mention Clinton corruption in every speech.

ROSS PEROT JOINS THE FRAY

In the midst of all of the hoopla, the Reform Party came to Atlanta for its annual convention. I knew the state director, Anne Merkl, who had given Congressman Barr an award for opposing fast track at one of the town halls I attended. I had also met some of the other members during my election eve experience at *Talk Back Live* in 1996. I had never been to a political convention before, so I decided to attend.

I found the platform debate interesting but noticed a large controversy over the issue of qualifying delegates from the State of New Jersey. I ended up spending a lot of time talking to the New Jersey delegates. I concluded that Vice President Pat Benjamin, who was from New Jersey, had heisted control of the delegation in a power play that was supported by President Russell Verney. I noticed that Russell Verney had lost the respect of many of the members and that was part of the reason why membership was dropping. While I was there, I tracked down Dale Barlow and asked her to run for President. I had remembered her from watching the last Reform Party convention.

I sized up the situation quickly because I had my own experience with Verney when I tried to get Ross Perot to speak at our National Town Hall on Impeachment. I sent Citizens for Honest Government videos to Ross Perot by way of Verney, but they were never acknowledged. Verney, a former Democrat Party state chairman, had told me at the time that "Whitewater was a two-bit land deal", and I challenged him on it. I was sure that was a lie because of the clear evidence that Bill Clinton assisted James McDougal in bilking what eventually cost us $60,000,000 of taxpayer money from Madison Guaranty after being told by his State Department and the Federal Home Loan Bank Board about Madison's insolvency in advance of its closure. A couple of members at the convention confirmed to me that they were not surprised since they had similar experiences with Verney's credibility.

The highlight of the convention was the Saturday evening speech by Ross Perot, which was carried live on C-Span. I got to sit on the third row. He spoke mostly about the need for Bill Clinton to resign and got about 15 standing ovations in roughly

20 minutes. I was bobbing up and down like a jack-in-the-box. He questioned Clinton's ability to lead, his sexual immorality, his drug usage and his potential threat to this nation.

I shook his hand afterwards and told him what a great speech it was, but inside something still seemed strange. Missing from the speech were virtually all of Clinton's serious crimes, including criminal activity in Arkansas, treason and bribery with the Communist Chinese government, abusive use of government agencies to persecute political adversaries and the obstructions of justice involving drug trafficking and organized crime.

Shortly thereafter, Perot went on the *Larry King Live Show* again to announce a campaign to force Bill Clinton to resign. I was suspicious because Perot never mentioned the serious crimes and never sought the impeachment of Bill Clinton, only his resignation. Many organizations had already collected millions of impeachment petitions, but Perot wanted to start collecting resignation petitions and take them to Washington on Pearl Harbor Day. I would show up there on Pearl Harbor Day, but Ross would be nowhere to be found. He later turned the petitions over to Senator Joseph Lieberman, a Connecticut Democrat who voted to dismiss the case against Bill Clinton without even hearing the evidence. This convinced me that the Ross Perot and the Reform Party leadership were not really on our side.

NATIONWIDE RALLIES

By now the impeachment inquiry had triggered a series of rallies across the country. Citizens for Honest Government had done one in Los Angeles that drew thousands of people and had to be run twice back to back to accommodate everybody. There were three rallies in the San Fransisco Bay area that also drew thousands to each one.

I got involved with these when a future friend named Dan called Citizens for Honest Government and told them he was putting on a rally in San Diego. They asked me to call and see if he needed any assistance because I had helped organize the National Town Hall on Impeachment. I called Dan, related some of my experiences to him, and we became good friends.

He already had most everything under control and was planning a fabulous event in the heart of Balboa Park, complete with props, guest host and a superb Ben Franklin impersonator. Since I had been closely supporting the Presidential impeachment effort of Bob Barr, he invited me to bring a message from him and speak. I simply could not turn that invitation down. I loved San Diego, could not wait to see the event and had years of thoughts balled up inside of me that were dying to get out.

I had done many presentations around town, but these were technical in nature and let the audience make up their own minds based on the facts that I assembled. A public speech at a rally was something different because it had to stir the crowd into a frenzy of emotion. I was not satisfied with many of the speeches that I had heard and wanted mine to be stronger and more factually based. I struggled to come up with a workable structure that would not be a boring recital of facts. I had also heard many great lines and seen many catchy signs by now and wanted to share them with the audience. Finally I came upon a concept of presenting the case against Bill Clinton in single bullet fact points with some props to support my case and related applause lines dispersed throughout after every two or three points.

Dan had assembled a great array of speakers and drew several hundred people. I was scheduled to go later in the program, but a couple of speakers were a little behind schedule in showing up, so Dan wanted to move me up to second speaker. I was sandwiched between Mason Weaver, the dynamic talk show host who authored *It's OK to Leave the Plantation* and former Congressman Bill Dannemeyer, another superb speaker who was to draw a standing ovation. It was a pressure situation, but I never knew it. I was so fired up to get out on the stage that I could barely wait. The speech concept worked great; I was able to have one of the most factual presentations with many rounds of applause. Dan had a fabulous rally. I spent the night at his ranch and was hooked on public rally speaking after that.

After I got back, I left a message for another organizer that I tracked down on the Free Republic web site to see how her rallies had gone. Her name was Jennifer, and when I got her return voice mail message, I was stunned. She was so articulate, sincere and passionate about her cause that I played her message over and over. She had organized two rallies that had drawn several hundred people each. It would be just a short time before I got to meet her and see her in action.

In the meantime, Jim Robinson received another call from Gary Aldrich, who after talking with Bob Barr, asked him to do another rally in Washington for the Judiciary Committee hearings. It was on short notice, less than a month after the first one, but Jim agreed and another 500 people returned for a rally at the Capitol steps. Most of the same speakers returned to make it another great event. Jennifer also attended and requested that her name be added to the agenda. Since it was a smaller event, they agreed, and when her turn came, she stole the show, proving that passionate citizens make the best speakers.

A MARCH FOR TRUTH

When had I talked to Jennifer on the phone, she mentioned to me that someone from the Atlanta metro area was organizing a rally in Washington for Pearl Harbor Day, December 7, the Monday after the second Free Republic rally. I was stunned because I didn't know about the rally, and I did not know the organizer, whose name was Michelle. I was still on a high from San Diego, so I called her to find out if she needed another speaker or any other help.

She told me that she had attended the National Town Hall on Impeachment, was frustrated with Clinton administration and felt that she had to do something about it. She already had a permit for Lafayette Square Park across from the White House. I was stunned to find out she had organized the rally with some other folks from different parts of the country, and they had marketed it exclusively through the Internet at a cost of next to nothing.

But Michelle had run into some problems and told me there was a lot of work left to be done. I found out that her funding was undependable and the agenda was still not together even though there were only a couple of weeks left until the event. Eventually the organization in Washington, D.C. that was to help sponsor it backed out, and we were left on our own. It was crunch time.

Michelle had done an incredible job in proving that a couple of people could organize a rally for a great American cause in remote location through the Internet. We could not let it fail. I helped her with the agenda and the funding, and we took up a collection at the rally to help offset some of the costs. Debbie from Virginia stepped in to handle the logistics and also contributed some funds. It was a true citizen-sponsored, citizen-organized and citizen-funded event.

The agenda turned out to be great. We got Howard Phillips to attend, along with Carmen Pate of Concerned Women of America and Paul Weyrich, who had established the Heritage Foundation, Free Congress Foundation, America's Voice TV channel and the *American Investigator* TV program. Pat Matrisciana just happened to be planning a visit to town that weekend. So he and John Wheeler spoke, and Pat filmed the event for his next video, *The Real Crimes of Bill Clinton*. He got great shots of the crowd chants at the event and filmed the long line parading in front of the White House, led by Piper George, our bagpipe player and by now, regular rally attendee. In the front of the line was a little girl carrying a sign saying "Lying is bad, Mr. President." She had figured out what 44 Democrat senators and over 200 Democrat representatives could not understand.

ARTICLES OF IMPEACHMENT

On the following Friday, December 11, the Judiciary Committee voted along party lines to move four Articles of Impeachment onto the House floor. The Articles were: perjury in Grand Jury testimony, perjury in the Paula Jones civil suit, obstruction of justice and abuse of power. Three articles passed 21-16 and one article passed 20-15, with Lindsey Graham casting the only dissenting Republican vote. All articles related solely to the charges in the Starr report.

While most people would expect that moving articles of impeachment out of the Judiciary Committee at long last, would be a great relief to those in the impeachment movement, many of us knew better. All of the evidence of the serious Clinton crimes collected in 10 other investigations authorized by the Republican Congress had been ignored by the Republican majority on the House Judiciary Committee. The evidence included criminal activity in Arkansas, abusive use of government agencies to persecute political adversaries, treason and bribery with the Communist Chinese government and a whole host of obstructions of justice with Janet Reno, even involving drug trafficking and organized crime.

The relatively pitiful Articles of Impeachment meant that the Republicans were helping the major media organizations to continue deceiving the American people into thinking that Bill Clinton simply had a personal problem and that the impeachment movement was just a matter about sex. Most Americans had been completely shielded from the real evidence, and many thought that the people who started the impeachment movement were some kind of sex police.

The Republican leadership helped the media mislead the American people into thinking there was no smoking gun in all of the rest of the evidence. I felt seriously betrayed because I knew better. It appeared that Republicans deliberately wanted the impeachment to fail in the Senate. The only question was: "Who made this decision and why?" Former Congressman Dannemeyer had asked Chairman Hyde several times but never gotten a straight answer, even though they were friends. Hyde had publicly claimed that those decisions were "above my pay grade." I was determined to find out what happened.

The next day, Saturday, December 12, Newt Gingrich was having his final town hall before his resignation became effective. I decided that I could get my answer from him. I had already asked Congressman Barr why the evidence was excluded, and he dodged my question by saying that, "We are concentrating on these charges for now." While I thought that Barr represented our interests much better than Newt, Barr was a little more reluctant to field pointed questions openly, perhaps because of his CIA background prior to becoming a U.S. attorney. One of the things I liked best about Newt was that he would always give his constituents a straight answer even if he did not agree with them.

I went to the town hall, wearing my impeachment button and peach ribbon that Roger had given me at the first large

Free Republic rally. I had made many friends there because I had passed out indictments at many previous town halls. The town hall attendees paid Newt Gingrich many compliments and touted his accomplishments. I noticed that one participant had already asked him why the China evidence was not included in the Articles of Impeachment. Newt's reply was that the Cox Committee was looking into that and the investigation was not yet finished.

When it was my turn, I wanted to start with a compliment, so I told Newt that I hated to see him go, but there was some poetic justice in the fact that he would still be Speaker the next week when "I believe that the House or Representatives will stand with the citizens of this country and against the media and vote to impeach President Bill Clinton." The crowd applauded.

I then followed up on the China question by mentioning that there was already enough evidence collected by the Burton and Thompson committees to prove both treason and bribery. In addition, evidence from a total of 11 other Congressional investigations showed criminal activity in Arkansas, abuses of power in Washington and a whole host of obstructions of justice. "I'd like to know why all of this evidence was left out of the Articles of Impeachment." I concluded by saying, "And, Newt, I ask this question because many people within the impeachment movement are concerned that the Republican Party leadership has done this in a deliberate attempt to fail the impeachment process in the Senate."

I had begun to walk away from the mike when Newt brushed the question off by replying "Go ask Bob Barr". Despite all of the confrontations that he had with the major media organizations, it was the first time that I had ever seen Newt not answer a question candidly. I was particularly surprised since I was his constituent, but I knew that I had struck a real nerve.

Since it was Newt's special day, I didn't want to come back and tell him that I already asked Bob Barr and we had asked Henry Hyde, too. Their response and Newt's evasive answer made me realize that the House Republican leadership and not the House Judiciary Committee majority had ultimately made the decision. Impeachment manager, Lindsey Graham, also confirmed this to me later and I believe he told me the truth.

Newt's unwillingness to address the question and his ultimate position of power as the leader of House Republicans led me to a reluctant but rather obvious conclusion. I realized that the John Birch Society had been right all along and it was Newt who had held up the evidence all of this time. The man who I once admired more than any other Congressman turned out to be the protector of perhaps, the most corrupt President in U.S. history.

CAN C-SPAN BE TRUSTED?

I was still contemplating the Republican designed impeachment failure the next evening, Sunday, the 13th, when I turned on C-Span and found out that it was broadcasting Newt's town hall. I was glad that my question would be made public and other Americans could reach the same conclusion that I had. I thought that it was strange that even though the audience cameras were in place during the shooting, the video focused on Newt the whole time and did not zoom in on any people asking the questions, as C-Span normally does. I watched the entire event carefully and saw myself first, sitting in the audience and then standing in line. When the time came for my question, all of a sudden the next person in line was asking his question. I had been cut straight out of the town hall in one of the most professional editing jobs I had ever seen. I was flabbergasted because I thought that C-Span did not edit events.

On Monday, I called C-Span and had a great deal of difficulty reaching the production department. I left my request for an explanation with viewer services and followed up on it after a few days. When I found out they had done nothing, I decided to get some help. I described what had happened in an Email to a national list that we had established and on the Free Republic web site.

The friends I had developed nationwide peppered C-Span with calls, faxes and Emails until we finally got a believable answer. At first, C-Span gave us several blatantly false replies. One C-Span representative said that they did not edit events until I explained that we had the tape and witnesses to prove otherwise. Another C-Span representative said it was a glitch in production until I explained how it was one of the most professional editing jobs I had ever seen.

Finally, when we persisted, a third C-Span representative checked the tape logs and found that there was a change of tape at the 74-minute mark of the town hall which was about when I asked my question. I was still suspicious, but I accepted that answer and E-mailed it back to all of the people who had helped me. I found out later in an Email reply that a friend in South Carolina had a similar experience when his live question for Brian Lamb was edited out of the posted transcripts. These occurrences, added to my experience with C-Span during our National Town Hall on Impeachment, made three strikes for the only network that I depended on to tell me the truth.

CLINTON IMPEACHED

The following Thursday, December 18, was supposed to be impeachment eve. By now many American citizens were communicating via Email and web sites like www.FreeRepublic.com, which had been created by software developer, Jim Robinson, in his spare time. The citizens had visited local offices of their representatives and bombarded them with faxes, Emails, calls and letters. The Capitol switchboard numbers were frequently jammed with their calls. Millions of petitions had been signed, collected and sent to Congress by dozens of civic organizations. Many concerned citizens participated in town halls and talk shows, explained facts to their friends and even attempted to pressure media organizations to tell the truth. Although all of this effort was almost totally unreported by the major media organizations, it was the final key to impeachment passage. More and more uncommitted representatives were forced to announce their support for impeachment.

Reports indicated that in the morning Bill Clinton was told he did not have the votes to stop his impeachment. Less than four hours later he issued a bombing strike against Iraq, which had been cooperating with weapons inspectors for several months and had even let inspectors enter Baath Party headquarters just days earlier. Iraq had been out of compliance with weapons inspections months before, and Bill Clinton had done nothing. Former U.N. weapons inspector, Scott Ritter, confirmed that Iraq had shuffled its weapons during that period and had begun cooperating again.

Bill Clinton had needlessly jeopardized the lives of American troops just to save his position of power. The Democrats screamed that our troops were now in harm's way; therefore, we should support them by postponing the impeachment vote. In a heated internal meeting, the Republicans decided to delay beginning the impeachment debate for one day until Friday.

On Saturday, December 20, the full House of Representatives continued the impeachment debate from the previous evening and held the impeachment vote. Bob Livingston, the prospective Speaker Elect who was expected to be the victim of a Clinton "scorched earth" attack for secret sexual escapades, challenged the President to resign. Some of the House Democrats, acting almost like a band of demons, began yelling "you resign" as he was speaking. Livingston then stunned America by saying that he would set an example for the President and resign. He read the rest of his prepared speech, which outlined the terms of his resignation.

After a few more hours of debate, votes were taken. The first article, perjury before a Grand Jury, passed 228-206; the second article, perjury in the Paula Jones civil suit, failed 205-229; the third article, obstruction of justice, passed 221-212; and the fourth article failed 148-285. The brave Democrats who voted for the passed impeachment articles included Reps. McHale (PA), Goode (VA) Steinholm (TX), Hall (TX) and Taylor (MS). Republicans who voted against the first impeachment article included Reps. Shays (CT), King (NY), Houghton (NY), Morella (MD) and Souder (IN). Souder voted for the third article of impeachment which passed despite the fact that Republican dissenters were joined by Reps. Johnson (CT), Boehlert (NY), Regula (OH), Castle (DE), Kim (CA), Leach (IA) and McHugh (NY)

Many of the Democrat members of the House walked out briefly during the first vote for a pre-staged press conference just outside the Capitol. They wanted an unconstitutional censure motion that would criticize the President with no consequences. After the votes, the morally bankrupt Democrat House members assembled on the White House lawn for a pep rally where Vice President Gore proclaimed Clinton to be "one of the greatest Presidents" ever.

Nevertheless, there was some relief. The House had finally impeached Bill Clinton, and we had achieved a major objective even if it was for the wrong reasons. We overcame a massive media distortion campaign that was protecting the most powerful person in the world. The House then voted for the Republicans on the Judiciary Committee to become the managers of the prosecution's case. These included: Barr (GA), Buyer (IN), Bryant (TN), Canady (FL), Cannon (UT), Chabot (OH), Gekas (PA), Graham (SC), Hutchinson (AK), Hyde (IL), McCollum (FL), Rogan (CA) and Sensenbrenner (WI).

Roger, Victoria, my wife and I celebrated with Victoria and her family at her house. It was supposed to be a Christmas party, but it turned into more of an impeachment party. The rest of the guests seemed happy with House vote as well. None of us were out to put an indelible stain on Bill Clinton's record; we were out to save America from what we believed may be the most corrupt President in U.S. history. We also knew that the Republican Party had left us a procedure designed to fail the required two-thrids majority Senate vote, but we still did not know why.

SENATE TRIAL

While the new year brought on anticipation of the Senate trial, the media wasted no time in formulating its attack. One strategy was to imply that Republicans had to cater to Democrats for the sake of bipartisanship while the other was to force a premature conclusion and prevent the evidence from being exposed. The major media organizations only had one question before the trial: "When will it end?" They never asked questions like "How will you determine the truth?" or "How will you ensure that all of the evidence is presented?" They simply wanted it to end before it began. NBC, under tremendous pressure, even delayed its interview of Juanita Broaddrick until after the impeachment trial was over, claiming that it needed more time to check facts. Broaddrick explained in the interview how Bill Clinton had raped her while he was running for Governor in Arkansas.

The Senate trial had not even begun before it was corrupted when the Republican-led Senate unanimously adopted procedures to redefine the Constitutional concept of a trial that is used in courtrooms throught America today. They set artificial time limits and decided to vote on what evidence they would hear and what witnesses they would call. They implemented numerous delaying tactics such as making their own motions, debating on the motions, debating on what witnesses to call and the re-deposition of all witnesses before they testified. They even decided to keep the testimony closed to the public. They ignored all of the precedents set in previous impeachment trials, including those of judges and of former President Andrew Johnson.

The senators, led by a 55-45 Republican majority, then used those procedures to sabotage the House managers' case by eliminating all of the potentially hostile witnesses. The Senate demanded that Hyde reduce the witness list, and he seemed to comply eagerly. Only Monica Lewinsky, Vernon Jordon and aide Sydney Blumenthal, all relatively supportive of the President, testified. The managers had requested only two weeks to present their entire case, including the brief questioning and cross examination of about 10-12 witnesses that they felt were essential to their case. The impeachment trial of Andrew Johnson similarly called 25 witness in just over five days. All of this was done under the phony argument of bipartisanship, a thinly veiled excuse that allowed compromised Republicans to pander to corrupt Democrats who were trying to destroy the Republic.

Although 27 of the Democrats had already voted to convict Judge Walter Nixon on the same charge, perjury before a grand jury, the Senate actually attempted to dismiss the case without hearing any witnesses. The motion to dismiss was made by Robert Byrd, who was frequently known to walk around with a Constitution in his pocket. The motion failed 56-44, with Democrat Russ Feingold crossing party lines to hear witnesses and the rest of the evidence. The unprecedented, unconstitutional motion that contradicted the sole power of impeachment provided to the House under the Constitution, exposed Byrd and most of the remaining Senate Democrats as Constitutional frauds.

Even more stunning was the refusal by Senate Republicans to uphold their Constitutional duty and hear the case. After eliminating all hostile witnesses and potentially damaging evidence, they decided to take the vote. Naturally, both articles failed. The first article of perjury failed, 46-54 with surprise "no" votes from Senators Fred Thompson, John Warner, Slade Gorton and Richard Shelby.

Arlen Specter, whose wife had received an appointment from Bill Clinton, actually referenced a provision of Scottish law to vote "not proven" instead of not guilty. It was somewhat fitting since he and the rest of the Senators had voted not to allow the House managers to prove their case fully. However, he did not explain when he was sworn to uphold Scottish law instead of the U.S. Constitution.

The second article of obstruction failed at a 50-50 vote with Republican Senators Collins, Jeffords, Chafee, Snowe and Specter voting with the Democrats, as was somewhat expected. It was particularly interesting that Specter, who was one of the last few Senators to vote, did not invoke his Scottish law claim but instead cast a straight "no" vote that prevented the second article from at least having a majority in favor of it.

Most of us knew that the handwriting was on the wall for the Senate trial before it started because of the trial procedure vote. Some of us had held out some hope since we knew that if Bill Clinton was to be removed, it would have to be by surprise because of the danger he posed in bombing countries to avoid his impeachment.

After witnessing the behavior of the House Democrats, the Senate Democrat votes were no surprise. The Democrat Party had become morally bankrupt and a threat to the freedom of every American citizen. It officially condoned anti-American activities of Bill Clinton involving tyranny, fascism and communism. Democrats were perfectly willing to subvert the Constitution, Declaration of Independence and Pledge of Allegiance by implementing an unprecedented double standard of justice in America for:

- A President vs. a judge who would be impeached;
- The commander in chief vs. a military officer or soldier who would be court-martialed;

- A government executive vs. a corporate executive who would be fired;
- An elected official vs. a private citizen who would be jailed.

THE REPUBLICAN BETRAYAL

The Republicans were even more stunning. They could have gotten the necessary 12 Democrat Senate votes for the two-thirds majority needed to convict Bill Clinton at any time simply by conducting a REAL trial and using the Congressional investigation evidence of criminal activity, abuse of power, treason and bribery in the Articles of Impeachment. Even a threat to use the evidence would force Democrat Senators to convict Bill Clinton on perjury and obstruction or be forced to dismiss real crimes such as treason, which would expose them as frauds.

I began to reflect on the incredible Republican betrayal. Despite overwhelming detailed evidence that Bill Clinton, Janet Reno and many Democrats implemented a treasonous, fascist regime, Republican leaders, after conducting reasonable investigations, established a systematic, multi-year cover-up of Democrat crimes. Ironically, two Republicans portrayed as heroes of the conservative and impeachment movements were responsible for much of the protection for Bill Clinton.

In early 1997, after many of the investigations were complete, Congressman Barr wrote a letter to House Judiciary Chairman, Henry Hyde (IL), suggesting an impeachment inquiry. Hyde, who is proclaimed as a hero of the impeachment movement for his elegant speeches in the Senate, stated that an impeachment inquiry was "premature" and delayed action on the inquiry for almost a year.

On November 5, 1997, Congressman Barr filed the H. Res. 304 impeachment inquiry with 17 co-sponsors. Speaker Newt Gingrich, a key adversary of Bill Clinton and acknowledged hero of the conservative movement, worked behind the scenes to prevent additional co-sponsors from signing onto the inquiry. Congressman Barr estimated that he would have probably had 150 co-sponsors had it not been for his friend, Newt Gingrich. Based on the eventual House impeachment vote, it is fairly easy to tell that Barr was correct.

After the Republican-led House voted to begin an impeachment inquiry in October, 1998, the House Judiciary Committee, chaired by Henry Hyde, elected to use only evidence from the Starr report for the impeachment. Hyde, who said that the original inquiry was "premature", now claimed that there was not enough time to investigate the more serious charges against Bill Clinton.

Newt Gingrich resigned after suppressing Clinton corruption through the 1998 election and then recommended Denny Hastert (IL) for his replacement as Speaker of the House. Hastert concurred with Hyde and avoided any confrontations by continuing protection for Bill Clinton from any charges based on the more serious crimes. Therefore, when the Republican House Judiciary Committee finally acted on the impeachment inquiry, it left out all of the evidence of serious, freedom threatening, impeachable offenses including the criminal activity in Arkansas, treason and bribery with the Communist Chinese government, abusive use of government agencies to persecute adversaries and a whole host of obstructions of justice involving drug trafficking, money laundering and organized crime.

Much of the drug trafficking and money laundering evidence was suppressed by House Banking Committee Chairman, Jim Leach (IA), who conducted an investigation into Mena, Arkansas, activities but never produced a report. Likewise, incriminating evidence regarding the FBI file case was collected by the Senate Judiciary Committee, but Chairman Orrin Hatch (UT) never produced a report. Evidence regarding Whitewater criminal activity and the death of Vince Foster was produced in a set of volumes by the Senate Banking Committee and its Chairman, Alfonse D'Amato, but no action was taken.

Republicans on the House Judiciary Committee were reluctant to deal with the more serious crimes since they had no support from the Republican leadership. In December of 1998, the House Judiciary Committee voted to send the Articles of Impeachment, based exclusively on the Starr report, to the House floor for a vote. The House of Representatives passed two of the four articles, and the charges were sent to the Senate where the Republican Judiciary Committee members served as case managers.

When the Articles of Impeachment reached the Senate, all 100 Senators, led by a 55-45 controlling Republican majority, voted to establish procedures that allowed them to refuse to hear the hostile witnesses and damaging evidence that would be presented in a normal impeachment trial. Henry Hyde, under pressure from Republican Senate leader, Trent Lott, then dealt the case a fatal blow by personally reducing the witnesses list from at least 12 to three, all supportive of the President.

Four Republican Senators from New England, Jeffords (VT), Chafee (RI), Snowe (VT) and Collins (ME), spoke out against conviction during the trial proceedings, and the Democrats, knowing that the Republican led Senate was preventing the evidence from being presented, held firm for acquittal. Thus, the failure to convict Bill Clinton rested almost exclusively on the shoulders of the "opposition" Republican party.

The Republican betrayal continued after the impeachment trial was over. As more evidence from the Cox Committee confirmed many likely acts of treason, the majority of Republicans did nothing about it. The Republicans refused to make Janet Reno accountable for justice obstructions, and they even let the independent counsel law expire, eliminating the last line of protection that American citizens have against collusion between Democrats and Republicans.

WHY THE BETRAYAL?

I had to know why the Republicans protected Bill Clinton so consistently. Conservative talk show hosts like to say that they are spineless and scared of the media. Some even say that they are stupid and inexperienced at majority leadership. These arguments are provably false, and I believe they are deliberate distortions.

Anyone who has watched Congressional business conducted on C-Span knows that Republican Congressional members are at least as intelligent and articulate as their Democrat counterparts and in many cases, more so. Most importantly, Republican (and even Democrat) Congressional offices were swamped with calls, faxes, Emails and letters supporting both impeachment and conviction by a wide margin. I personally verified non partisan letters collected on the internet and found them to be running as high as 10-1 or better for con-viction. Therefore, the Republicans knew that they had the support of their constituents if they voted to convict.

Another excuse frequently mentioned for Republicans is the fact that the Clinton administration held and used numerous FBI files against their adversaries, and this may have played some part in the reluctance of many Congressmen to confront the President. For Newt Gingrich, his unreported affair with Calista Bisek that dated to 1993 could be one factor since his FBI file was likely updated with information about the affair when he became Speaker of the House, and it is a near cer-tainty that the Clinton administration illegally obtained his file. But Henry Hyde continued to protect Bill Clinton even after a decades old affair had been exposed.

Henry Hyde originally stated that impeachment inquiry was "premature" then claimed that there was not enough time to in-vestigate the more serious charges against Bill Clinton, and he was eventually responsible for reducing the witness list from at least 12 mostly hostile witnesses to three supportive ones. His latter two actions came after his affair was exposed, thereby eliminating the FBI files as the likely excuse. Ironically, Hyde received a standing ovation at a dinner for the House im-peachment trial managers a few months after the trial.

It is also important to understand that Newt Gingrich, Henry Hyde, Jim Leach, John Chafee and Olympia Snowe are all members of the Council on Foreign Relations (CFR). My involvement led me to realize that CFR members control the national news media, Democrat Party agenda and key Republican leadership posts. The handful of Republican CFR members in Washington were instrumental in protecting Bill Clinton. Since there are only a few other Republican CFR members in Congress, this is more than just coincidence.

Since the number of Republican CFR members is relatively low, CFR membership cannot explain the consistent protection offered to Bill Clinton by all of the opposing Senators and even some members in the House of Representatives. I concluded that there had to be even more to it. I suspected what the real motive was after meeting Terry Reed and Col. Bo Gritz and re-ceiving the book, *White Out,* from my friend Chuck. I would soon meet former LAPD narcotics officer, Michael Ruppert, who led me to a gateway of additional information as I stumbled across one of America's best kept secrets.

CONCLUSION

We knew when the impeachment movement started that the Democrats would likely protect Bill Clinton at all costs and we would have to overcome them We also knew that the major media organizations would continue to distort nearly all political news about Bill Clinton to keep him in office, as they had done for almost two decades. We were prepared to fight a protracted battle to circumvent them. We suspected that Ken Starr would fail to find impeachable offenses in the FBI file case, the Travel Office firing scandal and Whitewater because he had likely covered up the murder of Vince Foster. We knew that the impeachment process could compensate for a corrupted independent counsel. What we did not fully realize was that there are no REAL opposing political parties.

If the Republican Party were a true opposition party, nearly every member of the party would have explained on national television how Bill Clinton had jeopardized the freedom of our friends and family. If the Republican Party were a true opposition party, Bill Clinton would have been forced to resign in 1995 when Republicans gained control of Congress. If the Republican Party were a true opposition party, it could have destroyed the Democrat National Committee solely with evidence of bribery by the Communist Chinese government.

Republican leaders withheld nearly all of the serious evidence of wrongdoing by the Clinton administration in the House and refused to hear true damaging witnesses and evidence against the President in the Senate. Republican leaders proved that our two-party system is a fraud as knowledgeable Americans witnessed a total corruption of the United States government.

REFERENCES

Investigation of Illegal or Improper Activities in Connection with 1996 Federal Election Campaign 1-6, Hearing 1-10, Senate Governmental Affairs.

Investigation of Political Fund Raising Improprieties and
   Possible Violations of Law #1-4, House Government Reform
   and Oversight Committee.
Hearing on the Impeachment Inquiry of William Jefferson
   Clinton, House Judiciary Committee.
Alexander Hamilton, James Madison & John Jay,*The
   Federalist Papers*, (reprinted by) Mentor.
Byron Preiss & David Osterlund, *The Constitution of the
   United States*, (reprinted by) Bantam Books.
Ed Timperlake & Bill Triplett, *Year of the Rat*, Regnery
   Publishing.
Judicial Watch, Interim Impeachment Report to Congress.

II
The Real
Corruption

CHAPTER SIX
THE REAL CASE FOR
IMPEACHMENT

The impeachment movement was initiated in 1994 by dozens of civic leaders based upon evidence of serious wrong-doings that occurred while Bill Clinton was Governor of Arkansas. Between 1995 and 1998, the Republican-led Congress conducted more than a dozen investigations into the Clinton administrations in Arkansas and Washington. They confirmed many facts upon which the original allegations were based and in some cases, found even more. The following summarizes allegations that have been made against Bill Clinton along with supporting evidence, which the Republican led Congress either collected or had access to, but refused to use in the Articles of Impeachment:

EMBEZZLEMENT AT MADISON GUARANTY

Those who have been tricked into believing that Whitewater was a two-bit land deal need only to look at the case of Madison Guaranty to find the truth. James McDougal, Bill Clinton's close business associate, Whitewater partner and fundraiser, was convicted on 18 counts of fraud for bilking millions of dollars from Madison Guaranty Savings & Loan. The total cost to American taxpayers was more than $60,000,000 when it was shut down by the Resolution Trust Co. in 1989.

Evidence indicates that Governor Clinton was warned about Madison's potential insolvency in 1983 by aide Marlin D. Jackson. He was warned again on June 21, 1984, by Arkansas Securities Department chief, Lee Thalheimer, and the Federal Home Loan Bank Board whose limited investigation concluded that the "viability of the institution is jeopardized" because of "unsafe and unsound lending practices". So what did he do to resolve the potential problem before it got out of hand?

Bill Clinton replaced Thalheimer with Beverly Bassett, who came from a law firm that had worked for Madison Guaranty. She was also the sister of his Washington County campaign chief. Clinton got McDougal to retain Hillary Clinton and the Rose Law Firm to produce an accounting study that concluded Madison was solvent. The study was quickly accepted by the revamped Securities Department, and Madison was allowed to continue its existence until 1989. Without the assistance of Bill Clinton, James McDougal would likely not have been able to embezzle the Madison funds.

The federal government agency that exposed the problems with Madison Guaranty was called the Resolution Trust Company (RTC). RTC investigator, Jean Lewis, submitted the first criminal referral, which helped convict Arkansas Governor Jim Guy Tucker in September of 1992. She submitted nine more criminal referrals later. Afterwards, procedures were changed to shift responsibility to the Legal division, and the case was transferred to the Rose Law Firm with its lead billing attorneys, Webster Hubbell and Vince Foster. Lewis was eventually removed from the Madison case. She and her supervisors, Richard Lorio and Lee Ausen, both lifelong Democrats who supported her investigation, were given a two-week administrative leave and escorted from the office. White House Associate Counsel, William Kennedy, another former Rose partner, was finally forced to release notes revealing that the White House had acquired inside knowledge of the criminal referrals.

In March of 1992, all files on the Mena drug trafficking investigation were removed by Clinton staff members from the Arkansas Attorney General's office, just before Freedom of Information Act requests could be filed by local news organizations. In 1994, one week after prosecutor Fiske was appointed to investigate Whitewater, the Rose Law Firm began shredding documents, despite protest demonstrations outside the building. Two employees resigned, and one stated that he saw many files being shredded with Vince Foster's initials. During the same week, a fire destroyed records on the 14th floor at the Worthen Bank, which was co-owned by the LIPPO GROUP, a major Clinton donor.

EXTORTION OF THE SMALL
BUSINESS ADMINISTRATION

David Hale who made Small Business Administration backed loans through his company testified that Bill Clinton pressured him to make a $300,000 "disadvantaged persons" loan to Susan McDougal because the Clinton Whitewater partnership would receive some of the proceeds. Susan McDougal was the wife of James McDougal, owner of Madison Guaranty. She was certainly not a "disadvantaged person" unless admiring Bill Clinton would qualify her for that status. Her loan was never repaid, and McDougal was also charged but acquitted of stealing $150,000 from Zubin and Nancy Mehta, a California couple for whom she worked. Susan McDougal was eventually convicted in regards to the Small Business Administration loan, but a judge freed her from prison a few months after the conviction using the grounds that back problems warranted her release on medical conditions.

Bill Clinton testified that he had no knowledge of the loan to Susan McDougal. His testimony was contradicted by James McDougal, David Hale and Trooper L.D. Brown, the former president of the Arkansas State Police Association. Susan McDougal was jailed for refusing to answer whether or not Bill Clinton had knowledge of the loan and actually demanded immunity from perjury for her testimony.

Clinton's testimony that he has no knowledge or connections to Madison Guaranty other than the Whitewater loan with McDougal also appears to have been contradicted by McDougal, Madison chairman John Latham and Rose attorney Richard Massey. McDougal stated that Bill Clinton stopped by his office one morning while jogging and asked him to give Madison business to Hillary Clinton at the Rose Law Firm, and he did as requested. But Hillary Clinton claimed that a junior partner, Richard Massey, brought in the Madison account. Massey testified, "That is NOT my recollection." Latham confirmed that McDougal made the decision, and McDougal also provided documents to support his claim and contradict both Clintons.

James McDougal stated that Clinton asked Hale about the loan after a meeting between Hale and McDougal concerning

Madison Guaranty. Arkansas Trooper L.D. Brown, a former Clinton bodyguard who was also a past president of the Arkansas State Police Association, told the FBI and Whitewater prosecutors that Clinton said to Hale in a tunnel under the state Capitol steps, "You're going to have to help us out. We're going to need to raise some money." Brown told the Associated Press, "There's no question that Clinton was pressuring Hale." Brown reported a bribe offer to change his testimony in June of 1997 while in London. McDougal joined the Clinton death count when he had a heart attack under mysterious circumstances while in prison.

GRAND LARCENY AND MONEY
LAUNDERING AT ADFA

As Governor, Bill Clinton established the Arkansas Development Finance Authority, ADFA, to issue state bonds for projects such as school and college construction. Webster Hubbell, the Rose Law firm partner, drafted and introduced Act 1072, the legislation that created ADFA. Larry Nichols, ADFA marketing director, stated that the first loan provided by ADFA was $2.85 million to a company named Park-O-Meter, which among other things, allegelly retrofitted airplane nose cones to carry drugs. Webster Hubbell was the secretary/treasurer of Park-O-Meter, which was owned by his father-in-law, Seth Ward.

Larry Nichols explained how ADFA was used by Bill Clinton to reward friends and campaign contributors with many times more than their contributions in the form of loans that were never to be repaid. For example, Nichols stated on *The Clinton Chronicles* video that Don Tyson, the Tyson Foods owner who was investigated as a major drug traffic suspect, contributed over $600,000 to Clinton and received $10,000,000 from ADFA. Bill Clinton totally controlled ADFA by appointing all board members.

Larry Nichols also explained how ADFA was used as a money laundering agency for Barry Seal's drug trafficking operation that ran between 1982 and 1986 from the airport in Mena, Arkansas, where family members of deceased Colombian drug lord, Pablo Escobar, lived. Then Governor Clinton issued $664,000,000 in bonds to Lasater & Co., which was owned by Bill Clinton's campaign contributor, fundraiser and convicted cocaine distributor, Dan Lasater. Former Clinton bodyguard, L.D. Brown, went on a flight where drugs were flown back to Arkansas. He stated during an interview that when he told Clinton about it, Clinton was aware of Seal's operation and knew that it was "Lasater's deal."

As much as $100,000,000 a month was reportedly transferred between ADFA and other banks, including Bank of Commerce & Credit, BCCI, which created one of the worst scandals in savings and loan history when it collapsed in 1985 and was shut down in July, 1991. As President, Clinton dismissed charges against the head of BCCI, Clark Clifford, who was the former LBJ Defense Secretary. Bank records show that the laundering abruptly ended when Barry Seal was assassinated in February of 1986 after he was ordered to be confined at a Baton Rouge Salvation Army halfway house just before he was scheduled to testify before a grand jury. Seal's attorney was Richard Ben Veniste, the Lead Democratic Counsel for the Senate Whitewater hearings.

THE KEVIN IVES AND DON HENRY MURDERS

On August 23, 1987, a train ran over the bodies of Kevin Ives and Don Henry as they lay across railroad tracks in Saline County, Arkansas, during the middle of the night. Fahmy Malak, the Arkansas State medical examiner, ruled that the deaths were accidental because the boys were under the influence of drugs and had fallen asleep on the tracks. The parents did not believe the examiner and spent over a year trying to get a second opinion while Malak did not comply with court orders for information. Finally during a second autopsy, Atlantan Joe Burton and six other forensic experts determined that Don had been stabbed in the back, and Kevin's skull was crushed before it was mutilated by Malak during the initial autopsy.

The *L.A. Times* found nearly 20 suspicious or obviously inaccurate death rulings by Malak, even ones that favored Clinton's mother, a nurse anesthetist who apparently had two patients die while under sedation for minor surgery. Other questionable death ruling examples include a suicide ruling for

Raymond Albright, who was shot in the chest five times, and a natural cause death ruling for James Milam, who was decapitated. Malak reported directly to Jocelyn Elders, who instead of firing him, gave him approximately a 40 percent raise. When the citizens held protest demonstrations and forced his resignation in 1992, Clinton created a new position in the state health department for Malak. Clinton told reporters that Malak was "stressed out", and Elders stated on video that "Arkansas owes Dr. Malak a great debt and a real apology."

Further investigation revealed that Ives and Henry had stumbled across a drug trafficking drop point known by the drug pilots of Barry Seal as A12. The drugs were dropped regularly out of planes flying from Colombia to Mena, Arkansas, and then picked up by ground crews that frequently included local government officials and policemen. Police deny the existence of the rifle that was the possible murder weapon used to kill Kevin Ives, even though it was videotaped as it was collected from the scene. They also deny the existence of the tarp that engineers saw covering the bodies of Ives and Henry as they lay on the tracks. From 1988 to 1995, seven people with knowledge of the death of Ives and Henry, including some of those who were on the tracks that night, have also been murdered. No one has ever been charged in any of the murders.

ABUSE OF POWER IN THE
FBI AND TREASURY

Clinton White House Counsel, Bernard Nussbaum, appears to have authorized Craig Livingstone, White House Personnel Security Office Director, to acquire confidential FBI files of over 900 officials using a list of names he gave the FBI. By contrast, in the Nixon administration Charles Colson was indicted and convicted on one count of possession of an FBI file. Livingstone was identified in reports as a former bouncer with a history of drug use and no qualifying experience for his position.

Livingstone and his supervisor, William Kennedy III, a former Rose Law Firm partner, testified that they did not know who hired Livingstone. I found this particularly amazing since I know of no one who has ever gotten a job without knowing who hired him. FBI agents Dennis Sculimbrene and Gary

Aldrich stated that Kennedy told them Hillary Clinton had hired him. A document leter uncovered by Judicial Watch also confirmed that Hillary Clinton hired Livingstone.

Livingstone claimed in June 1996 testimony that the list of names he gave the FBI was left over from the Bush Secret Service agents, since it contained many key Republican adversaries. However, Secret Service agents testified that no such list was left over. Livingstone's executive assistant, Mari Anderson, who apparently hid in fear for three months in Georgia, testified that Livingstone and Anthony Marceca had unrestricted file access. She also stated that six months of entries in the file check out logbook were missing. Marceca, a White House Personnel Office employee, invoked the 5th Amendment and refused to testify. Bill Clinton has maintained that this was "a completely honest bureaucratic snafu".

During the FBI file investigation by the Senate Judiciary Committee, Secret Service agents Libonati and Undercoffer provided testimony refuting Craig Livingstone's claim that the list of 900 names he gave the FBI was left over from the Bush administration. On October 2, 1996, after their testimony, Treasury Department Inspector General Valerie Lau opened an investigation into the agents' notes, as indicated by the testimony, and Email message of Assistant Inspector General James Cottos. The investigation was based on a memo from Donald Goldberg, a Congressional staffer, who was hired in 1997 by the White House Office of Legislative Affairs. The *Washington Times* reported that Emily Coleman, head of Eastern region investigations, admitted that on October 9, 1996, she destroyed the original case-tracking document, created a new one without the names of the agents and backdated it to October 2, 1996. Afterwards, Lau told Congress on two separate occasions that the agents were not under investigation. Senator Grassley called for and received her resignation.

Former Clinton aide, George Stephanopoulos helped to conceal damaging information in a related Judicial Watch lawsuite. A federal judge found that his testimony was "not truthful" and his memory loss was "not believable". His untruthfulness apparently qualified him to join Sam Donaldson, Barbara Walters and others at ABC where he was hired as a commentator.

BLACKMAIL AT THE IRS

Since the election of Bill Clinton, the IRS has made politically biased rulings and audited over a dozen organizations and individuals that have opposed Clinton policies or exposed corruption in his administration. Some organizations that have been audited include:

- Heritage Foundation,
- National Rifle Association,
- Christian Coalition,
- Citizens Against Government Waste,
- Freedom Alliance,
- Western Journalism Center.

Paula Jones also was audited immediately after her lawsuit was filed even though she was not working and her husband made only $30,000 a year. IRS agent Thomas Cederquist told the Western Journalism Center that their audit was not random, but political, and the outcome would be determined in Washington. The IRS also requested extensive detail on the publishing of articles about the death of Vince Foster, even though it had nothing to do with income. The Heritage Foundation was forced to produce a 75-foot stack of paper in response to IRS questions that wanted detailed data on each seminar, lecture and publication from 1994 through 1996. After a four-year wait, the National Policy Forum was denied tax exempt 503(c)4 status by the IRS even though it operated almost identically to the Democratic Leadership Council which had the status.

No known pro-Clinton organizations were audited during this period. The discrepancy in audit targets perhaps can best be explained by the fact that the person appointed by Bill Clinton to head the IRS during many of these audits was Margaret Richardson, a close family friend and 1992 Presidential campaign worker.

IRS audit abuses also continued in the Travel Office scandal. David Watkins, Clinton's director of the Office of Administration, fired Billy Dale and the Travel Office staff on May 19, 1993. Multiple communications by Watkins, Mack McLarty and William Kennedy from May 12-17 revealed that

Hillary Clinton ordered the firings to provide business for TRM, Inc., a travel agency partially owned by Harry Thomasson, a campaign fundraiser.

On May 20, 1993, Dale's air charter service, UltrAir was visited by three IRS employees who showed up to perform an audit. Mari Anderson, Livingstone's executive assistant, testified that around the same time, Livingstone asked her to check out Billy Dale's FBI file for White House personnel. In December 1993, after banning Dale from the White House, Livingstone's office requested and received his raw background file from the FBI, under the grounds that he was "being considered for access." The Clintons later brought against Dale, embezzlement and mismanagement charges, which were dismissed by a federal jury in two hours of deliberation. The taxpayers reimbursed Dale's attorney $400,000.

In 2000, a bi-partisan congressional committe finally determined that the White House had made illegal requests for information from the IRS on at least two occasions. One request came directly from the office of Vice President Al Gore.

VOTER FRAUD AT THE INS

The Immigration & Naturalization Service (INS) typically registers about 300,000 immigrants per year for citizenship. In 1996, it registered 1.1 million before the election, including 180,000 illegal immigrants and 70,000 criminals. In an April 4, 1997 House Appropriations Committee meeting, INS head Doris Meissner, confirmed that the INS was working closely with the Vice President and his office to register the immigrants. Meissner and other INS employees also acknowledged the existence of Email messages from the Vice President's office to the INS stating Bill Clinton's frustration and concern that the registration process may be going too slowly. His concern seemed to be that it would be completed in time for the election.

MORE WASHINGTON SCANDALS

The Clintons spent about $1,700,000 of taxpayer money to build and maintain a database of contributors at the White

House under the direction of Hillary Clinton. Many of the data sources were illegally collected from White House public property. In addition, Bill Clinton used 103 White House coffee klatches to raise nearly $27,000,000 from over 1,500 individuals who attended. The Pendleton Act, as well as Sections 600, 607 and 641 in Title 18 of the federal criminal code, prohibit the use government property or taxpayer funds to solicit personal or political contributions. Bill Clinton claimed that visits took place in his residence; however, videos released in October 1997 showed that many occurred in the Oval Office.

Dozens of other contributors received overnight stays at the White House for no apparent reason other than that they were a donor. This was confirmed in a 1995 memo from Clinton to then DNC finance chairman, Terry McAuliffe that said, "Ready to start overnights right away." for those who contributed "50,000 or more".

In March 1994, Webster Hubbell, a former Rose Law Firm partner, quit his appointment as Associate Attorney General, the third highest U.S. Justice Department position, to stand trial for embezzling $482,410 from Rose clients and evading $143,747 in taxes. Hubbell is the individual most knowledgeable about the Clintons' Arkansas activities and even kept the Whitewater partnership files. Between March and December when he was convicted, Hubbell received over $700,000 from 10 contributors, such as the LIPPO GROUP, and has no plausible explanation of what work he did for the money. During this time he also had over 70 meetings with 20 different Clinton administration officials, including three with the President. Officials, including Mickey Cantor, Mack McLarty and Erskine Bowles, solicited money and favors for Hubbell from many sources.

DRUGS AND DRUG TRAFFICKING

Bill Clinton's brother, Roger, told undercover agents, when he was videotaped snorting cocaine and busted for distribution by the DEA, "I have to get some for my brother. He has a nose like a vacuum cleaner." Witness Sharline Wilson stated that she had seen then Governor Clinton snorting cocaine at a party with his brother Roger. Larry Nichols stated that Clinton was hooked on cocaine. Dr. Samuel Houston, former physician of Bill Clinton's father-in-law, stated on *The Clinton Chronicles* video that Clinton was admitted to the Little Rock Medical Center and treated for a drug overdose. He also noted that Clinton was regularly treated for a sinus condition that could be caused by the destruction of membrane from snorting cocaine. Bill Clinton consistently refused to release all of his medical records.

As Governor and President, Bill Clinton maintained close relationships with drug traffickers. Dan Lasater, his friend, campaign contributor, fundraiser and suspected supplier, was convicted on cocaine distribution charges in a case that involved giving cocaine to teenage girls in exchange for sex. He was sentenced to 30 months in jail but was quickly pardoned by Clinton after five months. Another Clinton associate who owned a lumber company, was reportedly caught transporting cocaine in a truck with a lumber facade. Jorge Cabrera, a convicted felon who donated $20,000 to the DNC, had his picture taken with Al Gore at the 1995 White House Christmas party. Twice In the 1980s, Cabrera plea bargained after being indicted on charges of drug trafficking, racketeering and managing a continuing narcotics operation. In January of 1996, undercover agents arrested Cabrerra, a Cali cartel operative, with over 5,800 pounds of cocaine, most likely from the Cali cartel.

As President, Bill Clinton took amazing steps to facilitate drug trafficking within the U.S. In 1997, he decertified Colombia in the "war on drugs". In 1995, his DOD appointee removed radar tracking on planes coming from Colombia and Peru. From 1993 to 1994, Clinton eliminated the money laundering division of the U.S. Justice Department, cut over 80 percent of the White House Office of National Drug Control Policy, cut 355 Drug Enforcement Administration members, cut customs drug interdiction budget by one-third and cut $500,000,000 from Defense Department, anti-drug and other drug treatment and prevention budgets.

COMMUNISTS BRIBE THE DEMOCRATS

Senate campaign finance investigation testimony confirmed that many illegal large foreign contributions were accepted by the Clinton inaugural fund, Clinton defense fund and Democrat National Committee (DNC), in conjunction with Presidential fundraisers. Many of the illegal revenue streams were traced to individuals and organizations connected to the Communist Chinese military. The pattern of repetition and deception for illegal foreign contributions showed that they were not accidental. Here are some reported examples:

- Indonesians Sonya and Arief Wiriadinata, who were sent to a White House meeting by Mr. Riady, donated $450,000 even though they filed no U.S. tax return.
- Charles Yah Lin Trie donated $350,000 to the DNC and $640,000 to the legal defense fund in sequentially numbered money orders received from various cities by people who strangely have the same handwriting.
- Ted Seong, head of the Communist controlled Pagoda Red Mountain Cigarette Co., donated $400,000 to the DNC before Democrats attempted to implement anti-tobacco legislation, against American companies.
- Yogesh Gandhi donated $325,000 to the DNC despite having liens filed against him for non-payment of taxes.
- The Cheong Am American Co. donated $250,000 to the DNC, despite having raised no funds ever in the United States.

Nearly $1,000,000 in funds raised by Bill Clinton's long time friend, Charlie Trie, was traced through the Communist controlled Bank of China to a Chinese resident of Macao named Ng Lap Seng, also known as Mr. Wu. Senate testimony from the FBI showed that Ng was involved with the People's Consultative Congress, a panel that advised the Chinese government and Communist party on business and economic matters.

The investigations have resulted in more than 100 non-cooperative witnesses including:

- over 35 witnesses pleading the Fifth Amendment,
- over 20 witnesses requiring immunity for their testimony,
- over 10 witnesses leaving the country and
- over 10 foreign nationals refusing to be interviewed.

John Huang, the former U.S. President of the LIPPO GROUP, was the DNC's Asian fundraiser for most of the illegal campaign contributions. The Indonesian based LIPPO GROUP had a partnership with the Chinese Communist government controlled China Resource Holding Co. to own the Hong Kong Chinese Bank jointly, also known as Hua Ren Jituan in China. Under Hong Kong law, the partnership provided China Resources with access to all Lippo corporate information. China Resources was found by the Cox Committee to be an agent of "political, economic and military espionage" according to investigators from the Defense Intelligence Agency and Senate Governmental Affairs.

Huang left Lippo with a $780,000 bonus and took a large pay cut to join the Commerce Department. While at Commerce, he was given a top secret clearance, received over 100 intelligence briefings and reviewed dozens of top secret documents. To join the DNC, Huang took another large pay cut and was reissued a new security clearance. He also maintained a separate office at Stephens, Inc., owned by Jackson Stephens, the LIPPO GROUP's Worthen Bank partner who made a $3,000,000 loan to the Clinton campaign in 1992.

Huang's security clearance was issued by the Commerce Department Chief of Personnel Security and reissued by the Defense Industrial Security Clearance office without the standard full-field FBI background checks. Commerce Department phone logs showed that he made nearly 400 calls to Lippo or its subsidiaries. DNC Finance Director Richard Sullivan testified that Bill Clinton urged him to hire John Huang, former U.S. President of the LIPPO GROUP. Nolanda Hill, a business associate of Ron Brown, testified in a Judicial Watch that Bill Clinton pressured Brown to hire Huang at the Commerce Department.

The Senate Campaign Finance investigation and the House Government Reform and Oversight investigation found that the Clinton / Gore campaigns and the DNC had seven sources of revenue traceable through 11 revenue streams to Communist Chinese controlled companies or individuals connected to the People's Liberation Army. These money streams provided millions of dollars in illegal campaign contributions dating back to when Bill Clinton was still Governor of Arkansas. An April 17, 1996, DNC memo indicated that Bill Clinton was overseeing the fundraising efforts.

TREASONOUS TECHNOLOGY TRANSFERS

What did the Communist Chinese government get for its money? Bill Clinton transferred export technology decisions from the State Department to the Commerce Department in 1996. This weakened export controls and increased security risks. During his administration, *American Investigator* reported that over 1,000 dual use and military technologies were transferred to the Communist Chinese government. U.S. exports to China included:

- top-secret encryption
- missile guidance
- MIRV technology
- 46 supercomputers
- fighter bomber "hot section" range technology
- nearly complete missile and strategic bomber factories
- global satellite positioning
- patent database information

Bill Clinton became the first President in history to transfer military technology to a Communist nation over the objections of his own government agencies. Some of the transfers raised objections from the:

- Defense Department
- National Security Administration
- State Department
- Justice Department
- Judiciary Committee
- Congressional members

Bill Clinton apparently even allowed encryption technology to be transferred to China after he had prevented it from being transferred to Australia, one of our allies.

Clinton also met Long Beach, California, officials at the White House in September 1995 and visited them in August 1996 to support the Communist controlled, China Ocean Shipping Co. (COSCO) takeover of the Long Beach naval station. American military intelligence believes COSCO, which has a business relationship that controls both sides of the Panama Canal, is a front for Chinese military operations. No national security review of the takeover was conducted even though COSCO had been caught shipping 2,000 illegal AK-47s into the Oakland port.

The weapons came from Poly Technologies, just days before Wang Jun, the chairman of their parent company, China International Trust Investment Company, met with Bill Clinton at the White House. Wang Jun, who gained White House access without a backround check, is a renowned arms dealer and son of Wang Zhen, a general involved in the Tiananmen Square massacre.

After the House voted on impeachment, the Cox Committee determined that the technology transfers and policy changes of the Clinton administration were massive. A separate chapter of this book is allocated to describe them in detail.

REPAYING THE CONDUIT

The conduit for much of the Communist Chinese money flow was the LIPPO GROUP, an Indonesian company owned by the Riady family, who are ethnic Chinese. They have many business investment interests such as the financing of coal mining in Indonesia and China through their Hong Kong Chinese Bank.

A leading export of Indonesia is a unique form of clean burning, low sulfur coal, that is mined in the coal fields of Kalimantan Island, formerly known as Borneo. This super compliance coal is the only coal that meets the U.S. Clean Air Standards Act, and the largest deposit of it in the world is at the Kaiparowits plateau in southern Utah. The plateau area included 62 billion tons of coal valued at over a trillion dollars, about four billion barrels of oil and approximately three trillion cubic feet of natural gas.

Three million tons of coal that would produce 1,000 Utah jobs were about to be mined by the Kentucky-based company, Andalex Resources. However, Bill Clinton made the coal-mining project unfeasible by declaring 1.7 million acres in southern Utah as the Grand Escalante National Monument. The area is larger than the states of Delaware and Rhode Island combined.

The declaration was kept secret from Utah officials until midnight of the night before Clinton made the announcement, which actually occurred in northern Arizona instead of Utah. In protest of the declaration, the people of the Utah district immediately voted Democrat Rep. Richard Orion out of office and replaced him with Republican Chris Cannon, who went on to serve as a House manager in the impeachment trial. Twenty-nine counties also filed suit against Bill Clinton's decision which was based on the 1908 Antiquities Act. Kathleen McGinty and Linda Lance, the head and associate director of the Council of Environmental Quality, stated in Emails that the lands were "not really endangered" and "not threatened", respectively. It seems obvious that Bill Clinton did not make the declaration because he was concerned about the enviroment.

This New Attorney General

After the nominations of Zoe Baird and Kimba Wood had failed, Bill Clinton was able to have the U.S. Senate confirm Janet Reno as Attorney General of the United States. One of her first actions was to file a brief in the U.S. vs. Knox case. Reno sought to reverse the conviction of a child pornographer on the grounds that child pornography is a form of free speech rights protected by the First Amendment of the Constitution. She received a rebuke from the U.S. Senate by a 99-0 vote.

Around that time, Janet Reno appeared on CNN's *Larry King Live* and stated that her major objective was to make the Justice Department more accountable. This was pleasant news after the recent fiascoes at Ruby Ridge and Waco. However, she established an immediate track record that was diametrically opposed to any accountability.

WACO

When Janet Reno took office she was faced with a stand-off between federal agents and the Branch Davidians at Mount Carmel, near Waco, Texas. The ATF had brought in dozens of agents in an attempt to serve a search warrant on David Koresh, allegedly for having an automatic weapon. House Waco Investigation testimony in 1995 revealed that the ATF could have picked up Koresh while he was out several times in the days before the February 28, 1993, raid. The ATF falsely told the military that Davidians were manufacturing drugs and received military training in violation of the Posse Comitatus Act. Federal agents later accused Koresh of abusing children, although Texas Human Services had found no such abuse in two investigations.

More disturbingly, no substantial evidence was ever presented that indicated the ATF attempted to serve the warrant peacefully. In fact, the ATF had even contacted press reporters and indicated that there may be a major shoot-out when it served the warrant. The Davidians claimed that the ATF shot first. Most videotapes of the raid and the front door, which contained bullet holes that could validate or disprove the Davidian claims, were either lost or destroyed by the ATF and FBI. The videos that were provided showed that the ATF was not under fire as they climbed onto the roof using ladders and stood behind cars firing at the Davidians.

On April 19, 1993, after a stand-off with the Davidians, the FBI attacked the church and living complex with tanks, helicopters, automatic weapons and deadly CS military tear gas, which is internationally banned in warfare. The CS gas powder was dissolved in methylene chloride and propelled by carbon dioxide, both potentially suffocating agents. This dissolution method releases a deadly hydrogen cyanide. Reno approved the CS military gas attack that led to the deaths of over 80 men, women and children who had never committed any crime.

Videos, debris, Forward Looking Infrared (FLIR) tape and testimony from the survivors corroborate that the FBI started the fire that killed most of the Davidians on April 19. The FLIR tape shows pyrotechnic explosions immediately after the last gas insertions at the gym and second floor right front corner, the areas where fires first started. Pyrotechnic M-651 gas canisters, which disperse gas by burning and are fired from an M-79 grenade launcher, were found at the gym and right front corner of the Davidian property. Survivors Derek Lovelock and David Thibodeau saw fireballs igniting their paths while racing through the property from the gym and second floor of the right front corner, respectively.

The FLIR tape clearly showed heat images from automatic weapons fired at the Davidians as they tried to escape from the burning kitchen / dining area in back of the complex. FLIR creator and former Defense Department Night Vision Lab Manager, Edward Allerd, stated that "nothing in nature could duplicate the thermal signature" of the automatic weapons' fire shown. Infraspection Institute confirmed Allerd's findings after being contracted to analyze the tape for *60 Minutes*, whose producers then withheld the Institute's analysis from the American public

At least three Delta Special Forces members, two tanks, helicopters, communications equipment and 40-50millimeter military ammunition were part of the assault. Over 360 military ferret rounds of gas were fired into all windows of the Davidian buildings, despite manufacturer warnings that the ferrets could kill anyone that they struck. An aerial videotape also showed one tank destroying a Davidian building while people were still inside. Autopsy reports indicated that six bodies found in the rubble of that building were crushed to death.

Despite all of the evidence, Reno stated that she "could not find anything wrong" with FBI actions in Waco. She confirmed the FBI claim that the Davidians set themselves on fire based on a barely audible recording of the Davidians that had no supporting evidence. Janet Reno also could find no violation of the Posse Comitatus Act which expressly prohibits the use of military equipment and personnel to enforce laws against American citizens unless authorized by the U.S. Constitution or an act of Congress.

RUBY RIDGE

Janet Reno refused to support the conclusion of a Justice Department investigation that found an FBI sniper shot which killed Vicki Weaver at Ruby Ridge, Idaho, in 1992 was unconstitutional. Senate testimony showed that an FBI sniper killed Vicki Weaver by shooting her in the head as she held her baby while standing with the door open on her front porch. The FBI snipers were shooting at the Weavers from over 200 yards away using rifles with 10 power scopes.

In bone chilling Congressional testimony, the snipers and Assistant FBI Director Larry Potts, stated that they had the right to shoot and kill anyone if that person was holding a gun. Chairman Arlen Specter pointed out that such a situation did not warrant the use of deadly force according to FBI policy. On the House floor, Idaho Representative Helen Chenoweth called for the resignation of Potts, who was also responsible for the Waco disaster. Potts is a personal friend of FBI Director Freeh, who was appointed by Reno. Randy Weaver's attorney called for Lon Horiuchi, the sniper who killed Vicki Weaver, to be tried for murder based on the Justice Department investigation. Instead, Horiuchi and Potts received paid leave for over two years. The State of Idaho decided to pick up the ball and charge Horiuchi with manslaughter in the shooting, but he was eventually found not guilty, as expected, after his case was moved to a judge in federal district court. Some accountability was achieved through the judicial system when Randy Weaver was able to obtain a $10,000,000 settlement in a wrongful death suit. However, Horiuchi was later put in charge of a Waco sniper post that the full tape indicates fired on the Davidians.

CREATING THE DEPARTMENT
OF INJUSTICE

Another one of Janet Reno's first acts as Attorney General was to fire all 93 United States attorneys, a move unprecedented in American history. She stated that the replacement of all U.S. attorneys was a "joint decision" with the White House. Her liaison with the White House was the third highest ranking Justice Department official, Associate Attorney General, Webster Hubbell, who is now a convicted felon.

In another historically unprecedented move, Janet Reno fired FBI Director William Sessions on a trumped up charge of transportation misappropriation. Sessions was forced to leave immediately on July 19, 1993 and the next day the body of Chief White House Counsel, Vince Foster, was found in Fort Marcy Park. Sessions was eventually replaced with Louis Freeh, based on a recommendation from Robert Fiske, one of Clinton's former lawyer partners.

THE FEDERAL BUREAU OF INVESTIGATION

Under Freeh, the FBI entered the most incompetent, unaccountable period in its history as illustrated by the following evidence, most of which was collected in Congressional investigations:

- Louis Freeh promoted his close friend, Larry Potts, despite the Assistant FBI Director's responsibility for both the disastrous Waco and Ruby Ridge sieges;
- Freeh's FBI illegally gave Clinton administration personnel over 900 files, including those on political adversaries. Freeh's FBI General Counsel, Howard Shapriro apparently even briefed White House Counsel, Jack Quinn, on the information;
- Freeh's FBI failed to process criminal background checks on citizenship applications resulting in over 70,000 criminals' being granted U.S. citizenship in time for the 1996 elections;
- Freeh ordered agents to read Richard Jewell his Miranda rights while Jewell was cooperating to supposedly film a training video. The order was issued by phone over the unanimous protest of all involved Atlanta FBI agents;
- Freeh's FBI was cited along with the ATF by 13,500 Oklahomans who were granted a new grand jury investigation into the alleged government cover-up involving the Oklahoma City bombing;
- Freeh's FBI crime labs were accused by agent Fredric Whitehurst of tainting evidence in high profile cases including the Oklahoma City bombing case;
- Freeh's FBI agents interrogated agent Gary Aldrich about his book, *Unlimited Access*, as well as agent Dennis Sculimbrene about his Craig Livingstone background inquiry that linked the Livingstone hiring to Hillary Clinton;
- Freeh refused to get the FBI involved in the Vince Foster death investigation, which was handled by the park police, despite the fact that Foster was the highest ranking government official to die of unnatural causes since the assassination of John F. Kennedy.

THE VINCE FOSTER MURDER

Vince Foster, the chief White House Deputy Counsel and the Clintons' personal lawyer, allegedly committed suicide in Fort Marcy Park by placing a gun into his mouth and literally blowing his brains out. The conclusion was reached by independent prosecutor Robert Fiske, who happened to be the lawyer for International Paper, Inc., which sold land to the Clinton / McDougal Whitewater partnership. However, FBI lab analysis, witness testimony and other physical evidence illustrate that Foster could not have committed suicide in the park or anywhere else. Some examples of the evidence are:

- Although the coroner's report showed a skull exit wound, no exit wound fragments or bullet were found in the park.
- Foster's fingerprints were not on the gun, but another print was on it.
- Foster's family stated that he did not own the gun which had been untraceable since 1913.
- A search of Foster's ammunition showed he had no bullets for that type of gun.
- No powder burns were on his mouth, but there were powder burns on both of his forefingers.
- There was abnormally little blood at the scene.
- His glasses had no powder burns, and they were found almost 20 feet from his body.
- No grass or dirt was found on Foster's shoes even though he would have walked over 100 yards through the park to the point of the suicide.
- Foster's suit, shirt, tie and underwear were covered with carpet fibers.

Evidence indicated that Bernard Nussbaum, White House Counsel, turned over Foster's briefcase to the authorities. However, three different witnesses said that they saw the briefcase in Foster's car at Fort Marcy Park. So how did it get back to the White House? Did it fly or walk? On the third search of the briefcase, a suicide note, supposedly written by Foster, suddenly appeared in it. The suicide note was declared a forgery by several different handwriting analysts. The forgery was so obvious that anyone could see many letters that had several pen dots indicating the letters were drawn. No fingerprints were found on the note even though it was torn into 28 pieces.

OBSTRUCTIONS OF JUSTICE FROM THE DEPARTMENT OF JUSTICE

Janet Reno failed to implement a 1993 FBI investigation recommendation to prosecute Chuck Banks, the former Arkansas U.S. attorney who was to be tried for obstruction of justice for shutting down a federal drug investigation that implicated many people within the state and local governments. The investigation found compromised local judges and prosecutors, drug trafficking at Mena, money laundering through ADFA, suppression and distortion by the media and information about the murder of Kevin Ives and Don Henry, as well as five other subsequent deaths.

Assistant U.S. Attorney Bob Govar, who resigned in protest of the shutdown, received much information from Jean Duffey, the head of a drug task force investigation that was also shut down by Judge John Cole. Duffey was attacked with 200 false press articles, threatened with imprisonment on an illegal warrant issued by the same judge, pressured to turn over her investigation to the people she was investigating and forced to flee the state temporarily when her mother received a tip from a police dispatcher that she would be killed if imprisoned.

Despite confiscation of task force evidence, Dan Harmon, a prosecutor that she implicated, was tried and convicted in Arkansas during June of 1997 on five drug-related felony counts, each carrying a maximum of 20 years in jail and a $150,000 fine. Harmon was convicted in 1990 on tax evasion but had his suspended law license reinstated after Winston Bryant, the Arkansas Attorney General under Governor Clinton, testified on his behalf. To date, no one has been charged in any of the murders, despite contentions of the task force undercover agents that the murders were easily solvable.

THE JUSTICE DEPARTMENT AND
ORGANIZED CRIME

The Reno Justice Department shut down the prosecution of Arthur Coia, the head of Laborers International Union of North America, who was investigated by the Justice Department over several years for corrupt labor union practices such as extortion, conspiring to prevent free elections and even death by fire bombing. The National Legal and Policy Center reports explained how Justice concluded in its 1994 complaint that Coia was "associated with, influenced from and controlled by" organized crime.

His union political action committee, Laborers' Political League, contributed over $4.5 million to the Democrat National Committee and its candidates. In February of 1995, Coia helped Hillary Clinton raise millions of dollars in a Miami Beach fundraiser at the Fountainbleau Hotel for the top officials of his union. In February of 1995, the Justice Department suddenly dropped the complaint against Coia, signed a consent decree, withheld his prosecution and told him to clean up his own union. Officials of the Janet Reno-led Justice Department declared that the consent decree was "the finest, most practical resolution that's ever been reached in a case of alleged mob influence." Coia thanked them by being vice chairman of a May 1996 gala that raised over $12,000,000 for Democrats. Coia was eventually convicted on an unrelated felony.

ATTORNEY GENERAL OR CLINTON
DEFENSE LAWYER?

Soon after her Senate confirmation, Janet Reno became the defense lawyer for President Clinton. She began her clever defense by appointing Robert Fiske as a special independent prosecutor to investigate the Clintons' Whitewater dealings even though Fiske was a lawyer for International Paper Inc., the company that had sold land to the Whitewater partnership of Clinton and McDougal. Fiske was also a lawyer for the Bank of Commerce and Credit, which received laundered drug money transfers from the Arkansas Development Finance Authority (ADFA), according to ADFA marketing director

Larry Nichols. Questions concerning the impartiality of Fiske mounted after he ruled that Vince Foster committed suicide. In 1994, he was replaced by Ken Starr, who was selected by a three-judge panel, despite the fact that Starr had been on Janet Reno's short list when she appointed Fiske.

During 1994, Janet Reno barred expansion of the probe into the affairs of Agriculture Secretary Mike Espy so that it would not include Don Tyson, the Clinton campaign contributor who was accused of bribing Espy. The investigation of Mike Espy, conducted by independent prosecutor Donald Smaltz, is believed to have revealed evidence that Don Tyson may have been involved in drug abuse, drug distribution, money laundering and even murder for hire. Much of the evidence already existed in Arkansas State Police intelligence files as shown on *The Clinton Chronicals* viedo. Tyson, owner of Tyson foods, had contributed over $600,000 to various Clinton campaigns. Tyson Foods counselor, James Blair, was the individual who turned a $1,000 cattle futures investment into $100,000 for Hillary Clinton.

During 1997, Reno filed amicus briefs with the Supreme Court in an attempt to support the claim by Bill Clinton that he should be shielded from the Paula Jones sexual harassment civil suit until he left office on the grounds that he was the commander in chief of the U.S. armed forces. The Supreme Count ruled unanimously, by a 9-0 count, against Reno.

Also in 1997, Reno attempted to compromise the Kenneth Starr investigation by challenging an 8th U.S. Court of Appeals ruling that found the Hillary Clinton personal attorney client privilege claim did not apply to White House lawyers who were paid by American taxpayers. The ruling, which was challenged in the U.S. Supreme Court, involved Vince Foster and Rose Law Firm billing record matters that Hillary Clinton discussed on July 11, 1995, with White House Counsels Miriam Nemetz and Jane Sherbourne. The Supreme Court refused to hear the case.

COVERING UP FOR COMMUNISTS

For almost the entire Clinton term, the Reno-led Justice Department repeatedly attempted to stymie Judicial Watch in its freedom of information suit against the Commerce Department, even though the Justice Department's role was to make sure that the Commerce Department responded properly. The Judicial Watch suit was responsible for the John Huang deposition, which led to the exposure of millions of dollars in illegal contributions to the Democratic National Committee and Clinton campaigns. In February 1996, Judicial Watch also subpoenaed Ron Brown, who was killed in the plane crash in Croatia during April 1996, while he was preparing for the deposition. An assistant U.S. attorney in the Justice Department filed numerous motions to delay the case, made repeated objections that were overruled during testimony and terminated a deposition against orders of the judge, who ruled that his conduct was "totally improper" and "totally scandalous."

The cover-up continued into 1997 as Reno also refused to grant immunity to four Buddhist nuns who had contributed $5,000 apiece to the Democratic National Committee at a fundraiser in the Hsi Lai Buddist temple in Hacienda Heights, Califorina, during April 1996. The event was attended by Vice President Al Gore who claimed he did not know it was a fundraiser even though evidence showed that virtually everyone on his staff knew it was a fundraiser, and dozens of early 1996 documents confirmed it.

The nuns, who like Buddist monks, are sworn to poverty, were unwilling to testify as to where they got the money unless granted immunity. Reno admitted that the Justice Department would not prosecute the nuns but refused to grant immunity which helped conceal the illegal foreign source of the contributions. The Senate committee granted immunity to the nuns by votes of 15-1 and 13-3. The nuns testified that the related temple financial documents had been shredded.

Pictures showed two Communist Chinese agents sitting beside Al Gore and a Buddist monk at the fundraiser. The agents were, Maria Hsia, who helped John Huang with several fundraisers and Ted Sioeng, the head of the Communist controlled Pagoda Red Mountain Cigarette Co. Hsia was convicted an all five counts of campaign finance violations against her. Sioeng, who was also connected to Asian organized crime, gave $400,000 to the DNC just before the Democrat Party launched its anti-tobacco legislation against American companies under the guise of preventing teen smoking. Were they really trying to prevent teen smoking or were they repaying the Communists by giving them a foothold into the American cigarette market?

Janet Reno refused three separate House committee requests in 1997 to appoint a special counsel to investigate the Democratic National Committee and Presidential fundraising scandal, despite clear evidence of treasonous policies made by Bill Clinton in exchange for contributions. The requests were made by the Judiciary Committee in March and September, as well as the Government Reform and Oversight Committee in August.

In addition, FBI director Louis Freeh recommended an independent counsel, but Reno ignored him. Justice Department investigator, Charles Labella, who was hired and after a preliminary study, also recommended an independent counsel. Reno refused again, and Labella eventually resigned from the Justice Department. The House Government Reform and Oversight Committee, chaired by Dan Burton, requested the Freeh and Labella memos, and Janet Reno refused to comply. The committee voted to hold her in contempt, but the House never brought the contempt finding to the floor. Finally, Janet Reno allowed the House Judiciary Committee counsels, both Democrats, to review the memos at the Justice Department but not to take any notes about the content. Reno refused to let House Judiciary Committee members see the memos without redaction.

The Burton and Thompson Committees found that the Clinton / Gore campaigns and the DNC had seven sources of illegal revenue traceable through 11 revenue streams to individuals and organizations connected with the Communist Chinese government. For example, nearly $1,000,000 in contributions from Charlie Trie was traced by the FBI to Ng Lap Seng, who advised both the Chinese government and Communist party on business and economic matters. Several sources were known Communist Chinese agents and/or members of Asian organized crime.

Testimony revealed that Bill Clinton helped the Asian fundraiser, John Huang, get hired at the DNC and Commerce Department, even though he was a former U.S. president of the LIPPO GROUP, which has a partnership with goverment controlled Chinese resources to run the Hong Kong Chinese Bank and its affiliate in China. Before he was hired, Huang received a top secret military clearance which allowed him to attend over 100 briefings and review dozens of classified documents.

Consequently, Bill Clinton relaxed U.S. export restrictions to China for several types of military technology through his executive orders. For the first time in history, a President gave sophisticated military technology to a Communist government over security objections from government agencies. In Clinton's case, the Department of Defense, Department of State, Department of Justice and the National Security Administration had all objected to one or more of his technology transfers.

Bill Clinton also assisted Indonesia, a conduit for much of the Communist Chinese money, at the expense of American economic development. He ensured Indonesia's monopoly on new low sulfur, super compliance coal when he declared 1.7 million acres in southern Utah as the Grand Escalante National Monument and made U.S. mining of the world's largest deposit of that coal there unfeasible.

Despite all of this, Reno said she could see no evidence that a special prosecutor was needed and even failed to notify the White House when the FBI informed her of Chinese attempts to influence the 1996 presidential elections. Assistant Attorney General, Joel Klein, added the final insult to American intelligence after the Justice Dept. received an initial favorable ruling in the Microsoft anti-trust case. He stated that "no person or corporation is above the law".

In summary, the evidence presented here is not just an indictment of President Bill Clinton and his administration. It is also an indictment of the Republican-led Congress which collected much of this evidence in Congressional investigations and then opted to protect Bill Clinton by not using it.

REFERENCES

Investigation of Whitewater Development Corporation and Related Matters #2-4, Senate Banking Committee.
Inquiry into U.S. Park Police Investigation of the Death of White House Deputy Counsel Vincent Foster, Senate Banking Committee.
Investigation into the Activities of Federal Law Enforcement Agencies toward the Branch Davidians - 1995, House Government Reform & Oversight Committee & House Judiciary Committee.
Investigation of Illegal or Improper Activities in Connection with 1996 Federal Election Campaign 1-6, Hearings 1-10, Senate Governmental Affairs.
Investigation of White House Travel Office Firings and Related Matters, House Government Reform and Oversight Committee.

Investigation of Political Fund Raising Improprieties and
    Possible Violations of Law #1-4, House Government
    Reform and Oversight Committee.
Behind Closed Doors: The Abuse of Trust & Discretion in
    Establishment of the Grand Escalante National Monument,
    House Resource Committee.
Senate Judiciary Committee Investigation into FBI Background
    Files (videos), C-Span.
Senate Governmental Affairs Committee Meeting 11/3/97.
House Appropriations Sub-committee Meeting 4/4/97.
Judicial Watch, Interim Impeachment Report to Congress.
Human Events - Case For Impeachment.
Ethics Watch Vol. 3 No. 1 - Vol. 5 No. 1, Ken Boehm & Peter
    Flaherty, National Legal & Policy Center.
Eugene Methvin, "The Clintons and the Union Boss," *Reader's
    Digest* 4/96.
London Sunday Times, 2/2/97.
Washington Times 2/9/97, 4/5/97, 12/26/96-12/30/96, 4/11/97-
    4/18/97, National Weekly Edition 3/23/97, Vol. 4, No.25.
American Spectator, 7/97, 10/97.
China Trilogy (videos), American Investigator, Free Congress
    Research & Education Foundation.
Quid Pro Coal (video), American Investigator, Free Congress
    Research & Education Foundation.
The Clinton Legacy (video), Accuracy in Media.
The Clinton Chronicles (video), Citizens Video Press.
The Mena Cover-up (video), Citizens for Honest Government.
The Death of Vince Foster (video), Citizens for Honest
    Government.
Obstruction of Justice (video), Integrity Films.
William Gazecki, Michael McNulty, Dan & Amy Gifford,
    Waco, Rules of Engagement (video), Somford.
Martin Gross, *The Great Whitewater Fiasco,* Ballantine Books.
Jack Thompson, *The Truth About Janet Reno* (video),
    American Forum.
Christopher Ruddy, *The Strange Death of Vince Foster*, Free
    Press of Simon & Schuster.
Linda D. Thompson, *Waco: The Big Lie* (video), American
    Justice Federation.
Linda D. Thompson,*Waco II: The Big Lie Continues* (video),
    American Justice Federation.

TREASONOUS TECHNOLOGY TRANSFERS

COCOM- Coordinating Committee on Multi-Lateral Export Controls

ACEP- Advisory Committee on Export Policy
ACDA- Arms Control Disarmament Agency

Strategic Defense Initiative

Aegis Missile Tracking

Peter Lee

Energy Dept

Nuclear Weapons Labs

Energy Intelligence

Sub Detection

Heat Shield

Reentry Vehicle

Electromagnetics

Missile Guidance

W56 Minuteman2

W62 Minuteman2

W76 Trident C4

W78 Minuteman3

W87 Peacekeeper

W88 Trident D5

COCOM

FBI

Wen Ho Lee

Justice Dept

CIA

stolen by

reinstated security clearance for

removed color coded security badges at

stopped briefing to Congress by

suspended background checks at

briefed in April 1996

vetoed in 1994 by

restricted by

withdrawal made by

granted waiver during

briefed in 1996

investigated illegal transfer to

refused phone tap for

theft suspect is

impeded requests by
briefed in 1996

briefed 1th 1996

data stolen for
data stolen for
data stolen for
data stolen for
data stolen for
data stolen for
data stolen for
data stolen for

given to
given to
given to
given to
given to
given to
given to
given to

President Bill Clinton

CEO gave $10K to party

briefed in 1997

issued

elevated export intelligence releases by

stopped reviewing

Executive Order 12981

Executive Order 13020

State Dept

National Security Admin

Executive Order 12981

Loral

did not provide vendor product class requests to
claimed privilege to

claimed not briefed until 1998 to

impeded interviews by

Cox Committee

Review Committee

Defense Tech Sec Admin

Hughes

conducted

approved

prepared

conducted

gave briefing aboutCox questions to

objected to

chaired

cited 18 violations by

objected to transfer of

objected to transfer of

1996 Launch Crash Analysis

1992 Launch Crash Slides

1995 Launch Crash Analysis

Communication Encryption

Fiber Optic Equipment

Satellite Encryption

Launch Insurers

revealed loss of

released to

illegally given to

not returned by

Defense Dept

ACEP

ACDA

Machine Tools

Super Computers

Fighter hot sections

Commerce Dept

approved transfer of

objected to transfer of

approved export of

objected to transfer of

moved export authority to

raised PRC export limit from 12 to 7000 mbps

approved

objected to

Peoples Republic of China

Saudi Arabia

North Korea

Pakistan

Iran

given to
given to

600 given to

gave CSS8 missiles to

gave weapons assistance to

gave CSS7 and M11 to

gave CSS8 and DF807 missiles to

illegally given by IRC to

stopped release of

HOW THE CHINESE COMMUNIST GOVERNMENT INFLUENCED THE AMERICAN POLITICAL SYSTEM

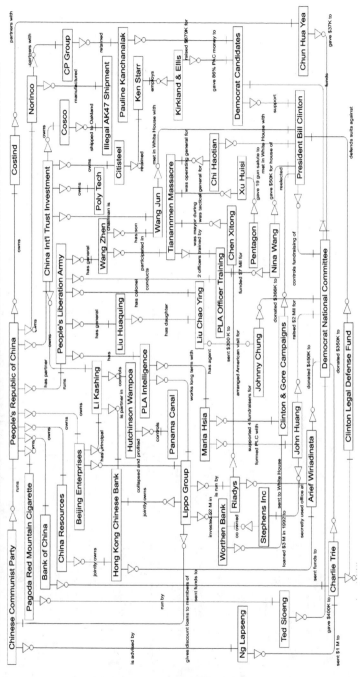

CHAPTER SEVEN
THE UNHOLY
NATO ALLIANCE

MARCH ON WASHINGTON '99

As the Senate trial came to an end, I was somewhat disillusioned since the Republicans literally sold out their base of support to protect the opposition party. More evidence of the treasonous China scandal was being detailed and reconfirmed by the Cox Report. Bill Clinton was never tried for a single one of the serious crimes that initiated the impeachment movement. An incredibly dangerous double standard of justice now existed for the Clinton Administration vs. American citizens. Worse yet, I feared there might be no limit to what Bill Clinton would do now that he was operating totally above the law. We could not simply let the Senate desecrate the Constitution and get away with it unchallenged.

I wanted to do another rally, but I knew what was involved based on the last one, and I just was not up to it. One day I was scanning Free Republic and found that a citizen named Andrew already had the same idea and the initiative to do something about it. Andrew had been active in picketing NBC and helping force them to air the Juanita Broaddrick interview they had delayed during the impeachment because it indicated that Bill Clinton was a rapist. I Emailed him to offer help with the agenda, and he quickly accepted. He had also joined forces with another citizen named Pat of the True Blue Patriots from Ohio, and together the three of us organized another rally. Andrew had some very good press contacts and got us very good Internet coverage on sites such as World Net Daily, News Max and Capitol Hill Blue. Pat worked very hard to coordinate the rally with many groups and individuals.

I set up the agenda that included Bill Triplett, co-author of the *Year of the Rat*, Larry Klayman of Judicial Watch, Cliff Kincaid representing Accuracy in Media, Pat Matrisciana, Herb Titus and some great citizen speakers. Dan Olsen produced a web site solely dedicated to the May 1 rally that Andrew named March on Washington '99.

I was particularly pleased to invite Michael Ruppert to explain the real impeachment scorch that Bill Clinton was holding over the heads of the Republicans. Michael, the former LAPD narcotics officer who had confronted CIA Director Deutch in a famous L.A. town hall, exposed three CIA drug trafficking operations that implicated George Bush. Michael discovered that Volume II of the CIA Inspector General's report on drug trafficking allegations was released to the web an hour after the Judiciary Committee voted to begin an impeachment inquiry. He also had found that Ken Starr, while in the Justice Department, helped draft a memo to the CIA that alleviated CIA reporting requirement responsibility for any knowledge it may gain about drug trafficking operations.

THE BOMBING OF YUGOSLAVIA

As we were getting things organized, one of my worst fears was realized when on March 24, Bill Clinton began bombing countries again. In December, four hours after he was told he did not have enough votes to stop his impeachment, Bill Clinton had issued a bombing strike against Iraq. In August, when the sex scandal broke, Bill Clinton bombed Sudan and Afghanistan without consulting a single one of his Joint Chiefs of Staff during the planning. Iraq was bombed despite the fact that two weeks earlier, Iraq had begun complying again with U.N. weapons inspections. The bombs in Sudan were dropped on what was proven to be nothing more than a pharmaceutical plant. The ones in Afghanistan were in retaliation for the bombing of African embassies, which the national news media told us was the responsibility of an alleged Muslim terrorist named Osama Bin Ladin. However, this time Bill Clinton had actually joined Osama Bin Ladin in support of the Kosovo Liberation Army (KLA), which was trying to force the province of Kosovo to secede from Yugoslavia.

The bombing of Yugoslavia was much worse since it was not an isolated strike, but a sustained bombing campaign. In addition, Bill Clinton had solicited and received the support of the North Atlantic Treaty Organization, (NATO). Nine of the 19 countries in the NATO alliance agreed to support the physical attack but America was doing about 90 percent of the bombing. Not a single country would have agreed to the attack without American initiation and leadership. The bombing was initiated exactly one month before the 50th anniversary celebration of NATO, held in Washington, D.C.

Andrew, Pat and I decided that we must include in the March on Washington '99, an additional objective to stop the bombing in Yugoslavia. The original objectives were to demand equal justice for all citizens including Bill Clinton, to help preserve national security by emphasizing the China scandal and to force the media to start telling the truth. I had already invited Bob Djurdjevic of Truth in Media to join the agenda. Bob, a Serbian computer consultant, founded his Truth in Media web site in the early '90s because of the inaccurate reporting of world events, particularly in the Balkans. Therefore, he was perfect to address the war on Yugoslavia.

I also added to my speech some startling information I had discovered regarding how we were being deceived about the war. The march drew several hundred people but was somewhat superseded the previous week when thousands of anti-war protesters showed up in Washington on April 24 for the 50th anniversary of NATO. Naturally, both marches were blacked out by most of the national news media; however, C-Span carried a few minutes of the anti-war protest to balance its coverage of NATO's 50th anniversary.

Until now our concern had focused on criminal activity in Arkansas, treason and bribery with the Communist Chinese military, abusive use of government agencies to persecute adversaries and obstructions of justice involving drug trafficking and organized crime. Suddenly those crimes paled in comparison to initiating a bombing attack on a sovereign nation. I predicted in some of my presentations that there could be a world destabilization because of bombing attacks by Bill Clinton and the media deception surrounding them; however, I could not foresee precisely how it might occur.

Now I was learning how grossly Bill Clinton, NATO and the national news media had misled Americans about the war on Yugoslavia. Yugoslavia would become the fourth country to fall victim to American bombs impeccably timed near the peak of a Clinton scandal. The thought of Bill Clinton once again killing innocent foreign civilians to cover his own scandals repulsed me more than anything else he had done. This time the unholy alliance with NATO meant that the killings would be continual.

THE PHONY WAR TRIGGER

In his March 24 speech, Bill Clinton justified the bombing of Yugoslavians by referring to a "massacre" where Serbian police allegedly lined up Albanians in a ditch and shot them. I was familiar with the lies about this incident, thanks to my friend Will Grigg, who wrote a tremendous cover story about it for *The New American* magazine in the previous month.

The alleged incident occurred at Racak on January 15th when the Serbian police forces were accompanied for the entire day by an Associated Press TV crew and two journalists, who saw no such massacre. The television footage reportedly showed Serbian police entering an empty town that was controlled by the KLA, engaging in a fierce battle with the KLA, who were dug into hillside trenches and then withdrawing from the town in the afternoon. Remaining KLA members then immediately returned to the town, but no bodies were seen. The bodies appeared the next day in trenches with little blood and few cartridges around them. The battle timing and fierceness of the battle indicated that THE TRENCHES WERE NEVER CONTROLLED BY SERBS WHEN THE BODIES WERE PLACED THERE.

The "massacre" was announced by Clinton administration official William Walker, whose account was denounced by French news sources, Le Figaro and Le Monde, based on the evidence they reported. Belarus and Finnish forensic experts who came to Yugoslavia could not verify the claims of massacre. Thus, America began bombing Yugoslavians based on false reports about an event that was likely staged. America entered the Vietnam War in much the same way after what are now considered false reports about a North Vietnamese attack on American ships in the Gulf of Tonkin. The false attack led Lyndon Johnson to create the Gulf of Tonkin resolution, which he used to place 550,000 troops in Vietnam, 58,000 of which never returned alive.

THE FALSE NATO CLAIMS OF GENOCIDE

NATO, and particularly Britain Prime Minister Tony Blair, backed up Clinton claims to the hilt with additional charges of genocide. Genocide against Albanians by Yugoslavian leader Slobodan Milosevic was the excuse that NATO used for bombing Yugoslavians. But when pressed for "ethnic cleansing" numbers in a March 25 Senate briefing, the Clinton administration stated that about 2,000 people, including 700 Serbs, were killed in the year before the bombing. Only a few dozen people had been killed during 1999 before the bombing.

In reality, there was a civil war between the Yugoslavian government and the KLA, who wanted Kosovo to secede from Yugoslavia against the will of Serbs and even most Albanians. Serbian hostilities were directed at the KLA, not Albanians, 100,000 of whom live peacefully in Belgrade as one of 26 Yugoslavian cultures.

Even after extensive residential area bombing drove hundreds of thousands of Kosovars from their homes and un- leashed para-military forces that the government could no longer control, Kosovo Democratic Initiative spokesman, Fatmir Seholi, stated "As an Albanian, I am convinced that the Serbian government and security forces are not committing any kind of genocide."

I soon found out that false claims of genocide or oppression were used several times in the 20th century to justify invasions. In 1931, Japan invaded and occupied Manchuria allegedly to protect it from Chinese terrorists. In 1935, Mussolini invaded Ethiopia to free Ethiopians who were allegedly enslaved by their emperor. In 1938, Hitler invaded the Czech Republic to end alleged ethnic violence against native Germans there, just before he committed genocide against the Jews. NATO took chapter, page and verse directly from the Hitler and Mussolini war tactics.

THE ILLEGALITY OF THE WAR

NATO was established as an alliance of mostly European nations and chartered only to defend them against invasion, not to attack other sovereign countries. NATO violated three of its own articles as well as United Nations and Geneva convention principles when it bombed Yugoslavians, who have never at- tacked another country. Despite the illegalities, the U.N. Security Council failed to pass a resolution condemning the bombing, and the U.N. war crimes tribunal gathered "ethnic cleansing" evidence on Slobodan Milosevic during the bombing, while doing nothing to hold NATO leaders accountable for their breeches of all fundamental international law. Thus, the U.N. proved itself far too prejudiced to mediate any international crisis.

NATO conducted a sustained bombing campaign, which any rational person would agree is clearly an act of war. Bill Clinton violated Article 1, Section 8 of the U.S. Constitution by participating in the war without approval by Congress, which holds exclusive power to declare war. Thirty-one Congressmen filed an unsuccessful suit when, without their approval, Clinton also violated the 60-day limit for introduction of any hostilities in the War Powers Act. In fact, not one parliament of any nation in the entire world passed a resolution endorsing the war, thus NATO acted outside the will of all governing bodies, even those of its own participating countries.

THE FALSE MEDIA PORTRAYAL OF THE KLA

What kind of organization would stage a massacre? The media repeatedly portrayed the Kosovo Liberation Army as a group of freedom fighters attempting to liberate the ethnic Albanians from Kosovo. Will Grigg of The *New American* magazine and several other sources reported that they were actually drug funded Muslim terrorists who received arms, equipment, money and training from forces of Osama Bin Ladin, the terrorist who was accused of bombing two embassies in Africa. This KLA profile is based on our own State Department, FBI and military intelligence reports, as recently as 1998, a year before the bombing started. The reports of drug allegations were also confirmed by the German, Swedish and Czech Republic police forces as well as the Strategic Research Institute of the U.S., which stated that it believed more Albanians may have died at the hands of the KLA than at the hands of the Serbs. Despite all of these reports, our Senators wanted to arm the KLA, and our President essentially gave them our air force.

In addition, America and other NATO countries supported the KLA covertly before and during the war. *PBS News Hour* reported on July 15, 1998, that selected Vietnam War veterans were training the KLA in Albania. After the bombing started, the *London Sunday Telegraph* reported on April 18 that the British special forces SAS unit had two training camps near the Albanian capital of Tirana. Jane's *Defense Weekly* publication confirmed on April 20 that France, Britain and U.S. special forces were working undercover in Kosovo. Canadian Parliament member, David Price, confirmed on April 19 that 50 Canadian soldiers were also working with the KLA in Kosovo to assist in bomb guidance. Apparently, they did not understand that water supplies, television stations and commercial power plants are not military targets.

Perhaps the most interesting report was released on April 8 from Jurgen Reents, spokesperson for the German PDS Party. It claims that the CIA founded the KLA by funneling funds through drug smuggling operations in Europe. It also says that the CIA formed a joint operation with the German Secret Service, to sow ethnic divisions in Yugoslavia and encourage its break-up. This effort to destabilize Yugoslavia, called Operation Roots, has been going on since the beginning of the Clinton Presidency, according to the report. The report also states that when Milosevic and Rugova were close to an agreement in 1998, the CIA stepped up KLA attacks on Yugoslavian police units. This is reminiscent of the fate of South Vietnamese President Diem when he wanted to reach an agreement with the North Vietnamese.

The German report was somewhat corroborated by additional reports indicating that Osama Bin Ladin was a CIA operative during the conflict in Afghanistan and that Richard Armitage was in the Balkans negotiating oil leases a few months before the bombing started. Armitage was implicated by Col. Bo Gritz and other authors regarding Southeast Asian drug operations originating in Burma during the late 1970s. Armitage, the former Assistant Secretary of Defense in the Carter and Reagan administrations, was supposed to be in charge of POW recovery at the time.

THE ARTIFICIAL RAMBOUILLET PEACE PLAN

Although our own government intelligence reports indicated the KLA was a drug funded terrorist organization, that was attempting to get Kosovo to secede from Yugoslavia, the

KLA was seated as representative of Kosovo Albanians at the Rambouillet conference. In reality, it appears that the majority of Albanians did not want Kosovo to secede from Albania. Two weeks before the bombing started, Doug Bandow, Senior Fellow at the Cato Institute, testified for the House International Relations Committee that on his recent visit to Kosovo, he could not find any Albanians who wanted to secede from Yugoslavia.

Nevertheless, NATO organizations made no serious attempt to negotiate peace at the Rambouillet conference and, in fact, attempted to goad Yugoslavia into a war, as shown in the Rambouillet accords. The accords specify that NATO and the European Union have final authority on all civilian matters, including how the Kosovo economy will run and that NATO personnel have total immunity, unrestricted access and use of nearly all services in Kosovo free of cost. These stunning accords clearly outline a colonization and occupation of Kosovo as shown in the following Chapter, Section and Article samples:

- **Chapter 4a, Article I**—"The economy of Kosovo shall function in accordance with free market principles." (Kosovo has vast mineral resources, including the richest mines for lead, molybdenum, mercury and other metals in all of Europe. The capital to exploit these mainly state owned resources would undoubtedly come from the U.S. and western Europe.)

- **Chapter 5, Article V**—"The CIM shall be the final authority in the theater regarding interpretation of the civilian aspects of this Agreement, and the Parties agree to abide by his determinations as binding on all Parties and persons." (The CIM is the Chief of the Implementation Mission, to be appointed by the European Union countries.)

- **Chapter 7, Article XV**—"The KFOR [NATO] commander is the final authority in theater regarding interpretation of this Chapter and his determinations are binding on all Parties and persons."

The following appendix sections further illustrate the unreasonable demands of NATO:

- **Section 6a**: "NATO shall be immune from all legal process, whether civil, administrative, or criminal."

- **Section 6b**: "NATO personnel, under all circumstances and at all times, shall be immune from the Parties' jurisdiction in respect of any civil, administrative, criminal or disciplinary offenses which may be committed by them in the FRY." (Federal Republic of Yugoslavia)

- **Section 7**: "NATO personnel shall be immune from .... arrest, investigation, or detention by authorities in the FRY."

- **Section 8**: "NATO personnel shall enjoy, together with their vehicles, vessels, aircraft, and equipment, free and unrestricted passage and unimpeded access throughout the FRY including associated airspace and territorial waters."

- **Section 11**: "NATO is granted the use of airports, roads, rails, and ports without payment of fees, duties, dues, tolls, or charges occasioned by mere use."

- **Section 15**: "The Parties (Yugoslav & Kosovo governments) shall, upon simple request, grant all telecommunications services, including broadcast services, needed for the Operation, as determined by NATO... free of cost."

One likely commercial motive for NATO member demands was control of the multi-billion dollar Trepca mining complex, 22 state owned mines and processing plants of Stari Trg, the third leading producer of zinc and lead in the world. Under the plans, the silver, gold, lead, zinc and $17 billion in coal reserves would be exploited by conquering NATO invaders. Mining director, Novak Bjelic, summed it up when he said: "The war in Kosovo is about the mines, nothing else."

AMERICAN TAXPAYER FUNDED MURDER OF CIVILIANS

Day after day, Americans were befuddled to find that much of the NATO bombing was directed not at the Yugoslavian military, but at the Yugoslavian citizens. The civilian targets hit by NATO included dozens of city bridges, water purification facilities, power generation stations, television stations, market-places, buses, a heating plant, a hotel, a refugee convoy, a passenger train, an engine factory, the Chinese Embassy and dozens of residential areas.

Many facilities were struck deliberately based on NATO claims that they were military targets. Even we Americans who are victims of a dumbed-down education system should be able to tell that the previously mentioned facilities are not military targets. For example, power plants do not provide energy for tanks, bomber fighters or warships, and only a fraction of one percent of plant output might actually be used by a military base. In addition, nearly all military bases have back-up generation capability for their critical functions, so bombing a power station serves nothing more than turning the lights out for civilians. Thus, I believe NATO blatantly lied by claiming that these and other bombings were for military purposes.

Over 2,000 civilians were killed in two months, three times the number of apparent Serbian military deaths and far more than the number that Milosevic was accused of killing in the year before the bombing. The web site, *www.truthinmedia.org*, posted pictures of the atrocities to allow visitors to draw their own conclusions. Over 90 percent of this death and destruction was conducted with American equipment, troops and munitions.

A series of incidents that clearly illustrated the evil of NATO, began on April 14 when a refugee convoy was bombed. NATO and our news media outlets reported that Yugoslavia bombed the convoy, despite obvious total air supremacy of NATO forces. Serbian television, which replayed parts of American newscasts nightly to explain how Americans were being deceived, proved that NATO had bombed the refugees. On April 23, after admitting that it had bombed the convoy, NATO then bombed the Serbian television building, killing innocent civilians whose only crime was that they had told the truth.

NATO spokesmen claimed that the "propaganda" of the Serbian television justified the bombing, and then later appeared to lie under pressure by stating that the TV station was a military target. A Yugoslavian television station is no threat to American citizens. When NATO decided to kill people who said things that it did not like, it proved to those of us who still have a brain and access to the truth, that NATO had become an evil, fascist alliance.

MARCH ON THE PENTAGON

Fortunately, there were still some people left in America who knew what was actually happening and cared enough to try and stop it. Thousands of them descended upon Washington again on June 5, 1999, for a March on the Pentagon. The march appropriately began at the Vietnam Veterans memorial, where Bob Djurdjevic was joined by a host of Orthodox Christian ministers and other Serbian speakers such as Sladjana Dankovic, who had recently returned from Yugoslavia. After a couple of hours there, we marched across the Memorial Bridge carrying signs such as "Clinton, Blair and NATO are war criminals".

As we marched across the bridge and down a Virginia highway that led to the Pentagon, the effect was stunning. For as far as the eye could see, there was nothing but a mass of humanity occupying the bridge and roadway that had been closed to traffic. Some marchers played instruments, and most shouted many different slogans during the brief journey which took a little less than an hour. While crossing the bridge, I thought about the many Yugoslavians who went to stand on their own bridges in hopes that NATO would avoid bombing the bridge and killing more civilians.

When we got to the Pentagon, Sara Flounders and Brian Becker of the International Action Center led another large rally with many speakers. Particularly effective speakers included former Attorney General Ramsey Clark, who summarized how the conflict really started; Pacifica Radio talk show host, Amy Goodman who exposed many media lies; and professor Brian Lituchy, who provided interesting details on Western involvement in the creation and destruction of Yugoslavia over several decades.

Despite having about 5,000 people present, the rally was blacked out by most media outlets. However, C-Span, which had also broadcast Serbian television newscasts, decided to carry the Pentagon portion of the rally live and on tape delay. Despite its coverage, many Americans never knew that the largest anti-war protest since the Vietnam era had just taken place.

It was interesting to note that the entire political spectrum was in attendance, from military veterans and proponents all the way to anti-Pentagon Communist Party members. Regardless of political philosophy, everyone knew that what we were doing was wrong. The widespread backlash against the war may have had an impact. Within a week, the 72-day bombing campaign stopped, and I felt a sense of gratification for having attended. However, throughout the afternoon there, I noticed the distinct smell of pesticide and could not help but wonder if the Pentagon area had been sprayed with some sort of potentially hazardous chemicals. Another year would pass before I begane to learn about the long history of chemical experiments such as "Chemtrails" that have been conducted on American citizens without their knowledge.

THE NATO "PEACE" PLAN

The peace plan that was accepted by the Yugoslavian parliament was not much different than the Rambouillet accords and basically called for NATO occupation and colonization of Kosovo. As Serb troops withdrew from Kosovo, the military damage assessment became obvious. As expected, NATO had lost almost no casualties and a few airplanes and NATO bombs had killed over 2,000 civilians, 3-1/2 times the 600 Yugoslavian soldiers who lost their lives, mostly as a result of ground fighting with the KLA. In addition, the Serbians had lost only three tanks that they left in Kosovo, and they had perhaps another 10 out of their total of 300 that had sustained some damage.

The military casualties were so light that it raised the question of why Milosevic decided to surrender, since he and the Yugoslavian government accepted what was close to the original NATO terms. The casualty count also raised the question as to whether NATO was actually targeting the Yugoslavian military at all. There were no reports of military bases being struck by bombs, yet NATO bombs did billions of dollars in damage to civilian facilities. It appeared that the portrayal of Slobodan Milosevic as a villain by NATO and the national news media was a scam.

As the bombing stopped, the news media continued to portray Milosevic as a villain by entering Kosovo and repeatedly documenting claims of genocide against him and the Yugoslavian army. However, there were a couple of problems with these claims. All of them occurred AFTER the bombing started and were conducted by PARA-MILITARY forces that the Yugoslavian government could not control during the bombing. Other than Racak, I could not find a single one of the daily claims of genocide, that occurred before the bombing started and was traceable to Slobodan Milosevic.

WHY THE MEDIA LIED

Yugoslavian leaders repeatedly claimed that they were victims of two wars, one of bombs and the other of false words used by the media to justify the bombing. The national news media reported virtually anything that NATO said, unchallenged. They reported that Milosevic had ordered the killing of Albanian leaders who were later found to be alive. They reported that Serbians had slaughtered Albanians and buried them in mass graves, which were later found to be individual graves with flowers on them. They reported that Yugoslavians had bombed a refugee convoy that was actually bombed by NATO. They reported that city bridges, water supplies, television stations and power plants were military targets.

American news media likely deceived Americans about the war to maintain domestic support for it and satisfy their vested interests. CBS and NBC are owned by Westinghouse and General Electric, respectively, which are two of the largest American defense contractors. News network parents can frequently profit from war by gaining new munitions and technology contracts. Likewise, CNN benefits tremendously from global conflicts that increase ratings and profits handsomely whenever America is involved in war. In addition, the immediate parent company of ABC is Capital Cities, which had on its board, a former director of the CIA, an organization specialising in masters of deception.

Consistent nightly misinformation cannot simply be excused as incompetence. Chinese General Sun stated thousands of years ago that "All war is based on deception." The military, CIA and CFR connections of the media obviously played a significant role in the daily media deception.

AMERICA DEMILITARIZED

The result of the war was devastating to America as well as Yugoslavia. The Yugoslavian war increased America's reputation as a terrorist country while draining our cruise missile supply. Nuclear warheads on the remaining cruise missiles were replaced under emergency contract with traditional warheads so that they could be used to bomb Yugoslavians. America was now forced to supply thousands of troops to Kosovo, even though our troops were already spread out all over the world.

Many of our existing troops were placed under the command of NATO or the United Nations, neither of which had any regard for the U.S. Constitution or American law. *The New American* and other sources reported that NATO Secretary General Javier Solana, who directed the fascist attack on Yugoslavians by our military, was actually a Spanish Marxist.

Without nuclear cruise missiles and domestic troops we are vulnerable to attack. I am convinced that the degradation and subordination of our military is no accident. It is a deliberate, long term effort by Bill Clinton, his predecessors and many globalists in his administration and Congress to demilitarize America so that it can be subordinated to a one world government body controlled by a global fascist regime, that is staffed by non-elected rulers.

AMERICA MOVED TOWARD FASCISM

As a result of the war on Yugoslavia and many other Presidential scandals, America moved far past Lyndon Johnson socialism and deep into Bill Clinton fascism against the will of most American citizens. It started when Bill Clinton was not held accountable for using the FBI, IRS, INS and Treasury to persecute his adversaries. It continued as Bill Clinton ruled America by unconstitutional Executive Orders and was not challenged by the Republican opposition. It was completed in a shammed impeachment effort when:

- House Republicans ignored Congressional evidence of his more serious crimes;
- Senate Republicans set up procedures to avoid hostile witnesses and damaging evidence against him; and
- Senate Democrats admitted that he was guilty but established a new double standard of American justice by refusing to hold him accountable for charges that were presented.

Worst of all though, were the bombings that covered his political scandals. The bombings, particularly in Yugoslavia, occurred against the will of the American people, who lost total control of their government.

THE THREATENING GLOBAL FASCIST PRECEDENT

When Bill Clinton and NATO joined forces to bomb Yugoslavians, it established a new precedent for a threatening global fascist dictatorship. NATO, a global organization, manufactured a "Hitleresque" excuse to invade a country, bombed hundreds of its civilian facilities, killed thousands of its citizens and created hundreds of thousands of refugees from the people it claimed to be helping. NATO did so by breaking the basic principles of international law without the consent of a single legislature in the entire world. NATO participants aligned themselves with KLA terrorists attempting to overthrow the government for the apparent purpose of eventually exploiting the mineral resources of the victims and establishing themselves as the sole world power.

The U.N., another global organization, did nothing to stop the aggression and is even attempting to prosecute the victims for war crimes, while imposing a double standard of justice for NATO to absolve it of guilt. These atrocities were committed under NATO and U.N. world leaders, none of whom are elected by citizens.

Those responsible for the atrocities include globalist leaders, who desire to form a worldwide, unaccountable, ruling class of elite, and the media organizations who deliberately misinform audiences to achieve that objective and their own vested interests. Our national news media missinformed Americans about NATO and key world events in the same manner that the German media misinformed Germans about Adolf Hitler.

REFERENCES

Independent Commission of Inquiry to Investigate U.S./NATO War Crimes against the people of Yugosalvia, Ramsey Clark, Independent Commission of Inquiry.

The U.S. / NATO War in Yugoslavia: Eight Myths, International Action Center.

The New American magazine, Vol. 15 No. 6.

The New American magazine, "Special Report: Are you Ready for the New World Army?"

NATO in the Balkans, various contributing authors, International Action Center.

The Recak Killings a Massacre?, archive of authors, Strategic Issues Research Institute of the U.S.

Richard Becker, The Rambouillet Accord, International Action Center.

Christophe Chatelot,Were the Racak dead really coldly Massacred?, Le Monde.

Bob Djurdevich, Daily accounts of the war on Yugoslavia, Truth in Media.

Sara Flounders, "Kosovo: 'The war is about the mines'," International Action Center.

Diana Johnstone,"The 'Racak Massacre' questioned by French Media," International Action Center.

Gloria La Riva, *NATO Targets* (video), International Action Center.

Jerry Seper, Some KLA rebels trained & financed by bin Ladin, *Washington Times*.

Tony Snow, Is Kosovo Really that Bloody?, NewsMax.com from Creators Syndicate, Inc.

Gary Wilson,Who is the KLA?, International Action Center.

Gary Wilson, The Balkans: Lies vs. Facts, International Action Center.

Benjamin Works, *Kosovo - Getting Worse?*, Strategic Issues Research Institute of the U.S.

CHAPTER EIGHT
AMERICA: THE BEST GOVERNMENT COMMUNISTS CAN BUY

THE COX REPORT

The bombing of Yugoslavia obscured much of the information in the Cox Report from the public. While the Burton and Thompson Committee investigations identified some key technology that the Communist Chinese government had received for its illegal contributions, they had only scratched the surface of what the Communist Chinese military had actually gotten.

The House Select Committee investigating technology transfers to China, provided more stunning details. The committee, referred to as the Cox Committee, after Committee chairman, Chris Cox produced the bi-partisan, unanimously approved Cox Report as an end product. The declassified version contained roughly 700 pages, while the classified version contained another 300 pages. Some of the factual highlights from the report by chapter are as follows:

THE COX REPORT - PRC Accquisition of U.S. Technology

The Chinese Communist Party controls all state, military, commercial and political activities in the PRC. The Communist Party's eight-member Central Military Commission heads the People's Liberation Army. General Liu Huaqing, the former vice chair of the Central Military Commission and father of Col. Liu Chao Ying, was involved with dozens of Hong Kong and western countries engaged in illegally acquiring advanced U.S. technology.

The PRC has more than 3,000 front companies in the U.S. with technology targeting and acquisition roles. The U.S. has no procedure in place to track PRC front companies and their technology acquisition activity.

In June 1993, Bin Wu and two other PRC nationals were convicted of smuggling third generation night vision equipment to the PRC. In 1997, Peter Lee passed classified techniques to the PRC regarding detection techniques for nuclear submarines. In 1985, he passed classified information to the PRC about laser created nuclear explosions.

THE COX REPORT - PRC Theft of U.S. Nuclear Warhead Design Information

The PRC has stolen classified information for over two decades on all the most advanced U.S. thermonuclear warheads, including all those currently deployed and several associated reentry vehicles. The thefts are continuing to the present. The thefts include the W-88 Trident D-5, W-56 Minuteman II, W-62 Minuteman III, W-70 Lance, W-76 Trident C-4, W-78 Minuteman III, Mark 12A and W-87 Peacekeeper. All are recent except for the W-70 design information the PRC stole in the late 70s from the Lawrence Livermore national labs.

The CIA learned about the thefts in 1995 from a Chinese informant who provided an official PRC document classified as secret. The CIA determined that the informant was directed by the PRC intelligence services. The thefts occurred primarily at Los Alamos, Lawrence Livermore, Sandia and Oak Ridge labs.

Peter Lee, a scientist at Los Alamos and Lawrence Livermore, admitted to passing submarine detection information to the PRC and was convicted in 1997 of passing classified data on miniature nuclear fusion explosions to the PRC.

A suspect in the W-88 theft, Wen Ho Lee, was identified in 1995 and investigated by the FBI beginning in 1996. However, he maintained his security clearance and continued to work in one of the most sensitive divisions at Los Alamos until 1998.

The PRC also may have acquired classified U.S. nuclear weapons computer codes from the labs.

Foreigners can visit labs even though a definitive assessment of risks vs. benefits has never been performed.

No procedures are in place to prevent or detect the movement of classified information to unclassified sections of the computer systems at the labs.

The Department of Energy briefed the Secretary of Energy about thefts in late 1995 and early 1996. The Department of Energy briefed the Deputy National Security Advisor in April 1996. It also briefed the CIA director, FBI director and Attorney General during this period. The deputy, Sandy Berger, who was promoted to National Security Advisor, stated in writing that the President did not learn about the successful PRC espionage until early 1998.

PDD 61, issued in February 1998, required the Energy Department to implement counterintelligence measures that would not even be minimally effective until 2000 according to the Cox Committee.

THE COX REPORT - High Performance Computers

High performance computers appear to have been diverted by the PRC for these unauthorized military uses:

- Upgrading and maintaining nuclear weapons
- Equipping mobile forces with high technology weapons
- Building a modern fleet of combat support aircraft and submarines
- Conducting anti-submarine warfare
- Developing a reliable accurate ballistic and cruise missile force
- Equalizing a battlefield with electronic information warfare
- Improving command, control communications and intelligence capabilities

The PRC may have received over 600 high performance computers since 1996, all over 2,000 million theoretical operations per second (MTOPS) and two over 10,000 MTOPS.

High performance computers recently sold to the PRC could be used for:

- Nuclear weapons development
- Information warfare
- Cryptography
- Military command and control
- Intelligence collection
- Intelligence instrument research and development
- Development of high technology
- Ballistic and cruise missiles
- Ballistic missile defense
- Mobile force development
- Designing submarine nuclear reactors
- Combat simulation

The PRC is seeking high performance computer software for:

- Satellite launch and missile guidance simulation
- Computer assisted design and manufacturing systems
- System simulators
- Applications of artificial intelligence

Three dimensional nuclear explosion simulation requires a computer capacity of one million MTOPS without test data for advanced nuclear weapons. These numbers decrease for more rudimentary nuclear weapons or depending upon how much test data exist.

Prior to 1994, licenses were required for computers over 195 MTOPS. In February of 1994, Japan and the U.S. agreed to raise the limit to 1,500 MTOPS.

Between 1993 and 1995 the NSA withdrew from high performance computer licensing reviews.

Export Administration Regulation revisions in 1996 made exporters responsible for determining whether a license is required.

The 1998 National Defense Act required exporters to notify Commerce of any computer over 2,000 MTOPS shipped to tier three countries such as the PRC.

In June 1998, the U.S. and PRC agreed on relatively useless conditions to verify post shipment computer use in the PRC. Some flaws in the agreement are:

- The PRC considers the request to be non-binding;
- The PRC insists that the verification be conducted by its own ministries;
- The PRC does not allow U.S. Embassy and Consulate personnel to attend verification unless invited;
- The PRC controls all scheduling of the verification;
- The PRC permits verification only for the first six months after the computer arrival.

A few examples of cases involving export violations are:

- On December 20, 1996, New World Transtechnology pled guilty to illegal export of a computer to a PRC nuclear equipment factory in August of 1992 and again in October, 1992. It paid a $10,000 fine and $600 assessment fee.
- On April 18, 1997, Compaq was fined $55,000 for alleged violations of computer export laws between September 17, 1992, and June 11, 1993.
- On June 12, 1997, Digital Creations Corp. of New Jersey was fined $800,000 for violating the Export Administration Act with regards to the PRC. It pled guilty in 1994 for exporting a DEC computer to the PRC illegally.
- On June 17, 1997, Lansing Technologies pled guilty to export violations for illegally exporting a DEC computer vector processor and data acquisition system in 1992.
- In July of 1998, IBM of East Europe and Asia was fined $8.5 million on 17 counts of violating U.S. export laws by shipping computers to a Russian nuclear weapons lab.

A Commerce Department license review between January 1, 1992, and September 23, 1997, showed:

- One export license to Hong Kong was rejected
- 100 licenses to the PRC were rejected
- 37 licenses to Hong Kong were approved, two of those in the 11,000 to 12,800 MTOP range.

THE COX REPORT - PRC Missile
and Space Forces

Qian Xuesen, a Chinese citizen trained in the U.S., worked
on classified missile systems including the Titan intercontinental ballistic missile (ICBM) program. He was born in
Shanghai in 1911 and left China in 1935 during Japanese occupation. He received a Masters from MIT and a Ph.D. from
CalTech where he worked in the jet propulsion laboratory and
became an expert. He was recruited by the U.S. Army Air
Force for its long range missile program and eventually began
working on the Titan. Qian was accused of spying for the PRC
but was not charged and was allowed to return to China, along
with four other Chinese members of the Titan design team. He
became the chief project manager of the CSS-4 ICBM (Long
March 2) which is targeted on the U.S. now. The CCP awarded
him an honorary rank of Lieutenant General in the PLA, and
President Jiang Zemin awarded him the highest honor a PRC
scientist can achieve in 1991.

The PRC has gotten much technology from Russia. The
Russian designer of the SSX27 claims that its advanced pene-
tration capability will allow it to penetrate any ballistic missile
defense.

The PRC proliferated complete ballistic missile systems or
components to Iran, Pakistan, North Korea and Saudi Arabia.

THE COX REPORT - Hughes Satellite
Launches in the PRC

China Great Wall Industries Corperation launched Hughes
Space and Communications International, Inc. satellites from
the PRC in 1992 and 1995, but explosions occurred before they
reached orbit. Launch failure investigations that determined
how to improve the rocket, resulted in the transfer of technical
information to the PRC when the transfer was approved by
government officials. Hughes' claim of government approval
in 1992 is not fully substantiated. In 1995, a Commerce
Department official improperly issued a clearance for Hughes,
which sought Commerce approval even though it knew that the
jurisdiction belonged to the State Department.

In the 12/21/92 Optus B2 failure the Hughes launch investigators, Peter Herron and Stephen Cunningham, submitted to the Defense Technology Security Administration (DTSA) view slides of a failure analysis paper prepared by Hughes' chief technologist, Al Wittmann, in June of 1993. The paper detailed how Wittmann believed that a fairing was the cause of the launch failure and how the fairing could be improved for a forthcoming launch. DTSA approval of the view slide transfer to the PRC appears in a 6/25/93 facsimile signed by Lt. Col. Coates, who said that he did not recall approving the transfer and did not have the authority to do so.

In the 1/26/95 Apstar 2 failure, the Hughes launch investigative team was composed of many of the same individuals. By July 1995, Wittman and Spencer Ku determined that the PRC had added some additional fairing rivets but did not re-structure the fairing based on the previous failure recommendation, and therefore, the changes were inadequate. Hughes Export Control Coordinator Leedle and others acknowledged that a State Department license was required to transfer failure analysis information to the PRC. However, Commerce licensing officer, Gene Chritansen, sent a letter to Leedle on 8/24/95 authorizing Hughes to release the detailed failure design analysis to the PRC. A 12/7/98 Defense Department report indicated that failure investigation transfer had damaged our national security.

Charlie Yah Lin Trie whose families and business contributed $220,000 to the DNC between 1994 and 1996, received $100,000 in May 1996 from CP Group, shareholders in Asia Pacific Telecommunications and the Apstar satellite program. During the same period that Trie made his contributions he received $1.5 million by wire transfer from foreign sources.

THE COX REPORT - Loral Satellite
Launch in the PRC

On 2/15/96 a Long March 3B carrying Intelstat 708 crashed after liftoff from the PRC, the third PRC launch failure in 38 months involving rockets carrying U.S. payloads. In April 1996, the Great Wall China Industry Corperation invited Dr. Wah Lim, Loral's Senior V.P. of Engineering and

Manufacturing, to chair an independent review committee that would conduct a failure investigation. The first meeting of the committee took place on 4/22/96 where William Schweickert, Loral Technology Control Manager, claimed he told the committee that Loral did not have a license for the meeting. The preliminary report of the investigation containing a conclusion that an inertial measurement unit within the rocket control system had failed, was faxed to the China Great Wall Industry Corperation on 5/7/96 by the committee secretary, Loral's Nick Yen, without any U.S. Government approval.

Around May 14, Robert Kovac, a DTSA Export Analyst read about the transfer in *Space News* and called Loral's Export Control Officer, who met with State and Defense Departments' licensing personnel the next day. In June of 1996, the U.S. Government issued a cease and desist letter regarding investigation activities to Loral and Hughes which had members on the review committee. In 1997, the Defense Department concluded that "Loral and Hughes committed a serious export control violation" and recommended referral to the Justice Department for possible criminal prosecution. Lim refused to be interviewed by the Cox Committee, despite Loral's agreeing to a voluntary disclosure.

In August 1996 the Defense Department prepared a classified assessment citing 18 violations of the Independent Review Committee. The State Department prepared a corroborating report, and the DTSA recommended referral to Justice for possible criminal investigation.

The crash into a mountainside occurred at 3:00 a.m. local time, but Loral and Intelsat employees were not allowed onto the debris field for 12 hours. The media reported that PRC officials were seeking out satellite encryption devices that protect the satellite from unauthorized messages once it is in orbit. Loral engineers determined that the satellite encryption devices were never shipped back to Loral at Palo Alto.

THE COX REPORT - Launch Site
Security in the PRC

U.S. satellite manufacturers hire a security force to provide physical security for the satellite prior to launch. Only one company has bid for the contracts, and the conduct, professionalism and abilities of the personnel of that company have been sharply criticized by Defense Department monitors.

If the PRC has unrestricted access to a satellite for two hours, it could gain valuable information that is not publicly available. The PRC could learn virtually everything about a satellite with unrestricted access for 24 hours. PRC could gain this information via sophisticated X-ray and other equipment while remaining completely undetected.

A Defense Department monitor stated that we, as a nation, cannot afford to allow an industry to police itself when it comes to national security, and that if restrictive measures are not levied against the industries, our technology will be compromised to such a staggering level that our highest level of technology advancements will be available to our international competitors before it comes off the research and development floor.

During 1993 to 1996, Commerce issued three export licenses for satellites to be launched in the PRC without Defense monitors present and without reimbursing the Defense Department for monitors.

After the Intelsat 708 crash, a Defense Department monitor advised Loral management to delay piece recovery until a meeting between Loral, the PRC and the monitor could be held to avoid technology transfers in the recovery effort. Loral upper management ignored the advice, and the satellite encryption technology was never recovered.

A former Loral security manager argued against having the Chinese program manager placed in charge of security during the Intelsat 708 launch because the manager's objective of launching the satellite took precedence over security. He was overruled by Loral management. The manager also had Chinese nationals photographed in front of the satellite, which is a violation of security rules.

Only Pinkerton Aerospace offers foreign launch security since Launch Security Services International went out of business in 1996. One Defense Department monitor reported that problems with security guard forces included:

- Sleeping on job;
- Reporting to work under the influence of alcohol;

- Poor reporting on daily logs and at shift changes;
- Routine bus trips into the town to meet prostitutes ;
- Overall lack of respect for management;
- Reporting to work with a sleeping bag.

Satellite companies also have a cost incentive not to hire an adequate number of security guards.

THE COX REPORT - Commercial
Space Insurance

China Great Wall Industry Corperation set up the review committee for the Intelstat 708 failure to provide adequate reporting so that it could stay in the launch business and prevent cancellations.

It invited Dr. Wah Lim of Loral (and formally of Hughes), to chair the committee. On May 13, 1996, Lim sent a copy of the preliminary report to Paul O'Connor, Vice President of Marsh and McLennan, one of the prospective insurers for the next launch of the Apstar-1A.

Lim hired Nick Yen as secretary for the committee. Yen advised O'Connor that "The IRC may require a technical export license for the subject matter which may result in a revised version in wording. However, the technical contents and assessment in the report as faxed in this package remain valid."

On May 31, 1996, O'Connor advised China Great Wall Industry Corperation of the formal State Department decision that the release of the IRC interim report was not allowed.

THE COX REPORT - U.S. Export Policy
Toward PRC

The 1979 Export Administration Act established control of American export regulations. The 1996 Economic Espionage Act provided additional regulations to the Export Administration Act.

In 1995, new CIV licensing exceptions were issued by the Commerce Department for items under export controls that were destined for civil use; a new CTP license exception raised the super computer export limit from 2,000 MTOPS to 7,000 MTOPS.

Key Executive Orders that loosened U.S. export controls included:

E.O. 12981 - 1995:

Eliminated need for Commerce referrals to State, Defense Energy and U.S. Intelligence;

E.O. 13020 - 1996:

Transferred commercial communication satellite and "hot section" range technology export authority from the State Department to Commerce;

E.O. 13026 - 1996:

Required Justice Department review of encryption applications from Commerce Department.

The Commerce Department failed to provide the Cox Committee with classification requests that vendors had submitted to determine licensing requirements for commodities they were preparing to export.

In the spring of 1996, Bill Clinton approved new NSC commodity classification procedures that transferred commodity jurisdiction to Defense and Commerce Departments and included an appeal process to the President.

The countries participating in the Coordinating Committee on Multi-Lateral Export Controls (COCOM) agreed on consistent export controls for items to China and the Soviet Union since 1972.

In October 1998, U.S. President Reagan approved a plan to permit the export of U.S. satellites to the PRC for launch on PRC rockets, provided the PRC followed conditions defined in an agreement signed in December 1998. The agreement specified security safeguards to prevent unauthorized technology transfers to the PRC, required the PRC to apply fair trade market principles, limited the number of launches and assumed responsibility and liability for any damage done by space objects.

In 1990, Congress passed the Foreign Relations Action with additional sanctions prohibiting exports of satellites, U.S. munitions list items and crime control and detection equipment as a result of the Tiananmen Square massacre.

George Bush authorized three waivers to the act, and Bill Clinton authorized nine waivers, including one on 2/18/98 to

Loral that bypassed Justice, which was investigating Loral for an earlier illegal transfer.

On 10/23/92, regulations were issued to transfer certain satellites from the State Department munitions list to the Commerce control list.

On 9/29/93, Commerce issued a report "Toward a National Export Strategy - Report to U.S. Congress" which quoted Bill Clinton in Chapter Five as saying, "One reason I ran for President was to tailor export controls to the realities of a post Cold War world."

The State Department's Warren Christopher objected to the March 1996 Clinton decision to transfer all commercial communication satellite export control from the State Department munitions list to the Commerce control list.

Commercial communication satellites having nine identifying characteristics were transferred from the State Department munitions list to the Commerce Department control list in October 1996. Commercial satellite authority was returned to State by Congress in 1999 under the Strom Thurmond Defense Act. Jet engine hot section range technology was transferred to Commerce in October 1996, and encryption item authority was transferred to Commerce during December 1996.

In May of 1992, the U.S. imposed foreign policy controls on super computers, defined as those above 195 million theoretical operations per second (MTOPS) in a bilateral agreement with Japan, the other exporter.

Prior to 1994, COCOM countries agreed that licenses would be required to export computers of more that 12.5 MTOPS to the PRC. In January 1994, COCOM raised the limit to 260 MTOPS, and that was published in the *Federal Register* on 2/24/94. On 3/30/94, the Clinton administration removed licensing requirements on computers up to 1,000 MTOPS exported to COCOM controlled countries.

In October 1995, the Clinton administration announced further export regulation changes that allowed the PRC to receive computers up to 7,000 MTOPS without a license. Commerce published these licensing requirements in the *Federal Register* on 1/25/96 as revised Export Administration regulations using a four-tier structure of countries based on their security risk. The Clinton administration also removed all supercomputer licensing requirements to most industrialized nations.

More favorable export controls, such as a 10,000 MTOPS supercomputer non-licensing limit, have remained for Hong Kong even after it was taken over by the PRC. The Cox Committee stated that "a sizable number of Hong Kong enterprises serve as cover for PRC intelligence services, such as the MSS."

Defense Intelligence Agency Analyst, Nicholas Eftimiades, and Senate Governmental Affairs Committee investigator, Thomas Hampson, stated that China Resources Co., a PRC owned corporation that is based in Hong Kong, is "an agent of economic, military and political espionage". It is also a partner of the LIPPO GROUP, whose principal executive in the U.S. was John Huang.

Huang left Lippo to join Commerce in late 1993 as Principal Deputy Assistant Secretary of Commerce International Economic Policy. He had a top secret clearance, and his superiors even requested him to increase it to the sensitive compartmented information clearance held by his predecessor.

Between October 1994 and November 1995, he received 37 briefings from the Office of Intelligence Liaison at Commerce and had access to dozens of classified cables each day. During his 18 months at Commerce, Huang made 394 calls to LIPPO GROUP headquarters, subsidiaries, consultants or partners.

For additional communications, Huang used a visitor's office across the street at the D.C. branch of Stephens, Inc., another LIPPO GROUP partner. He also met with PRC Embassy officials in D.C. on at least nine occasions. His other office and visits with PRC officials were unknown to anyone at Commerce.

THE COX REPORT - Manufacturing Processes

COCOM, Coordinating Committee for Multi-lateral Export Controls, restricted exports to the PRC of machine tools having a linear positioning accuracy no better than 10 microns because they could be used for nuclear weapons development.

In 1996, the Wassenaar Agreement and Nuclear Suppliers Group generally required export licenses for lathes and milling machines better than 6 microns and grinding machines better than 4 microns.

On 6/24/94 and 7/28/94, the export of McDonnell Douglas machine tools from a closing Columbus, Ohio, plant to the PRC was discussed by State, Defense, Energy, Commerce and an Arms Control Disarmament Agency (ACDA) at an Advisory Committee on Export Policy (ACEP) meeting. No agreement to export was given because of the concerns expressed by Defense and ACDA that the tools or other existing PRC tools would be diverted to the PLA. ACEP later voted to export the tools with 14 conditions.

China Aero Technology Import and Export Corp (CATIC) violated the conditions by distributing the tools to various unauthorized military locations. McDonnell Douglas reported this to Commerce on 4/4/95. No action was taken by Commerce until the Defense Technology Security Administration requested a formal investigation on 10/4/95.

Once an investigation began, the Commerce Department refused the November 1995 request from its L.A. field office to issue a temporary denial order against CATIC.

THE COX REPORT - Appendices

Loral employees were instructed by their lawyers not to answer questions and three Loral lawyers claimed attorney certain client privileges after Loral waived the privileges for voluntary disclosure.

The CIA impeded the Cox investigation by tipping off Hughes with a "courtesy" notice that the Cox Committee might interview Hughes employees. The CIA even detailed to Hughes the potential lines of questioning. The Cox Committee did not agree to the "courtesy" notification and was concerned that the CIA had given Hughes the opportunity to destroy evidence and pressure employees to be less candid.

Chairman Cox testified that the Justice Department attempted to insert itself as an intermediary for information requests between the committee and all government agencies because an investigation was in progress. However, Justice did not provide other agencies with necessary progress information about its investigation. The Cox Committee spent a major part of its resources retracing Justice Department steps despite protests of harm to the investigation. (Note: The sincerity of its investigation was demonstrated one day after the Cox Report was released, when Justice gave John Huang immunity for the entire campaign finance scandal in a plea bargain on an unrelated 1992 charge. Previous evidence indicated that Huang arranged most of the seven sources of revenue traceable through 11 streams from Clinton / Gore campaigns and the DNC to individuals and organizations directly connected to the Communist Chinese military.)

Defense Technology Security Administration (DTSA) employees testified that senior managers frequently overruled valid national security concerns regarding DOD positions on dual-use license applications. But the DOD refused to allow the Cox Committee to interview the six most senior DTSA managers, refused to let them interview DTSA employees unless a DOD observer was present and refused to allow DTSA employees to answer a survey by mail.

HIGH TREASON

As the media continued to focus only on the fact that the Chinese had stolen most of our classified nuclear design information, the real story that the media deliberately avoided was how government agencies and individuals, particularly in the Clinton administration, helped the Chinese Communists obtain the information and technology they sought. Slowly the facts became a little more obvious as to why Bill Clinton would strongly support an illegal, immoral, unconstitutional and fascist war against Yugoslavia and why he would even go to the extent of lying about genocide to initiate it. After considering the Burton, Thompson and Cox Committee investigations and statements from their members and other supporting sources, I compiled the following breakdown by department and individual of 50 reported unexplained potential acts of treason that I believe may have been committed by the Clinton administration.

TREASON AT COMMERCE

- The Clinton administration, primarily through Commerce, loosened export controls to transfer over 1,000 military and dual use technologies to Communist controlled companies and organizations in China.
- Commerce gradually raised the PRC supercomputer export limit from **12.5 to 7,000 MTOPS** (million theoretical operations per second), a near **600-fold increase** over the previous limit in force during January 1994. As a result, the PRC received over 600 supercomputers, which can be used for nuclear weapons design.
- Commerce approved the illegal release of a 1995 PRC launch crash analysis and approved export of sophisticated jet fighter "hot section" range technology that helps planes fly farther.
- Commerce refused the November 1995 request from its L.A. field office to issue a temporary denial order against CATIC after it violated the agreement conditions for distributing sophisticated McDonnell Douglas machine tools to various unauthorized PLA military locations.
- Commerce revised the Export Administration Regulations in 1996 to make exporters responsible for determining whether a license is required instead of the federal government.

TREASON AT ENERGY

- Former Energy Secretary, Hazel O'Leary, removed the color coded security badges for visitors at weapons labs.
- Hazel O'Leary, suspended background checks during 1993 and 1994 for visitors to at least of two nuclear labs.
- In 1995, Hazel O'Leary, overturned the decision of the Energy office in Oakland and allowed a former employee to retain his classified status after his status has been removed by the Oakland office for releasing sensitive classified information to unauthorized people.
- Hazel O'Leary gave a classified diagram of the W87 nucular warhead to a reporter for *U.S. News and Report* which published it in the July 31, 1995 issue.
- In 1995, an assistant to Energy Secretary O'Leary prevented Notra Trulock from briefing Congress about nuclear

lab security breeches because she thought it might hurt the President's China policy.

- The Intelligence and Arms Control director newly appointed by Hazel O'Leary removed Jay Stewart from his position as Foreign Intelligence Director and destroyed all documents from his "Russian Fission" program after it detected a loss of nuclear weapons control by the Soviets in 1993.

- Former Energy Secretary, Fredrico Pena, issued a "gag order" at a weapons lab to prevent any Energy employee from interacting with Congress or providing documents without formal approval.

- In October 1998, Energy, under Secretary Richardson **gave a Chinese national all of the key computer parts needed to create one of the most powerful computers in the world (150,000+ MTOPS). The parts, valued at $9,000,000, were sold for $30,000,** and the transaction was not exposed until the manufacturer was alerted when the Chinese national contacted them with questions regarding re-assembly.

- In 1999, Secretary Richardson claimed that security problems at Energy had been corrected despite Cox Report statements that it would require several years for the Energy Department to minimally address security concerns.

- In 1999, Energy Security Chief, Col. Ed McCallum, who pointed out many security lapses, was placed on administrative leave by Secretary Richardson, who claimed McCallum passed classified information while interviewing a whistle-blower.

TREASON AT THE CIA

- The CIA alerted Hughes about the questions that the Cox Committee would ask them against the will of the committee.

- A CIA intelligence officer was pulled from a panel drafting Presidential Decision Directive 25 after he objected to intelligence sharing in international peacekeeping efforts and opposed U.S. troop involvement in civil wars.

TREASON AT DEFENSE

- The U.S. Navy reversed Lt. Jack Daly's highest rating ever for a promotion, making it the worst evaluation of his career after he was struck in the eye by a laser while monitoring a Russian ship and notified a House Intelligence Committee member about the incident.
- The Defense Technology Security Administration (DTSA) refused to grant the Cox Committee private interviews of its employees and refused to allow its employees to fill out Cox Committee surveys.

TREASON AT STATE

- The State Department gave a 24-hour advance notice of American intent to search the Russian ship suspected of having the laser that injured Lt. Col. Jack Daly and his Canadian co-pilot.
- A government agency believed to be the State Department leaked advance notice of American intent to arrest Chinese officials for the smuggling of 2,000 illegal AK47 into Oakland by COSCO. This helped protect Wang Jun, who had recently met with Bill Clinton at the White House. Wang is the son of PLA General, Wang Zhen, and the head of the COSCO parent company, CITIC.

TREASON AT THE NSA

- The National Security Administration, NSA, withdrew from high performance computer licensing reviews between 1993 and 1995.
- After being briefed about major security breeches and theft in the nuclear labs in 1995, Sandy Berger failed to brief the President for two years.
- In 1995, the NSA assisted in producing NIE 95-19, a document that ruled out a rogue missile threat to the U.S. The GAO found the document to be overstated with numerous analytical shortcomings, while former CIA director, Robert Gates, who headed an independent review, found the document to be "politically naïve" and "foolish from every perspective" in regards to the threats posed to Alaska and Hawaii.

TREASON BY THE PRESIDENT

- Bill Clinton became the only President in U.S. history to give military technology to a foreign country over the objections of his own government agencies. He did this not once, but four times on three separate transfers over objections of four different agencies. The technology was not sent to an ally, but to a **Communist** government whose Communist Chinese Party and People's Liberation Army literature refers to America as its main enemy.
- In March 1996, Bill Clinton transferred all commercial communication satellite export control from the State Department munitions list to the Commerce control list over objections by State Department Secretary Warren Christopher.
- Bill Clinton issued Loral a waiver for a satellite launch over objections from the Justice Department while Loral was under investigation for illegal transferring launch crash analysis information to China.
- Bill Clinton approved the transfer of fiber optic communications equipment over objections from both Defense and the NSA.
- Bill Clinton issued Executive Orders 12981 and 13020, which moved much of the export authority to Commerce and eliminated intelligence referrals to other departments.
- Despite briefings by Energy in 1995 and the NSA in 1997, Bill Clinton initially claimed that he was not briefed until 1998.
- Bill Clinton terminated American involvement in the Coordinating Committee on Multi-Lateral Export Controls (COCOM), whose members had agreed on consistent export controls for items to China and the Soviet Union since 1972.
- Bill Clinton lobbied for COSCO to take over the Long Beach naval base after it was caught smuggling 2,000 illegal AK 47's into Oakland and after its parent company chairman, Wang Jun, son of PLA General Wang Zhen, met with Clinton in the White House.
- Bill Clinton orchestrated the illegal campaign fundraising scheme that produced **seven sources of revenue** traceable through **11 illegal** revenue streams to organizations and in-

dividuals directly connected to the **People's Liberation Army**, including three **Communist agents** and three members of **Asian organized crime**.

- Bill Clinton pressured Ron Brown to hire John Huang, the illegal campaign fundraiser, at Commerce despite his lack of qualifications.
- Bill Clinton pressured DNC Finance Chairman Sullivan to hire John Huang at the DNC despite his lack of qualifications.
- Bill Clinton repeatedly lied about national security, stating over 100 times that no missiles were pointed at the U.S..
- Bill Clinton said in March of 1999 that he had not been told about espionage at the labs after he had been briefed by several cabinet members.

TREASON AT JUSTICE

- Attorney General Janet Reno granted immunity for the entire campaign finance scandal to John Huang, key organizer of the 11 illegal revenue streams traceable from the DNC and Clinton / Gore campaigns to the Communist Chinese military.
- The Reno Justice Department refused several times to tap the phone line of nuclear design theft suspect Wen Ho Lee, the only individual whose phone tap was denied out of more than 2,000 FBI requests, even though the Justice Department had been briefed about the lab thefts in 1995.
- The Reno Justice Department delayed a search warrant for the computer and documents of Charlie Trie, thus giving him the time needed to remove key information.
- Janet Reno refused seven requests to appoint an independent counsel to investigate all of the numerous detailed allegations of illegal campaign contributions from the Communist Chinese military to the Clinton / Gore campaigns and the DNC.
- In 1996-7, Lee Radek of the Reno Justice Department's Office of Public Integrity sent cease and desist orders to the L.A. U. S. Attorney regarding the investigation of the Hsi Lai temple fundraiser attended by Al Gore.

- The Reno Justice Department attempted to impede information requests from the Cox Committee by demanding that all requests be routed through them.
- Justice Dept. lawyer Laura Ingersoll, and her boss Lee Radek refused to allow FBI agents Ivian Smith, Daniel Wehr, Kevin Sheridan and Roberta Parker to get a search warrant while Charles Trie destroyed business and travel records for four months;
- Laura Ingersoll allegedly told FBI agents "Not to persue any matter related to solicitation of funds to the president. That's the way the American political process works";

TREASON IN THE JUDICIAL BRANCH

- Judge Norma Holloway, a Carter appointee, bypassed the normal random selection of judges and assigned cases involving Webster Hubbell and Charles Trie to Clinton appointed judges;
- Clinton appointed Judge Paul Friedman ruled on Friday October 9, 1998 that it was not illegal for foreign nationals to contribute unlimited amounts of "soft money" political contributions used for general campaign purposes;
- Judge Paul Friedman threw out a total of 19 Justice Dept. campaign finance related charges against Charles Trie, Maria Hsia and Pauline Kanchanalak in addition to 6 other charges that were dropped as a result of his ruling;
- Judge Paul Friedman "erred" in his dismissal of charges against Maria Hsia according to a D.C. Circuit Court of Appeals ruling on May 18, 1999. Hsia was eventually convicted of all five counts against her.
- Judge Paul Friedman refused to jail Charles Trie to keep him from fleeing overseas after being informed by a federal prosecutor that Trie applied for a Taiwanese passport after being forced to surrender his U.S. passport when charged with campaign finance violations;

THE PAYOFF

Many of the technology transfers began occurring before the Clinton / Gore campaign and the DNC received illegal contributions from China. The contributions were documented

long before the impeachment votes by the House Government
Reform and Oversight Committee and the Senate Campaign
Finance Committee.

Eleven illegal streams of revenue were traced from the
Clinton / Gore campaigns and the DNC to individuals and organizations directly involved with the Communist Chinese
military. As a whole they form an incredible bribery scheme
that was obviously used by the Communist Chinese government to gain prohibited American technology. Some
reported examples of this intricate arrangement are:

- Charles Yah Lin Trie, a member of Asian organized crime,
  donated $350,000 to DNC and $640,000 to Clinton defense
  fund in sequentially numbered money orders from various
  cities sent in by different people who happened to have
  identical handwriting. The Trie funds were traced to the
  Communist controlled Bank of China and to Ng Lapseng,
  an advisor to both the Communist Chinese Party and
  Communist Chinese government;
- PLA Col. Liu Chao Ying, daughter of PLA General Liu
  Huaqing, gave Johnny Chung $300,000 from Chinese
  General Ji Shengde, who told Chung that he wanted to give
  it to Bill Clinton because "We like your President." Chung,
  who passed about $100,000 of that money along, also
  donated $366,000 to the DNC, a figure well beyond his
  personal means;
- Ted Sioeng, head of the Chinese Communist controlled
  Pagoda Red Mountain Cigarette Co. donated $400,000 to
  DNC. Immediately afterwards, the Democrats tried to help
  Sioeng get a foothold in the American market by introducing a significant amount of anti-tobacco legislation
  against American companies under the guise of concern
  about teen smoking;
- Sonya and Arief Wiriadinata donated $450,000 to the DNC
  but filed no U.S. tax return. Arief is the Indonesian gardener
  who can be seen on White House videos shaking the hand
  of the President and saying "Mr. Riady sent me." The
  Riadys own the LIPPO GROUP, which jointly owns the
  Hong Kong Chinese Bank with China Resources, an "agent
  of political, economic and military espionage" according to

investigators from the Defense Intelligence Agency and Senate Governmental Affairs Committee;

- The Worthen Bank, jointly owned by the LIPPO GROUP and (Jackson) Stephens, Inc., made a key $3,000,000 loan to Bill Clinton in 1992, which catapulted his Presidential campaign from near collapse to success;

- The Communist Chinese controlled arms company, Norinco, partnered with Thailand's CP group, which retained Pauline Kanchanalak, who raised nearly $600,000 for various Democratic Party candidates;

- Maria Hsia, a known Communist Chinese agent, supported four fundraisers for Vice President Al Gore and formed the Pacific Leadership Council with John Huang to raise money for the DNC. Hsia can be seen in a picture sitting with Al Gore at the Hsi Lai temple fundraiser;

- John Huang, the former Lippo U.S. President at the epicenter of Chinese espionage against America, raised about $2,000,000 for the DNC after Bill Clinton pressured DNC Finance Chairman Sullivan to hire him;

- Nina Wang, who gave $50,000 to help restore Bill Clinton's boyhood home, also funded $7,000,000 for American training of PLA officers, including two involved in the Tiananmen Square massacre;

- The Communist Chinese controlled company, Costind, partnered with Chun Hua Yea, who gave $37,000 to the DNC;

- Other mysterious illegal campaign contributions were also received. For example, the Korean company, Cheong Am American, donated $250,000 to DNC but never raised U.S. funds, and Yogesh Gandhi donated $325,000 to DNC but had liens filed against him for non-payment of taxes;

During the Congressional investigations, over 100 witnesses either pleaded the 5th Amendment, required immunity for testimony, left the country or refused to be interviewed because they were foreign nationals. In addition, China refused to provide bank records or allow Congressional investigators to enter the country. On the American side of the scheme, an April 17, 1996, DNC memo uncovered by the House Government Reform Committee investigation confirmed that

Bill Clinton oversaw all fundraising. As expected, Bill Clinton was not only aware of the freedom threatening fundraising scheme, he orchestrated it.

CONCLUSION

The sheer number of potentially treasonous acts involving the Clinton administration and the Communist Chinese government indicate Bill Clinton orchestrated a clear pattern of events that will jeopardize the security of American citizens for decades to come. His obvious motive was the 11 illegal revenue streams received from individuals and organizations directly involved with the People's Liberation Army. However, whether or not a quid pro quo existed is irrelevant since treason and bribery are independently impeachable offenses.

The known evidence may present the clearest case of treason and bribery that has ever existed in America. Therefore, perhaps even more stunning than these acts committed by a Democrat administration, is the unwillingness of the "opposition" leadership in the Republican controlled Congress, to protect the American citizens as China acquires the best government money can buy.

Equally disturbing is the fact that Chinese generals who had operational, tactical and general responsibility for the Tiananmen Square massacres such as Xu Huizi, Wang Zhen and Chi Haotian, have been welcomed to Washington by the Clinton administration.

The national news media outlets have attempted to convince the American people that only a couple of hundred pro-democracy students were killed at Tiananmen Square by repeatedly showing a picture of a tank stopping for a Chinese student. However, on June 3 and 4, 1989 the tanks did not stop as thousands of non-violent pro-democracy students were crushed to death and machine gunned by the PLA.

On the morning of June 4, the Chinese Red Cross announced that 2,600 people had already been killed. On the same day, the Swiss Ambassador who had diplomatic responsibility for the International Red Cross confirmed 2,700 civilian deaths. But the killing continued that day as NATO intelligence estimates eventually reached 6,000 deaths. One of the most knowledgeable organizations of all was the Hong Kong

Communist Party newspaper, Wen Wei Po, which reported that 5,000 people were killed and 30,000 injured.

However, it was not just the students that were murdered by the PLA, according to Toronto Globe and Mail reporter Jan Wong and London Observer correspondent Dr. Jonathan Mirsky. When parents of some students gathered in front of the Beijing Hotel on East Changan Ave. PLA troops opened fire killing dozens of them and even the white gowned nurses and doctors from Beijing's Capital Hospital who had rushed to the scene in an ambulance.

By nearly all accounts the PLA unit responsible for most of the killing was 27th Group Army, formerly commanded by General Chi Haotian, who met with Bill Clinton in the White House.

REFERENCES

The Select Committee on U.S National Security and Military/ Commercial Concerns with People's Republic Of China, House Select Committee (Cox Committee).

Investigation of Illegal or Improper Activities in Connection with 1996 Federal Election Campaign 1-6, Hearing 1-10, Senate Governmental Affairs.

Investigation of Political Fund Raising Improprieties and Possible Violations of Law #1-4, House Government Reform and Oversight Committee.

Bill Gertz, *Betrayal*, Regnery Publishing.

Ed Timperlake and Bill Triplett, *Red Dragon Rising,* Regnery Publishing.

Ed Timperlake and Bill Triplett, *The Year of the Rat*, Regnery Publishing.

China by any other Name (video), American Investigator, Free Congress Research & Education Foundation.

Low Road to China (video), American Investigator, Free Congress Research & Education Foundation.

Red Gold Rising (video), American Investigator, Free Congress Research & Education Foundation.

The New American magazine, "Special report: Treason in the White House," Vol. 18. No. 4.

CHAPTER NINE
THE DEATH TRAIL

The Clinton administration appears to be directly involved in the cover-ups of the murders of Kevin Ives, Don Henry and Vince Foster. Although two independent counsels ruled that Vince Foster committed suicide, it is obvious to any halfway intelligent human being that a man cannot shoot himself without getting some portion of his fingerprints or palm prints on the gun. All the other evidence I previously described in this book also debunks the suicide rulings. I believe the evidence clearly shows that Vince Foster was murdered and both independent counsels lied.

In regards to Clinton administration involvement in the cover-up of Vince Foster's murder, evidence indicated that Bernard Nussbaum, the White House Counsel, turned over Foster's briefcase to authorities. However, three different witnesses said that they saw the briefcase in Foster's car at Fort Marcy Park. On the third search of the briefcase, a suicide note, supposedly written by Foster, suddenly appeared in it. No fingerprints were found on the note even though it was torn into 28 pieces. The suicide note was declared a forgery by several different handwriting analysts. The forgery is so obvious that anyone can see many letters that have several pen dots indicating the letters were drawn.

In the case of Kevin Ives and Don Henry, after the parents proved that Fahmy Malak, the Arkansas State medical examiner, had made false rulings in their deaths, the *L.A. Times* documented nearly 20 suspicious or obviously inaccurate death rulings that he had made. Afterwards, Bill Clinton introduced lagislation to give an approximate 40 percent raise to Malak, who reported to Jocelyn Elders. When the citizens held protest demonstrations and forced his resignation in 1992, Bill Clinton created a new position in the state health department for Malak. Clinton told reporters that Malak was "stressed out", and Elders stated on the *Obstruction of Justice* video that "Arkansas owes Dr. Malak a great debt and a real apology."

Therefore, based on the protection that Bill Clinton gave Malak directly, I believe it is clear that he personally participated in the cover-up of the murders of Kevin Ives and Don Henry.

There are also many other mysterious deaths of individuals who in some direct or indirect way are related to the Clinton administration even though there is no direct evidence implicating anyone in the administration. The number of mysterious deaths has grown to the point where it even surpasses the approximate 55 mysterious deaths involving the assassination of John F. Kennedy. These strange reported deaths generally fall into four categories:

- Suicides;
- Unsolved Murders;
- Plane or car crashes;
- Heart attacks.

I have compiled the following partial list of about 70 individuals many of whom became adversaries of the Clinton administration. The list is in reverse chronological order beginning with the most recent incidents. It includes the date of death, official cause of death, their connection and the unusual circumstances surrounding their death:

Carlos Ghigliotti 4/2000 Unknown
Thermal image expert who told House committee FLIR video indicates federal agents fired shots at Branch Davidians and was to be retained for Davidian civil suit after first expert suffered a stoke. Decomposed body found at his home with no signs of a break-in or struggle.

Lt. Col. Mark Cwick 9/99 Car crash
HMX-1 helicopter pilot who transported Bill Clinton and other officials around Washington area. Died when a car he attempted to pass moved in front of him, causing him to swerve off the road.

Daniel Dutko 7/23/99 Bicycle accident
Co chair of DNC's Leadership 2000 fund raising, vice chair for DNC finance in 1996, vice chair of finance for Clinton/Gore in 1995. Died of multiple head injuries in bicycle accident.

David Drye 6/99 Plane crash
Friend of *The Clinton Chronicles* producer, Pat Matrisciana, who was scheduled to fly with him to Washington. Plane lost one engine on take-off and a second engine while immediately attempting to land.

Ann Drye 6/99 Plane crash
Friend of *The Clinton Chronicles* producer, Pat Matrisciana, who was scheduled to fly with her to Washington. Plane lost one engine on take-off and a second engine while immediately attempting to land.

Major Marc Hohle 4/99 Helicopter crash
Pilot for Bill Clinton during first year of Presidential term in 1993. Died In same HMX-1 Unit as Mark Cwick.

Cpl. Eric S. Fox 3/99 Suicide after car crash
Helicopter crewman in same Marine Corps HMX-1 Unit as Mark Cwick and Marc Hohle. Found in school yard with gunshot wound to head after car ran off the road and hit a guard rail earlier in the evening.

Johnny Franklin Lawhon 3/29/98 Car crash
Transmission shop owner who found $27,000 check from Madison Guaranty Savings and Loan to Bill Clinton in car trunk. Died in single car crash with no witnesses when run off the road by a semi for a second time in the weeks after turning over the check to Ken Starr's team.

James McDougal 3/8/98 Heart failure
Clinton Whitewater business partner and campaign fundraiser convicted of fraud. Prison staff apparently denied his nitroglycerin heart medicine, gave him a diuretic and prescribed a "near fatal" 60 milligram daily Prozac dose, according to examiner.

Ron Miller 10/12/97 Unknown
Gave Congressional investigators recorded tapes of Gene and Nora Lum's illegal campaign contributions. The Lums, who were sentenced to prison, hired Ron Brown's son, Michael, to funnel $60,000 to Ron Brown, according to Nolanda Hill's testimony.

Mary Caity Mahoney 7/7/97 Unsolved murder
Former White House intern who worked with Asian groups and in Clinton 1992 campaign. Shot five times in head while two co-workers shot once at Georgetown Starbucks in triple murder by men who left $4,000, in the store apparently used silencers and locked doors when they left.

Pamela Harriman 2/5/97 Heart failure
Top 1991 DNC fundraiser appointed by Bill Clinton as ambassador to France. Bill Clinton was chairman of her PAM PAC (political action committee).

Neil Moody 8/25/96 Car crash
Stepson of Vince Foster's ex-wife, Lisa Foster, who was remarried to Judge James Moody, on 1/1/96. Believed about to expose evidence from Lisa Foster's private papers and was last seen in an argument just before he drove off and crashed.

Aldo Frascoia 8/18/96 Plane crash
Secret Service agent who maintained White House security equipment. White House claimed pilot turned around and called for help before crashing in Tetons, but no such record exists at Jackson Aviation or FAA Salt Lake center.

Jeremy Boorda 5/16/96 Suicide
Admiral who knew of the naval technology China received for donations. Died days after giving officers' mess presentation that included the naval technology given to China under Clinton policy.

Niko Jerkic 4/5/96 Suicide
Head of Maintenance and Operations who was air traffic controller for Brown's plane at Cillipi airport in Dubrovnik. Died of shotgun blast to chest three days after Brown's plane crashed and before being interviewed by investigators.

Ron Brown 4/2/96 Plane crash
Commerce Department Director and former DNC chairman. Had perfect cylindrical .45 millimeter round hole in top of head; X-rays now disappeared; video shows Clinton immediately faked tears for camera after laughing while he was leaving Brown's funeral.

James Lewak 4/2/96 Plane crash
High level CIA officer who prepared the Daily Intelligence
Brief for the President. No investigation by FAA, NTSB, Air
Force safety report or airplane manufacturer into crash near
Cillipi airport at Dubrovnik, Bosnia, Croatia.

Adam Darling 4/2/96 Plane crash
Confidential assistant to Ron Brown. Familiar with investi-
gations of Ron Brown by Justice, FDIC, FBI, Commerce IG,
Energy, Senate Judiciary and Reform and Oversight
Committee.

Charles Meissner 4/2/96 Plane crash
Assistant Secretary of Commerce for International Trade.
Placed John Huang on a Commerce Department contract that
allowed him to retain his security clearance.

Shelly Kelly 4/2/96 Accidental death
Stewardess who initially survived the Ron Brown plane
crash. Dead on arrival at hospital after reportedly helping at
crash scene for nearly 12 hours.

William Colby 2/28/96 Accidental death
Ex-CIA director, Strategic Investment contributing editor,
head of Operation Phoenix in Vietnam. Helped expose fake
Foster suicide note, drug cartel control of U.S. Goverment, CIA
mind control project and Castro assassination attempt.
Drowned in canoe while wearing no life jacket and leaving a
particlly eaten dinner on the table.

Barbara Alice Wise 11/30/95 Natural causes
The 14 year Commerce Department employee who shared
suite with John Huang. Nude, bruised body found locked in her
Commerce Department office; autopsy results remained unpub-
lished.

Ken Michael Trentadue 8/1/95 Suicide
Held in the Oklahoma prison about the same time as
Timothy McVeigh. Garrotted with a bed sheet and violently
beaten so badly that body wounds prove suicide ruling is virtually impossible. Reno Justice Department has resisted
pressure from Senate Judiciary to get truth.

John Hillyer 7/10/95 Heart failure
Cameraman filming Arkansas drug activities and investigator with Citizens for Honest Government. Collapsed in dentist's office before his investigative information on ADFA could be produced.

Mike Samples 6/95 Unsolved murder
Witness in Ives and Henry grand jury investigation. Shot to death; 7th witness (or potential witness) in Ives/Henry murders to be killed.

Florence Martin 10/94 Unsolved murder
Accountant who reportedly had documents and PIN# to Barry Seal's laundered bank account. Shot three times in head; (Barry Seal's Cayman Island account at the Fuji Bank was reportedly worth $1.46 million.)

Calvin Walraven 7/28/94 Suicide
Informant in cocaine distribution trial of Jocelyn Elders' son. Died of shotgun blast to head 10 days after testifying against Jocelyn Elders' son.

Stanley Huggins 7/1/94 Viral pneumonia
Attorney investigating Madison Guaranty Savings and Loan. Principal of Memphis law firm heading investigation into Madison Guaranty Savings and Loan for Resolution Trust Co. agency.

Bill Shelton 6/12/94 Suicide
Fiance of Kathy Ferguson an Arkansas police officer critical of the Ferguson suicide ruling. Died of gunshot wound to back of head at her grave site.

Kathy Ferguson 5/11/94 Suicide
Nurse and ex-wife of Trooper Ferguson, who brought Paula Jones to Clinton; potential witness in Jones' civil suit. Found shot after packing bags to leave town; autopsy contradicted by six nurses, and Dr. Houston who stated she had a gunshot wound to BACK of head.

Dr. Donald Rogers 3/3/94 Plane crash
Arkansas dentist on his way to interview with foreign journalist about Bill Clinton. Rogers radioed that plane fuel read empty, apparently due to electrical problems since tank was determined to be nearly full.

Hershel Friday 3/1/94 Plane crash
Clinton Presidential Campaign Finance Committee member. Plane apparently exploded for unknown reasons.

Gandy Baugh 1/8/94 Suicide
Attorney for Dan Lasater, Clinton friend and fundraiser with access to Governor's mansion. Lasater was pardoned by Clinton after his drug distribution conviction. His company was allegedly used to launder money through ADFA.

Ed Willey 11/30/93 Suicide
Presidential Campaign Finance Committee manager. Husband of Kathleen Willey who was found dead in northern Virgina woods on the very same day that his wife was groped by Clinton, according to her testimony.

Jerry Parks 9/26/93 Unsolved murder
Presidential Campaign Security Chief. Ambushed and shot a dozen times while driving home from restaurant after files he compiled on Clinton's sex scandals were stolen from his home.

Stanley Heard 9/10/93 Plane crash
Appointed by Clinton as Chairman of National Healthcare Advisory Committee. Also personally treated Clinton's mother, stepfather and brother.

Steven Dickson 9/10/93 Plane crash
Counsel to Chairman of National Healthcare Advisory Committee. Was flying with Heard when they called to report fire on board aircraft they rented after Heard's personal aircraft developed trouble.

Jon Parnell Walker 8/15/93 Suicide
Senior RTC specialist investigating Whitewater. Fell from an apartment balcony.

Vince Foster 7/20/93 Suicide
Chief White House Counsel and personal attorney for Clintons. No fingerprints on gun; gun and ammo not his; no dirt / grass on shoes after walking in park; no blood at scene in park; clothes covered with carpet fibers; suicide note proved forgery.

Paul Wilcher 6/22/93 Suicide
D.C. attorney who delivered an approximate 100-page affidavit to Janet Reno detailing Mena, Arkansas, drug running. Cause of death still unknown.

William Barkley 5/19/93 Helicopter crash
Secret Service agent who was a former Clinton bodyguard. Escorted Clinton to carrier *U.S.S. Roosevelt* for Bosnia peace mission talks.

Brian Hassey 5/19/93 Helicopter crash
Secret Service agent who was a former Clinton bodyguard. Escorted Clinton to carrier *U.S.S. Roosevelt* for Bosnia peace mission talks.

Scott Reynolds 5/19/93 Helicopter crash
Secret Service agent who was a former Clinton bodyguard. Escorted Clinton to carrier *U.S.S. Roosevelt* for Bosnia peace mission talks.

Tim Sabel 5/19/93 Helicopter crash
Secret Service agent who was a former Clinton bodyguard. Escorted Clinton to carrier *U.S.S. Roosevelt* for Bosnia peace mission talks.

John Wilson 5/19/93 Suicide
D.C. Councilman attempting to expose Clinton corruption. Hanging.

Conway Lebleu 2/28/93 Murder
ATF agent who was a former Clinton bodyguard. One of four agents killed while attacking Branch Davidians. Killer is unknown.

Todd McKeahan 2/28/93 Murder
ATF agent who was a former Clinton bodyguard. One of four agents killed while attacking Branch Davidians. Killer is unknown.

Robert Williams 2/28/93 Murder
ATF agent who was a former Clinton bodyguard. One of four agents killed while attacking Branch Davidians. Killer is unknown.

William Robertson 2/23/93 Helicopter crash
V Corps Deputy commanding general Europe who   figured prominently in Bosnia-Serbia peacekeeping operations. With carrier *U.S.S. Roosevelt* before crash in Germany.

William Densberger 2/23/93 Helicopter crash
V Corps Chief of Operations and Plans who figured prominently in Bosnia-Serbia peacekeeping operations. With carrier *U.S.S. Roosevelt* before crash in Germany.

Robert Kelly 2/23/93 Helicopter crash
V Corps Chief of Intelligence who figured prominently in Bosnia-Serbia peacekeeping operation. With carrier *U.S.S. Roosevelt* before crash in Germany.

Gary Rhodes 2/23/93 Helicopter crash
V Corps Spec. crew chief who figured prominently in Bosnia-Serbia peacekeeping operations. With carrier *U.S.S. Roosevelt* before crash in Germany.

Ed Cauley 1/93 Unknown
Campaign Finance Chairman in Arkansas. Found dead in hotel room.

Jim Wilhite 12/21/92 Skiing accident
Vice Chairman of Arkla, whose Chairman and CEO was Mack McLarty, White House Chief of Staff. Smilar sking accident circumstances as deaths of Sonny Bono and Michael Kennedy.

Paula Gober 12/9/92 Car crash
Clinton speech interpreter for the deaf. No witnesses to single car crash.

Paul Tully 9/24/92 Unknown
DNC Political Director who authored Clinton and Democratic Party strategies. Was found dead in hotel room, and cause of death still unknown.

Victor Raiser 7/30/92 Plane crash
National Finance Co-Chairman of Clinton for President Campaign. Cause of crash undetermined.
Montgomery Raiser 7/30/92 Plane crash
Son of National Finance Co-Chairman of Clinton for President Campaign. Cause of crash undetermined.

Dan Casalaro 8/10/91 Suicide
Reporter investigating ADFA, Mena, PROMIS. Found in Martinsburg, West Virgina, hotel with wrists slashed over 10 times. Many other mysterious deaths have been related to the PROMIS scandal.

Jordan Ketelson 7/90 Unsolved murder
Potential witness in Ives and Henry grand jury investigation. Convicted drug dealer who knew Keith McKaskle.

Richard Winters 7/89 Unsolved murder
Witness in Ives and Henry grand jury investigation. Shot during apparent staged robbery attempt.

Keith Coney 5/17/89 Motorcycle crash
Potential witness in Ives and Henry grand jury investigation. Told friends he was at tracks when Ives and Henry were killed; Officers at scene believed his throat was cut before crash.

Jeff Rhodes 9/89 Unsolved murder
Potential witness in Ives and Henry grand jury investigation. Told parents he knew too much about Ives and Henry murders before being shot in head and set on fire.

Boonie Beardon 3/89 Disappeared
Potential witness in Ives and Henry grand jury investigation. Friend of both Keith Coney and Greg Collins who is believed to be dead; only the T-shirt he wore was found.

Greg Collins 1/89 Unsolved murder
Scheduled to testify at Ives and Henry grand jury investigation. Shotgun blast to face.

Keith McKaskle 11/7/88 Unsolved murder
Cooperated with prosecutor on Ives and Henry investigation. Stabbed 113 times.

Don Henry 8/29/88 Accidental death
Died at Mena, Arkansas, drug drop point A12. Second forensic exam found stabbing in back; *L.A. Times* documented 20 false death rulings by Arkansas medical examiner.

Kevin Ives 8/29/88 Accidental death
Died at Mena, Arkansas, drug drop point A12. Second forensic exam found skull crushed with rifle butt; examiner got 40 percent raise from Jocelyn Elders and new job from Clinton.

Barry Seal 1/86 Murder
Mena, Arkansas, drug ring head turned DEA informant. Shot to death after being forced by judge to stay at a Salvation Army halfway house before he testified about drug trafficking for Arkansas grand jury.

Judy Gibbs 1985 Accidental death
Penthouse cover girl who lured politicians into compromising sexual encounters. Burned to death in fire at her home after calling 911; was cooperating with investigators; Bill Clinton flew with state police over her house after it burned.

Susan Coleman 2/15/77 Suicide
Former Clinton law student who was pregnant. Shot to death while seven months pregnant, reportedly with Clinton's child.

It is mathematically unfeasible that these deaths could all have happened as they are described by the official causes. Eventually one must reach the inevitable logical deduction that there are individuals or an organization willing to systematically eliminate those people who pose some threat to Bill

Clinton, particularly those who have inside knowledge of more severely damaging evidence and threaten to use it.

This raises many questions as to who is ultimately behind the deaths and why it has been so important to keep Bill Clinton in office. Was he chosen and groomed to be President since his days in college and in Europe where he conducted anti-American demonstrations? Was he designated to disintegrate America in the same way that the Soviet Union was disintegrated? Why are the major media organizations keeping so much information secret? Why is the opposing political party protecting him? The answers to some of these questions can be found in the subsequent chapters.

REFERENCES

Christopher Ruddy, *The Strange Death of Vince Foster*, Free Press of Simon & Schuster.

Christopher Ruddy & Lt. Col. Steve Cogswell, *The Death of Ron Brown* (video), Vortex.

Kenn Thomas & Jim Keith, *The Octopus*, Feral House.

Vincent Foster: The Ruddy Investigation, United Publishing.

Bill Clinton's Rise to Power (video), Bozeman American Trust.

The Death of Vince Foster (video), Citizens for Honest Government.

Obstruction of Justice (video), Integrity Films.

Vortex Issues, Volume 1 Nos. 10-11, newsmax.com.

CHAPTER TEN
AMERICA'S DARKEST
SECRET

ONE OF AMERICA'S BEST KEPT SECRETS

As I was scanning the Free Republic web site after the impeachment trial one day, I ran across an article about Michael Ruppert and a link to his web site. Ruppert is a former LAPD narcotics officer, who confronted CIA Director Deutch about drug trafficking by the agency in a now famous L.A. town hall. He publishes a newsletter entitled *From The Wilderness* and has assembled information on several CIA-sponsored worldwide drug trafficking operations.

I had already met Bo Gritz and Terry Reed and received the book, *White Out*, from my friend Chuck, so I was well aware of CIA drug trafficking implications but was unaware of the details. I knew that the Mena, Arkansas, operation was set-up by CIA operative, Barry Seal. I suspected that the connections between George Bush and the drug operations were the ultimate reason for the Republican cover-up, but only a handful of others shared that view. When I contacted Mike Ruppert, I was fascinated to learn that Mike and I had reached the same conclusion from almost completely opposite angles. Although Mike was not involved in the impeachment movement, he was already convinced that it was compromised by Bush / CIA drug trafficking and had additional evidence to support his conclusion.

Over the next couple of months, I ordered videos, back issues of the newsletter and other published reports he produced. I found a gateway of information to numerous other authors and individuals who presented details of various operations. I read the material carefully and was surprised to find no significant conflicts of information presented among all of the different authors. The work of those authors, supported in part by three government investigations, fit together to form the pieces of an amazing puzzle that offers a clear picture illustrating one of America's darkest secrets.

I was particularly impressed by the videos that illustrated the remarkable credibility of all the authors, like Robert Parry, who broke one of the initial stories on CIA / Contra-related drug trafficking operations in Central America. The national news media generally portrayed those who believed in CIA drug trafficking as crazed lunatics, much the same way it portrayed those who wanted to hold Bill Clinton accountable to the same laws as the rest of the citizens. Suddenly I reached perhaps my most significant revelation: The controlled national news media was not just discrediting one political side but was deliberately discrediting honest people on BOTH sides of the political spectrum so that it could compromise the majority of politicians in Washington and implement its agenda.

DRUG TRAFFICKING HISTORY

Much to my surprise (and to the suprise of many fellow Americans who are victims of the controlled national news media), I found government-sponsored drug trafficking has actually been going on for hundreds of years. In fact, the recent turnover of Hong Kong to China has direct connections to drug trafficking, which has been almost totally unreported by our media.

When Britain colonized India in the late 1590s and early 1600s, Britain began to manufacture opium there in the mountainous northeastern regions. It used ships to distribute it to China where they traded it for items such as tea, silk and textiles, part of which generated funds to continue colonization. In the 1830s and 1860s Britain fought two wars with China as China attempted to stop the influx of opium into its destabilized country. Britain eventually won the right to lease Hong Kong from China for 99 years. Therefore, the historical roots of the fabulous economy in Hong Kong can be traced, at least in part, to opium profits.

The worldwide drug market has grown into an estimated $500 billion a year market, a number roughly one third the size of the U.S. government's total annual income. Americans are believed to spend $50 billion a year on drugs. American government involvement actually predates the CIAs beginning with its predecessor, the Office of Strategic Services (OSS).

Subsequent CIA and American military-related worldwide drug trafficking operations have code names such as Operation Amadeus, Pegasus, Watchtower, Triangle, Morning Gold and Burma Road. There have been several government investigations that have reached significant conclusions about government-sponsored drug trafficking operations, but these were primarily limited to Central American drug connections with the Contras.

THE CONTRAS AND COCAINE

The first major story linking the Contras, CIA and drug trafficking was written by Associated Press journalists Robert Parry and Brian Barger, who had begun a series of articles in 1985. It was suppressed by AP editors in the United States who had growing concern about its increasingly damaging content which included links to Panamanian head, Manuel Noriega. However, a Spanish language editor unknowingly translated the story and put it out on the AP Latin American wire, where it was picked up and run on the front pages of Spanish language newspapers throughout the world in December of 1985. Parry then convinced the AP to produce a watered down version on the English language wire. Thus, one of the most important stories of the decade was suppressed by the Associated Press and broken to the American public almost completely by accident.

The story led with the claim that "Nicaraguan rebels operating in northern Costa Rica have engaged in cocaine trafficking in part to help their war against Nicaragua's leftist government, according to U.S. investigators and volunteers who work with the rebels". It linked the Costa Rican drug trafficking to the Contra group of Edwin Pastora, a CIA-created group run by Aldofo Calero and Enrique Bermudez, and a Contra splinter group led by Sebastian Gonzales Mendiola, who was indicted in Costa Rica and a CIA-sponsored Cuban émigré group which oversaw the operations.

KERRY COMMITTEE

Parry and Barger were prohibited from writing any more stories about the Contras and drugs by the AP Washington Bureau chief, according to Parry. Both left the Associated Press; however, their articles triggered a 1986 investigation by the Senate Foreign Relations Subcommittee on Terrorism, Narcotics and International Communications. The subcommittee received testimony over more than two years about CIA-sponsored drug trafficking in Central America in conjunction with the Iran Contra affair that was supervised by Oliver North.

The investigation concluded that: "It is clear that the individuals who provided support for the Contras were involved in drug trafficking. The supply network of the Contras was used by drug trafficking organizations, and elements of the Contras themselves received financial and material assistance from drug traffickers". The drug traffickers had exploited "...the clandestine infrastructures established to support the war and that the Contras were receiving assistance derived from drug trafficking". However, the investigation, led by Senator John Kerry, reached few substantive conclusions regarding direct CIA or American military involvement other than conclusions such as "The military and intelligence agencies turned a blind eye to the trafficking."

DARK ALLIANCE

More recently, CIA drug trafficking attention was generated after the *San Jose Mercury News* published a three-part series called "Dark Alliance", written by Gary Webb, who had written previous articles on the danger of California asset forfeiture laws that allowed police to confiscate property without trial. The series, which began in a Sunday edition during August of 1996, linked the Nicaraguans to America's crack plague. It described how a group of Nicaraguan exiles set up a cocaine ring in California and established ties with the black street gangs of South Central Los Angeles who manufactured crack out of shipments of powder cocaine.

The series was summed up in the lead paragraph that stated: "For the better part of a decade a San Francisco Bay Area drug ring sold tons of cocaine to the Crips and Bloods street gangs of Los Angeles and funneled millions of dollars in drug profits to a Latin American guerrilla army run by the CIA." The drug ring was headed by Norwin Meneses (Cantarero), who was in charge of security and intelligence for the Contra FDN group, headed Adolfo Calero and Enrique Bermudez who were apparently installed in their positions by the CIA.

Meneses' contact in Los Angeles was Danilo Blandon, who left Managua just before Meneses did in 1979. Blandon had earned a master's degree in marketing from the University of Bogota in Colombia before heading an export program for the Somoza dictatorship that fell shortly after he left. Blandon had developed close ties to the U.S. Commerce and State Departments while in the position. Blandon hooked up with "Freeway" Ricky Ross through exiled Nicaraguan dealer Henry Corrales and by 1983 was passing as much as 100 kilos of cocaine a week at attractive undercutting prices to Ross, who distributed most of it in South Central Los Angeles.

In 1991, the DEA arrested Blandon for cocaine trafficking. Although the U.S. Probation Office recommended a life sentence, after cooperating in other cases he served only a little over two years. In the spring of 1995, the DEA approached Blandon to set up a sting operation against Ross, who had already been arrested, served time in an Ohio prison and had just returned to L.A. The sting was successful although it is not clear if Ross actually agreed to buy drugs from Blandon again, since he still had retained much of his property after serving his time. Blandon returned to Nicaragua, and Ross was back to prison when Webb went to see him and decided to do the story.

Webb, who eventually resigned from the newspaper after being transferred against his will, went on to author the book entitled, *Dark Alliance*. The book provided more details to the "Dark Alliance" series of articles, confirmed Parry and Barger's original AP stories and provided some evidence of CIA involvement in that:

- Contra FDN leaders Enrique Bermudez and Adolfo Calero were handpicked by the CIA and on its payroll;
- Blandon's federal grand jury testimony stated that he was instructed by Bermudez to raise money for the Contras and that "the ends justify the means";

- Meneses' admitted to Webb that he was involved with the Contras after being shown a picture of himself with Adolfo Calero;
- A 1986 FBI report indicated that Blandon and Lister were involved in drug trafficking and arms supply for the Contras;
- A police report stated that Blandon's arms supplier Ronnie Lister mentioned he "worked with Scott Weekly of the CIA" when his house was raided;
- Acknowledgment by Blandon's attorney acknowledged that the CIA "winked at this sort of thing".

CIA INSPECTOR GENERAL REPORTS

Despite the evidence, several conservative news media organizations attacked Webb and his book. However, most fundamental facts were confirmed and never substantially refuted in Volumes I and II of the declassified CIA Inspector General reports that were released by Frederick Hitz in January and October of 1998, respectively.

Although the reports denied any CIA involvement, the first part of Volume I admitted that:

- Blandon and Meneses donated thousands of dollars to the Contras;
- Blandon had a personal relationship with Contra leader, Eden Pastora,
- Blandon supplied Pastora with rent free housing and two vehicles in Costa Rica;
- Blandon met four times with Enrique Bermudez who solicited support for the Contras from him.

The second part of Volume I addressed the "Frogman Case" in San Francisco where swimmers were arrested with 430 pounds of cocaine as they attempted to swim ashore from a Colombian freighter in 1983. Also arrested were Nicaraguans Julio Zavala and Carlos Cebezas, who had some of their assets confiscated. Two Contra leaders sent letters requesting that $36,000 in seized funds be returned because the money actually belonged to the Contras. A CIA cable written shortly after a CIA attorney met with the responsible prosecutor, indicated that the money was returned at the CIA's request.

Hitz testified about the reports before the U.S. House Permanent Select Committee on March 16, 1998, and denied CIA involvement in drug trafficking. In his opening statement regarding the second part of Volume I, he told Congress: "CIA officials mistakenly identified one of the Contra members as a former CIA asset, and there was a concern that the depositions might expose a Contra support group in which the CIA had an operational interest." In regards to the meeting, he also told Congress that, "The CIA attorney cannot recall the facts of the case or the meeting in question." His testimony seems laughable if it were not for the underlying depth of corruption that exists.

In Volume II, the CIA acknowledged six cases where it was not deterred from using organizations or individuals involved in drug trafficking. Several pages are devoted to the activities of John Hull, who reportedly received cocaine at his airstrips, but the pages never identify whether or not he was a CIA asset. Hull and Oliver North were indicted in Costa Rica for drug trafficking.

The report also explained that Moises Nunez could not answers questions relating to his involvement in Costa Rican drug trafficking because he revealed that since 1985 he had engaged in a clandestine relationship with the National Security Council (NSC). Oliver North headed the Central American Contra operations at the NSC.

POWDER BURNS OF A DEA AGENT

Perhaps the most important aspect of Volume II was its tacit confirmation of some basic charges regarding El Salvador operations as raised by DEA Agent Celerino Castillo and later documented in his book, *Powderburns*. Castillo recruited an informant at the Ilopango air base in El Salvador, who recorded dates, times, pilots and plane numbers of drug trafficking and arms supply flights being flown by the Contra support network.

One hangar was operated by the CIA under control of Felix Rodriguez, and the other by the NSC under control of Oliver North. Both reported to Donald Gregg, the National Security

Advisor to then Vice President George Bush. Rodriguez set up operations at the air base immediately after meeting personally with George Bush on January 22, 1985. When Castillo raided the house of a cocaine pilot in San Salvador, he found weapons, vehicles and communications equipment belonging to the U.S. Embassy. He confronted Ambassador Edwin Corr and was told, "It's a White House operation, Cele, stay away from it."

But DEA agent Castillo went further than just accusing the CIA of involvement in drug trafficking. He produced a written statement claiming that the CIA was complicit in the murders of several individuals in Guatemala by Guatemalan Military Intelligence (G-2). He even cited names, dates and case file numbers of the people who were murdered.

In DEA file # TG-86-0005, Castillo stated that the trafficker, Jose Ramon Parra Iniguez (Mexican passport A-GUC-043), was tortured and murdered while his two daughters were raped and murdered "by CIA and DEA assets with the approval of the CIA." In addition, Colombian pilots, Adolfo Leon Marales-Arcilia (a.k.a. Adolfo Morales-Orestes), Carlos Alberto Ramirez, and Jiro Gilardo Ocampo were brutally tortured and murdered in the presence of both a DEA and CIA agent. In all cases the bodies were gruesomely dismembered. It seems that the CIA, DEA and Guatemalan military lost sight of the fact the murder and torture are far worse crimes than drug trafficking.

THE LEGNDARY BARRY SEAL

Terry Reed, a CIA operative and Contra co-pilot, extensively documented in his book, *Compromised*, how Contra shipments and drugs were being transported by pilots under the control of Barry Seal. Seal is considered to be the most notorious American drug smuggler of all time, but his CIA and military connections can no longer be credibly denied.

Seal served as a pilot for the U.S. Army Special Forces Division in the early 1960s where he was active in the CIA backed Bay of Pigs operation. The video, *In Search of the Drug Lords*, by Daniel Hopsicker, recently published an astounding January 1963 photograph of Seal in Mexico with CIA agents Felix Rodriguez and Frank Sturgis. Sturgis is also pictured in the House Select Committee investigation of the Kennedy assassination as he celebrated with Fidel Castro after they overthrew Batista in Cuba several years earlier.

In 1965, at the age of 26, Seal became a pilot for TWA. He lost that job when he was busted for smuggling 14,000 pounds of C-4 explosives into Mexico in 1972. He was not prosecuted after the CIA told the U.S. Attorney's office that a trial would threaten national security interests.

In the mid-1970s, Seal set up the bulk of a major drug and gun running operation between Colombia and America while becoming the chief link between the Medellin cartel and the Southeastern United States. In 1982, while facing the threat of prosecution in Louisiana, he moved his operation to the Mena, Arkansas, airport. Mena had been used for CIA drug operations as far back as 1972, according to Michael Ruppert, who interviewed two of the pilots.

In 1983, Seal was first nailed by the DEA for smuggling 200,000 Quaaludes into a Fort Lauderdale airport. He was convicted in 1984 and faced 10 years in prison but had his sentence postponed after the DEA refused, but then later agreed, to use him as an informant.

After he had relocated to Mena, the CIA approached Seal about carrying loads of supplies and guns to Central America. Seal's drug runs were a perfect cover for the covert operation, and Seal naturally agreed since it meant federal protection for his planes and pilots. The CIA also equipped his planes with the latest electronic gear, including remote control hidden cameras for the C123 that Seal soon purchased from CIA contractor, Harold Dean.

Seal provided some bonus cooperation when he arranged a sting of Nicaraguan Sandinistas by videotaping Fredrico Vaughn and some other Sandinista soldiers loading 1,200 pounds of cocaine into Seal's C123 at the Los Brasiles air strip in Nicaragua on June 25, 1984. The CIA claimed that Vaughn was an associate of Interior Minister, Tomas Borge, although it appears that Vaughn had CIA contacts as well. The Managua home phone number that Seal claimed belonged to Vaughn was actually used for U.S. military intelligence between 1981 and 1986. The photographs that Seal took were eventually used by Ronald Reagan in a dramatic nationally televised address that supposedly exposed drug trafficking in the Sandinista regime that the Contras opposed.

Seal's cooperation eventually netted him a sentence of six months' probation on the Florida smuggling charges after he received supporting testimony from DEA agents. However, in December of 1984, Seal was caught again, this time flying a load of marijuana into Louisiana.

On February 20, 1985, Emile Camp, Seal's best friend and co-pilot for many of his runs, was killed when his state-of the-art equipped Seneca plane crashed into a mountain near Mena. Terry Reed may have summed up the crash best when he said: "I still think his crash was sabotage. His plane left Baton Rouge with three hours of fuel. He crashes two hours later. There is no post crash fuel and no fuel in the engine lines. Couple that with the fact that he crashed in a heavily wooded area, miles off course, while executing an instrument approach to Mena in VFR conditions."

By the summer of 1985, Seal was exposed and the Medellin cartel knew that it had been taken. Seal sold the C123 back to Harold Doan, and it eventually ended up in the service of the Contra re-supply effort headed by Oliver North. The plane, nicknamed "Fat Lady" by Seal, was the same one that carried Eugene Hasenfus when it was supposedly shot down by the Sandinistas in October of 1986, just before expiration of the two-year old Boland Amendment, which prevented inter-ference in the Nicaraguan government.

According to Reed, Seal believed that he had an ace in the hole, which may have turned out to be a liability. Seal confided to Reed that he received documentation and videotapes from a DEA informant indicating Jeb and George W. Bush were also into drug use. Details subsequently revealed that they were caught on videotape in a DEA sting operation picking up two kilos of cocaine for personal use from a plane owned by Seal at the Tiamiami airport in Miami.

The tape has still yet to surface publicly; however, Daniel Hopsicker and Mike Ruppert found that the plane model type is a Beechcraft King Air 200, with FAA registration number N6308F and serial number BB-1014. They traced the own-ership of the plane through several individuals and organizations connected to various government officials and agencies. Its current owner is none other than the State of Texas, where it frequently was used by George W. Bush per-sonally, as Governor.

In a plea bargain arrangement on the Louisiana charges, Seal testified in three major drug cases during 1985, helping to obtain convictions on all three in exchange for an agreement that his sentence would not exceed that which was given in Florida. However, DEA agents did not testify on Seal's behalf at his trial in Louisiana.

On December 20, 1885, Baton Rouge U.S. District Court judge, Frank Palozola, effectively set Barry Seal up to be executed by sentencing him to probation having a nighttime confinement, in the Baton Rouge Salvation Army halfway house on Airline Highway. The sentence which prohibited personal body guards, was featured in a movie about Seal's life, entitled *Double-crossed*.

Seal was placed in a federal witness protection program that offered no protective agents. He was assassinated on February 19, 1986 by a Colombian hit team headed by Jose Coutin, a Miami-based CIA asset whose gun shop supplied weapons to the Contras, according to Daniel Hopsicker, who also made some other startling discoveries.

Seal's attorney, Larry Unglesby, told Hopsicker that he once challenged Seal by telling him that, "I cannot represent you effectively unless I know what is going on." Seal gave him a phone number and told him to identify himself as Seal to the answering party. Unglesby said, "I dialed the number and a pleasant female voice answered 'Office of the Vice President'." When Unglesby identified himself as Seal, he was transferred to an admiral who hung up on him when he identified himself as Seal's attorney.

Sam Dalton, a criminal trial attorney for the hit men who killed Seal, also had a corroborating story for Hopsicker. Dalton gained access to the trunk of Barry Seal's Cadillac through discovery. But the FBI entered the Baton Rouge Police Department and illegally seized the contents of the trunk.

Dalton was forced to start a legal battle to gain access to the trunk, but neither the FBI nor CIA would honor his subpoena for the evidence. Eventually a courageous state judge threatened to hold them in contempt, and the FBI returned the trunk after ransacking it. Dalton explained that, "Some of the things that had been in it, we didn't get back. But they missed a few things that indicated just how valuable the trunk was. That's where we found George Bush's personal phone number."

THE HASENFUS PLANE CRASH

Information about the Contra supply network that was established in violation of the Boland Amendment was exposed when Barry Seal's former C123 plane was shot down by the Sandinistas over Nicaragua in October of 1986. Pilots Bill Cooper, William "Buzz" Sawyer and a Nicaraguan were killed. Eugene Hasenfus, a "kicker" who pushed shipments out of the plane, parachuted to safety. However, the details of the crash are very suspicious, as explained to Terry Reed by Israeli agent, Amiram Nir, a former consultant to the Israeli Prime Minister on terrorism. For example:

- The plane flew miles off course directly over a Sandinista military camp;
- The plane contained documents from prior flights including flight dates, crew member names, descriptions of the munitions carried and the coordinates of the drop zones;
- Cooper was carrying his Southern Air Transport ID card, a direct link to the CIA against CIA covert operation procedures;
- Hasenfus was carrying a parachute over hostile territory against CIA covert operation procedures;
- Hasenfus, who stated that the plane was hit by a surface-to-air missile, would have no way of knowing that;
- There was no evidence of profuse bleeding normally associated with crash victims killed by impact, thus indicating the bodies were already dead prior to the crash;
- Nicaraguan autopsies indicated the bodies had been dead for up to 12 hours before the crash;
- The remains of the plane that was put on display in Managua indicated that the plane exploded from inside out;
- The Nicaraguan co-pilot had his throat cut.

Israel participated in Central American drug trafficking and arms supply operations as a partner of the United States. Nir claimed that CIA employee, Felix Rodriguez, was likely a double agent involved in killing the pilots before the plane took off. Reed confirmed that Hasenfus was capable of flying and bailing out of the C123 by himself, but Nir was unsure whether Hasenfus was a willing or unwilling accomplice. Rodriguez certainly would have no qualms about killing people since he reportedly was an assassinations manager in the notorious Phoenix program that may have killed as many as 40,000 Vietnamese who allegedly had Communist ties.

Nir's claim that the crash had been staged as a shoot down was further substantiated when the bodies of Cooper and Sawyer were never returned to America for autopsies and burial because of national security reasons. Therefore, it appears obvious that, at a minimum, the CIA protected the killer of its own operatives even if Rodriguez were not involved in the killings. Israel must also be a suspect in the downing of the C123, particularly considering its motives at the time and the Mossad track record of killing American agents in Operation Watchtower, as documented in this book and several other sources.

Nir mentioned that Israel wanted to end its involvement in the operation since key documents were stolen in a break-in at its embassy in Mexico City. Nir also said that Israel was concerned about the balance of power shift if Russia were ruined economically and Communism were destroyed. In the spring of 1988, Nir resigned and moved to London. He was killed in another mysterious plane crash in November of 1988 over Mexico.

The C123 is not the only plane crash in which Israel would have a motive for foul play. Just recently, EgyptAir Flight 990 crashed after leaving New York on Halloween morning 1999, carrying 30 Egyptian officers who had been trained in the U.S. on modern Apache helicopters. In July, the plane of John F. Kennedy, Jr. crashed on the third anniversary of the TWA 800 crash and the 30th anniversary of the car crash at Chappaquidick, where Senator Ted Kennedy left Mary Jo Kopechne in the car to drown. John Kennedy was in the process of interviewing Isreali Mossad agents for a follow-up article in *George* magazine on the assassination of former Prime Minister Yitzhak Rabin, as reported by Catherine Crier of Fox News.

Although *George* magazine normally treats politics somewhat superficially, the March 1997 issued contained a devastating investigative interview with the mother of assassin, Yigal Amir. She and journalist Linda Gradstein provided detailed evidence that he was encouraged to shoot Rabin by

Avishai Raviv, an operative of the Shin Bet, an Israeli equivalent of the FBI and Secret Service.

The article apparently caused some serious contention between Kennedy and Michael Berman, a key *George* magazine investor. Kennedy certainly had a special place in his heart for the story since most serious researchers into the assassination of his father have concluded that CIA elements involved with the anti-Castro Cuban movement played a direct role in his father's murder.

CHIP TATUM AND OPERATION PEGASUS

Much of the information authored by Terry Reed was further confirmed by Gene "Chip" Tatum, an Army helicopter pilot from 1982 to 1986 and a CIA agent from 1986 to 1992. Tatum was ordered to fly drugs from Fort Campbell, Kentucky to Mena, Arkansas. Tatum stated that he was a commander in the Contra supply operation called Pegasus and that Rep. Henry Hyde (IL) was responsible for finances of the unit.

On CIA orders, he had infiltrated the 3/498th Medical company without its knowledge. Tatum documented many flight plans where he flew Contras and civilians in "Medevac" helicopters to or from Pamerola air base in Honduras or Ilopango air base in El Salvador. The flights frequently contained cocaine disguised as medical supplies, which Tatum accidentally discovered one day when a cooler was dropped and had to be resealed. Tatum reported the find to Donald Gregg and Oliver North, both who independently told him that the cocaine was evidence of Sandinistas manufacturing drugs, and it was going to the world courts.

Tatum stated that the operation involved Oliver North, Felix Rodriguez, Gen. Manuel Noriega, Israeli Col. Michal Harari, Willam Barr, Donald Gregg, Bill Clinton and George Bush. Recipients frequently included Dan Lasater and Clinton security chief, Raymond "Buddy" Young, who were sometimes assisted by Jerry Parks, the security company owner who was later murdered.

Both Reed and Tatum describe separate meetings that they attended where the subject of missing drug money on the Panama to Arkansas route was discussed at the highest government levels. Reed stated a meeting occurred in Arkansas shortly after Barry's Seal's assassination in 1986. It included Oliver North, Felix Rodriguez, Bill Clinton, his aide, Bob Nash, and William Barr, an attorney for CIA proprietary Southern Air Transport, whom he did not know at the time.

Tatum stated that a meeting occurred during 1985 in Central America and included William Barr, CIA agent Joe Fernandez, Gen. Manuel Noriega of Panama, Gen. Gustavo Alverez of Honduras and Michael Harari. Tatum also stated that the amount in question was $100,000,000 and that Oliver North, George Bush and Bill Clinton all participated by phone.

At the 1986 meeting Reed stated that Barr accused Clinton of siphoning off extra money through the Arkansas Development Finance Authority and told him that they were moving the operations out of state. Barr, whose code name was Robert Johnson, was eventually appointed Attorney General of the United States by George Bush.

DRUG TRAFFICKING DISGUISED
AS POW RECOVERY

Government sponsored drug trafficking began long before the Contra movement. In 1978, Defense Intelligence Agency Director, Gen. Eugene Tighe, called Ross Perot and asked him to front a private sector effort to determine whether or not U.S. prisoners of war (POWs), those missing in action (MIA), were alive and being held against their will in Southeast Asia. Perot had gained fame for his rescue of EDS personnel in Iran just prior to the hostage crisis. The rescue was so dramatic and sur-passed the government handling of the hostage crisis so thoroughly that it was made into a famous TV movie entitled, *On Wings of Eagles*.

Perot contacted Col. Arthur "Bull" Simmons, who had rescued the EDS employees in Iran and Col. Bo Gritz, one of the most decorated soldiers of the Vietnam era. In April of 1979, Bo Gritz went to Southeast Asia and determined in one month that there were POWs left there. He sent Perot a TWX message on May 17 telling him "the problem is real".

His conclusion was since confirmed by refugee reports, in-telligence documents, numerous individuals in the intelligence community, DIA satellite photography and a famous picture taken on May 25, 1990 of three live prisoners of war still held in captivity. The Pentagon continually denied the authenticity of the evidence and disputed any testimony confirming live POWs, despite estimates that over 2,000 POW/MIAs were left in Southeast Asia after the Vietnam War. When confronted by the families of POW/MIAs at a National League of Families convention in July of 1992, George Bush replied, "Shut up and sit down."

Gritz spent the next few years attempting to track down POWs and bring them back to the United States. He had frequently arranged to do so, but each time his efforts were sabotaged by individuals within the American government. Gritz and Perot eventually suspected that Richard Armitage, who was in charge of the POW recovery effort, was not doing his job.

In 1986, Gritz made a journey to Burma to meet with General Khun Sa, who reports indicated, may have some MIAs or help in locating them. Khun Sa could not locate any for Gritz but provided some stunning information to him almost by accident.

Khun Sa had set up the world's largest heroin production capability in the mountainous Shan territories of the Golden Triangle within Burma. He had an army of people who protected the drug production and constantly fought Burmese Communists and occasional Thai incursions. However, Khun Sa offered to stop virtually all heroin and opium production and distribution at the Golden Triangle. In exchange, he asked for some American assistance in converting heroin and opium production to legitimate crops and for recognition of the Shan provinces as independent, so that they would no longer have to sell heroin to fight the Red Burmese.

Gritz knew that America was already prepared to recognize the Shan provinces. Although disappointed that no POWs could be located, he returned to Washington optimistically with a videotaped offer to eliminate 900 tons of opium and heroin annually from the world market and expose those U.S. government officials who had been dealing with Khun Sa for the last 20 years. Gritz was not only surprised to find out that there was no interest in Washington for the offer, but he and his partner, Scott Weekly, began to incur the wrath of the federal government, which seem to increase its support for Khun Sa's adversaries in Burma and Thailand.

Gritz went to see Khun Sa again in May of 1987, and even though he did not have concurrence from the U.S. Government, Khun Sa was willing to provide the names of previous U.S. government officials with which his organization had done business. Khun Sa assembled his generals who had just withstood a remarkably well-timed attack by the Red Burmese, and they provided some amazing names, probably without realizing the magnitude of the information. Several key top level CIA personnel stationed in Southeast Asia were named as well as:

- Santos Trafficante, head of the Miami Mafia;
- Ted Shackley, CIA Deputy Director of Covert Operations, who reported to George Bush;
- Richard Armitage, then Assistant Secretary of Defense for International Security Affairs in charge of POW recovery.

According to the generals of Khun Sa, Trafficante handled "civilian" U.S. distribution, Shackley handled international operational aspects, and Armitage handled financial transactions and money laundering.

VIETNAM WAR: FIGHTING COMMUNISM OR MOVING DRUGS?

If that were true, Armitage would be the last person to want POWs returned home, since some of them would likely have knowledge of the operations. Many of the POWs were in Laos covertly during the Vietnam War. Although America was not supposed to have any presence in Laos, it became the home of the largest covert operation in American history. American military personnel allowed drug shipments to pass from Burma through Laos. Laos became a gateway for drug distribution from Burma while some of the profits appear to be used to fund the Vietnam War.

America became involved in Vietnam to prevent the spread of Communism by Ho Chi Minh, a Communist connected North Vietnamese nationalist, who originally sought help from American President Dwight Eisenhower but was rejected. The Vietnam situation escalated into a war for America when North Vietnamese allegedly fired on American ships in the Gulf of Tonkin. Afterwards, Lyndon Johnson signed the Gulf of Tonkin

Resolution in the mid-60s and escalated American involvement to 550,000 troops, 58,000 of whom did not return alive.

It is now reasonably well-established that the North Vietnamese did not really fire on American ships. The Gulf of Tonkin situation was a false war trigger, nearly identical to the alleged massacre in Rajak that was used to justify NATO bombing of Yugoslavia. In reality, Yugoslavia was fighting a civil war with the KLA over the secession of Kosovo. The KLA was found to be a drug-funded terrorist group supported by America in much the same way as America supported the Contras.

Gritz's discovery raises a very disturbing question. We know that the Vietnam War was falsely triggered, and American officers have explained how the war dragged on because politicians never allowed Americans to fight to win. Laos, home to the largest covert operation in American history, is perfectly positioned between Vietnam and Burma drug production. Were we in Vietnam to defeat communism, or were we there to establish and control Southeast Asian drug trafficking?

BUSH: "GET BO GRITZ"

A stunned Gritz returned to America and shared the information of CIA and military drug connections with Ross Perot and officials in Washington. However, Washington was far from thrilled with his findings. Gritz, who naturally used special identification while traveling for his clandestine POW recovery efforts, found himself as a target of a Justice Department criminal prosecution. The charge was using a false passport WHILE HE WAS ON THE COVERT MISSION. The Justice Department spent two years attempting to prosecute Gritz for the operation that he was requested to perform by Defense Intelligence Agency Director, Gen. Eugene Tighe, through Ross Perot.

Gritz was eventually acquitted on April 21, 1989, before he could give a word of incriminating testimony about CIA and military personnel engaged in Southeast Asian drug trafficking. As he left the courtroom, U.S. Attorney William Maddox was pressured by TV news personnel to explain why the government had spent two years prosecuting a bogus charge.

Maddox admitted and even repeated to TV news reporters that he had gotten a call from George Bush who told him to "Get Bo Gritz".

WHY ROSS PEROT DISLIKES
GEORGE BUSH

Unbeknown to Gritz, the information he discovered also corroborated previously collected evidence by the Christic Institute. In addition, Ross Perot had apparently already verified Armitage's drug financing involvement through federal, state and local law enforcement authorities by October of 1986. Related articles subsequently were written by Ben Bradlee, Jr. for Globe News Co. on January 11, 1987, and by George Church, Jonathan Beaty and Bruce van Voorst of *Time* magazine on May 4, 1997.

The astounded Perot made a trip to the Pentagon, backed the 6 foot, 275 pound Armitage into a corner, confronted him with the allegations and demanded his resignation. Naturally, Armitage denied everything, and Perot, not satisfied with his answers, went to see his fellow Texan, George Bush, the Vice President of the United States. After Perot explained the details, Bush told Perot to see the "proper authorities". In reality, George Bush was the proper authority since Executive Order 12333 and Presidential Decision Directives 2 and 3 put Bush in charge of all covert operations not long after the assassination attempt on President Ronald Reagan.

When Bush ran for President and won the following year, Perot established United We Stand, the forerunner of the Reform Party, to oppose him in 1992. Perot constantly attacked Bush during the campaign even after Clinton pulled ahead in the polls, and he eventually cost Bush the 1992 election. He apparently could not reveal his true motive for fear of being destroyed by the CIA dominated national news media, which concealed the information from the American public.

Despite the videotapes from Gritz and the corroborating evidence assembled by Ross Perot from federal, state and local authorities, Armitage was protected at all costs by the very top level of the American government, including the Vice President of the United States, George Bush. His covert activities appear to have continued for decades. In 1998, the *Washington Times* reported that he was negotiating oil leases and development contracts for U.S. firms in Albania and "the former Yugoslavia". His timing is fascinating since the trip occurred the year before Yugoslavian refineries and production facilities were destroyed by NATO.

THE AMERICAN MILITARY AND ORGANIZED CRIME

The link that Gritz discovered between the CIA, Defense Department and organized crime was furthered by the discovery of Col. Albert Vincent Carone a few years after his death in 1990. His existence was not publicly known since virtually all records of his existence were electronically destroyed after his death. Carone was a New York Police Department detective and Colonel in the Army Reserve. Michael Ruppert pieced together much of the story of Albert Carone from Carone's daughter, Dee Ferdinand and other sources during his own exclusive research as publisher of the *From the Wilderness* newsletter.

Between 1940 to 1946, Carone was in the U.S. Army, Pacific Theater, where he received his first intelligence training. Between 1946 and 1966, he was a NYPD patrolman and detective who was issued badge number 3283 and assigned to the 81st precinct, the 42nd precinct in Manhattan and a Chinatown precinct during the course of his service. Carone was on periodic active Army reserve while he was with NYPD. He went on full time active reserve in 1956, was commissioned as a second lieutenant and eventually crossed over into the CIA, according to his daughter.

In 1980, Carone was apparently caught in sodomy with two twelve-year old boys which he said were provided to him. The book, *Franklin Cover-up*, by former Nebraska State Senator, John DeCamp, details just such a covert child sex slave operation beginning around that time. Carone retired after he was committed to and released from South Oaks psychiatric hospital which was run by his brother, Pat.

Immediately afterwards Carone went on active reserve as a commissioned officer, moved to Rio Rancho, New Mexico, in 1980 and began traveling worldwide. He had black, maroon, olive drab and navy blue passports, one of which was in the name of Albert V. Rodgers. His service number, 04639528 USAR, contains an 046 prefix believed to indicate he was an officer in military intelligence.

During this time Carone had frequent contact with James Robert Strauss, a CIA operative whose code name was Cherub. The Ferdinands believed that Strauss was the one who closed down many of the accounts and records of Carone after his death and before they could get to them. The offices of Senator Pete Domenici told the Ferdinands that Strauss was nothing more than a con-man and that they were advised by CIA that it had no connection with Strauss. However, a civil suit filed by American Airlines for non-payment of fares indicates that Strauss flew all over the world on what could only be a government travel account, considering the extensive charges accumulated.

Carone's personal phone book had several interesting entries discovered by Michael Ruppert who summed it up this way: "I visited Dee Carone-Ferdinand in New Mexico and while staying with Dee and her family I was allowed to examine Al Carone's personal phone book. It was closed with rubber bands and there were other loose pages inside. In the pages of the book proper, I found the home address and telephone number of CIA Director William Casey on Long Island. On a loose piece of note paper inside the book I also found the home address and telephone number of Pauley Castellano, head of the Gambino Mafia family." Carone also knew Joe Percilia, the Columbo family crime member believed to handle all CIA transactions.

In 1994, Dee Ferdinand confirmed Carone's mob contacts this way: "I knew Santos Trafficante as 'Uncle Sonny', Joe Percilia as 'Joe Pickles'. I grew up with them around all the time. My father knew Joe Black, Vito Genovese, Carlo Gambino, Benny Eggs, Matty 'the Horse' Aienello, Jimmy Bruno, Joey Lugosa and Pauley Castellano. Most of them were at my wedding. My father was an NYPD detective so we had two rooms full of people at my wedding, and no one from one room ever talked to the people in the other."

On the federal government side, Dee Ferdinand confirmed that Carone worked with Richard Stillwell and Paul Helliwell of the Army Intelligence Support Activity (ISA), which was reportedly disbanded for corrupt activities. She confirmed that

Carone knew Bill Casey, who lived in Locust Valley, Long Island, when Carone lived in Wantagh, Long Island, until 1980. She also confirmed that Carone knew Oliver North. Carone told her about a mission named Amadeus and that he mentioned North's alias "20 or 30 times" when talking about Nicaragua and Mexico. Coincidentally, there is an Amadeus restaurant directly across the street from a bank in San Juan, Puerto Rico, where Carone and the CIA conducted numerous financial transactions.

Dee Ferdinand was able to locate Strauss after visiting Mid-Valley airport, believed to be the destination for drug shipments. Mid-Valley is heavily populated by retired Air Force officers. It has a fascinating uncontrolled airport with two north/south runways less than a mile long and immediately adjacent to railroad tracks. In addition to standard hangars, there are 15-20 large homes with attached hangar garages, where it would be possible to taxi a multi-engine aircraft into them and close the doors for total privacy.

In 1985, Carone became depressed over a mission in Mexico where he told his daughter that innocent people and two DEA agents were inadvertently killed. The mission he referred to was later confirmed by Strauss to be near Veracruz. Carone suddenly became ill, was treated at Presbyterian and St. Joseph's hospitals in Albuquerque and eventually died of "chemical toxicity of unknown etiology" on January 7, 1990. After his death, nearly every record of his existence was lost or destroyed including:

- Military records;
- NYPD records;
- New York and New Mexico driver's licenses;
- Most medical records;
- Insurance policies given to his attorney, Robert Fuentes, who claims that he gave them back to the family;
- Bank accounts, including a joint account #3330690, held at Albuquerque Federal (now BOFA) with daughter Dee, who has some of the canceled checks.

Carone was buried with military honors including a 21 gun salute in a Santa Fe national cemetery, and his headstone was upgraded from Staff Sergeant to full Colonel after Carone's daughter, Dee Ferdinand, made contact with the offices of Ted Shackley. Later she received a letter from Patricia Moore, the Chief of Inquiries, dated November 26, 1991, stating that "Extensive searches at this Center and at the National Archives and Records Administration Center in St. Louis, Missouri, failed to locate Mr. Carone's military records." The Army's denial came despite the fact that Dee had in her possession:

- A diploma for successful completion of a Counter Intelligence Corps course dated 7/23/54;
- Several letters of commendation from the First Army Intelligence School, Ft. Slocum, N.Y., Post Intelligence Office, Fort Hancock, N.J.;
- Several Army course completion certificates including an Army Intelligence school certificate signed by Major John Murphy (MPC) and Col. Thomas Larner stating that, as a Sergeant, he successfully completed a AR-CIC Investigations Course from 10/16/56 to 10/26/56;
- Orders to Active duty and special orders from the New York military district;
- Oath of Office certificate from the New York Guard.

The need to destroy all of Corone's military and personal recoreds speak volumes about his involvement with the CIA and the mafia.

THE MURDER OF DEA AGENT "KIKI" CAMARENA

The Mexican operation that Carone referred to near Veracruz likely involved DEA agent Enrique "Kiki" Camarena and SETCO, a Honduran air freight company owned by Juan Ramon Matta (Ballesteros). Contra leader Adolfo Calero testified before Congress during the Iran Contra investigation that SETCO received funds from "bank accounts established by Oliver North".

Volume II of the CIA Inspector General's report stated that SETCO was selected to transport goods for the Contras from late 1985 to mid-1986 by the Nicaraguan Humanitarian Assistance Office of the State Department. SETCO apparently got this contract and others despite the known existence of a DEA profile indicating SETCO was smuggling cocaine into the U.S. and a 1983 U.S. Customs Service report stating that its owner was a "Class I DEA violator".

Juan Matta Ballesteros was a Honduran drug dealer who had been arrested and merely deported in 1970, after bringing 26 kilos of cocaine into Dulles International Airport. In 1975, he set up a partnership with Mexican drug lord, Felix Gallardo, and transported huge amounts of cocaine from Colombia to Mexico.

The Gallardo cartel included partners Ernest Fonseca Carillo and Rafael Caro Quintero. One DEA account indicated that it was the largest cocaine operation in history, moving as much as four tons of cocaine a month. All of the partners were being investigated by Camarena, who had already directed raids on two of their largest plantations and was unraveling their ties to Mexican politicians and the Mexican secret police (DFS), which received funds from the CIA.

On February 7, 1985, Camarena was kidnapped in front of his office by five gunmen who witnesses believed to be members of the Mexican secret police (DFS). Camarena and his pilot, Alfredo Zaval Avelares, who had also been kidnapped, were driven to a ranch owned by Felix Gallardo near Veracruz. The were brutally tortured the following day and then murdered the next.

Gallardo, Matta Ballesteros and Caro Quintero were eventually tracked down, arrested and convicted of various charges in the murder of Camarena and his pilot. One intriguing witness was Lawrence Harrison, a DEA informant who was hired by the DFS to install high-tech electronic bugging equipment. In their book, *White Out*, Cockburn and St. Clair describe DEA reports and testimony from the trial of Camarena defendants and two other trials in Los Angeles where Harrison stated that:

- He developed a system to monitor Camarena's office for the DFS;
- He installed and managed a bugging operation at the house of Guadalajara drug lord, Ernesto Fonseca, while on the DFS payroll in 1983;

- He recorded hundreds of conversations between drug traffickers and the Mexico City DFS;
- Fonseca made a drug deal with two Americans who claimed that they were being protected because they worked with Contras;
- Fonseca had a visitor named Theodore Cash, pilot of CIA proprietary, Air America, who had previously testified that he had worked for the CIA for ten years;
- Gallardo told him that they were being protected because they sent weapons and money to the Contras;
- The CIA used Gallardo's ranch to train Guatemalan troops, who slaughtered and tortured 19 Mexican federal judicial police officers during an unexpected raid on the ranch.

Witness Enrique Plascencia Aquila told the DEA that he saw Matta at Fonseca's house at a meeting where they passed around a photograph of Camarena and planned the details of his kidnapping. Therefore, the DEA knew that Matta was involved soon after the murder. The CIA Inspector General's Volume II report may have provided the final insult to the Camarena murders when it indicated that SETCO was selected by the State Department to transfer goods for the contras. AFTER it became clear that its owner, Juan Matta Ballesteros, was involved in plotting the murder of DEA agents.

OPERATION WATCHTOWER

Ted Shackley, the CIA deputy director who reported to George Bush and was implicated by General Khun Sa in Southeast Asian drug trafficking, had his own deputy named Thomas Clines. Shackley and Clines were assisted in Southeast Asia by CIA operatives, Ed Wilson and Frank Terpil. Shackley, Clines, Wilson, Terpil and Felix Rodriguez were eventually transferred to the JM/WAVE group in Miami, the largest CIA office in the country outside of the Washington headquarters. They focused on South American drug operations and were apparently involved in military related drug operations that have been pieced together by former LAPD narcotics officer Michael Ruppert, among others. Wilson and Terpil were implicated by several American military personnel as the controlling agents in Operation Watchtower, a series of three missions that took place between December of 1975 and March of 1976.

The operation established three electronic beacon towers beginning outside of Bogota, Colombia and continuing northeast to the border of Panama. The purpose of the operation was to guide aircraft carrying drugs so that they could fly undetected by normal air traffic control from Bogota, Colombia, into Albrook Air Station in Panama. The planes were met by Panama Defense Force officers led by Col. Manuel Noriega, Ed Wilson of the CIA and an Israeli national called "Mike", who was later identified by Pvt. William Tyree as Israeli Army Col. Michael Harari, a former Mossad intelligence agent who headed an assassination team.

Tyree was a U.S. Army Special Forces team member (SAG-7 & SAG10) who participated in Watchtower, provided details about it and subsequently identified the people meeting the planes. Upon completion of the missions, Tyree returned to Fort Devens, Massachusetts, where he lived in an apartment with his wife, Elaine, whom he married in December of 1977. Elaine was a U.S. Army member who was also an informant for the Army Criminal Investigative Division. She kept a diary of illegal activities happening at Fort Devens, according to affidavits by Bill Tyree and Elaine's friend, Tina Gregory. In October 1978, Bill and Elaine Tyree began to receive threats about the diaries, and on January 30, 1979, Elaine was murdered.

In April and May, 1979, Bill Tyree was investigated for the charge that he murdered his own wife, but no probable cause was found. Earl Michael Peters (SP4), who had befriended Tyree and then later admitted to Tyree that he killed Elaine, was charged with the murder. Apparently Peters was noticed at the scene, and there were even photographs of his entering and leaving Tyree's apartment at the time of the murder. Col. Edward Cutolo, Tyree's immediate superior, had put the apartment under surveillance after Tyree reported the threats to him. Erik Aarus, a drug dependent buddy of Peters, according to the affidavit of Kenneth Garcy, was also charged and subsequently convicted in February of 1980.

However, District Attorney John Droney attained a ruling from the Massachusetts Supreme Court that struck down the murder charge against Peters and reinstated the charge against Tyree. On the ruling, the Supreme Court actually granted itself exclusive jurisdiction to prosecute the Tyree case, in violation of state statues.

Droney was a target of Operation Orwell, where Devens military personnel conducted covert surveillance on the top Massachusetts politicians, judges and prosecutors to compromise them. Droney had apparently been compromised by a closet homosexual relationship where he admitted to his lover that his office had helped cover up the police murder of a convicted felon who had escaped from the East Cambridge jail. Tyree participated in Operation Orwell and was on the team that monitored Droney.

Droney sent a remarkable letter to Cutolo using Middlesex County, Massachusetts District Attorney letterhead, as illustrated in *The Tyree Papers* assembled by Michael Ruppert. The letter, delivered in person by Lt. Dywer, contained:

- An acknowledgment of an agreement between them;
- A commitment that Peters would not be arrested for the Elaine Tyree homicide;
- A request for the audio-visual material collected concerning the relationship between him and to the escaped convicted felon;
- A request not to mention the material related to his alternative lifestyle;
- A recommendation to destroy the surveillance material collected at the Tyree residence on January 30, 1979.

Tyree was subsequently convicted in February of 1980, based, in part, on the testimony of Aarus and the fact that Peters had befriended Tyree, asked to store a shotgun at his apartment and later got an apartment key from Tyree so that he could pick up the shotgun. Fifteen years after their conviction, in November of 1995, Aarus swore in an affidavit that Bill Tyree was not involved in the murder of his wife; however, Tyree remains in prison at Walpole, Massachusetts, today.

Nine additional key individuals with knowledge of Watchtower have subsequently lost their lives, including five Special Forces colonels, two National Security Administration employees and even a member of Congress. They are:

- Sgt. John Newby, who worked with Bill Tyree on Operation Watchtower and Operation Orwell, also received threatening phone calls in October of 1978 and died that same month when his parachute failed to open;
- Col. Robert Bayard, who supplied photographs of Michael Harari and Mossad operative, David Kimche, was murdered in Atlanta, Georgia, in 1977 as he went to meet David Kimche;
- Col. Edward Cutolo, Tyree's immediate superior at Fort Devens who also commanded the final Operation Watchtower phase, died in 1980 in a one-car accident while on a military exercise at Skullthorpe, England, just before he was to meet Harari;
- Col. A.J. "Bo" Baker, the original commander of Operation Watchtower, died shortly thereafter, while trying to determine if Harari had killed Cutolo;
- Col. James Rowe, who provided the picture that helped Tyree identify Michael Harari and provided drug trafficking information to the CBS *60 Minutes* staff, which declined to use it, was assassinated on April 21, 1989, in the Philippines three days after Harari arrived;
- Paul Neri of the NSA, who tried to help Rowe and Baker determine if Harari had killed Cutolo, died on April 29, 1989;
- Hugh Pearce of the NSA, who met with Col. Rowe and Congressman Larkin Smith about going public to call for a full investigation, died in June of 1989 in a helicopter accident;
- Congressman Larkin Smith (R-MS,5th), who met with Pearce and Rowe about conducting a Congressional investigation into the incidents, died in a plane crash on August 13, 1989;
- Col. Richard Malvesti, who was assisting Col. Rowe and Bill Tyree, died on July 26, 1990 after his parachute failed to open on a routine jump.

New evidence has since revealed that the Elaine Tyree diaries, taken illegally from her apartment, were kept and delivered to CIA headquarters by Col. Albert Vincent Carone, whom Tyree believed to be the paymaster of several drug operations. The evidence has triggered a civil suit by Bill Tyree who identified Carone, as did the daughter of Edward Cutolo. Named in the suit along with the CIA, are:

- Governor Paul Celucci, who ignored the recent appeals of Tyree, and coincidentally had a former law partner, William Kittridge, who defended Erik Aarus in 1980;
- Attorney General Scott Harshbarger, who defended Peters in 1987 and failed to comply with court orders to return the diaries in 1985 and 1987;
- George Bush, whom the suit claims provided "express direction" for Carone to retrieve the diaries.

Also named in the suit are Oliver North and Bill Clinton for their roles in facilitating various related drug operations that have been previously discussed.

The assistant district attorney who helped John Droney was none other than John Kerry, who went on to become a U.S. Senator from Massachusetts. In 1986, Kerry, in his role as chairman of the Senate Foreign Relations Subcommittee on Terrorism, Narcotics and International Communications, received testimony about CIA-sponsored drug trafficking in Central America. The investigation thoroughly documented Contra involvement in drug trafficking, but it did not reach significant conclusions about CIA and military involvement or ensure that those responsible were held accountable for their activities.

Cutolo attained his position by succeeding his superior, John Shalikasivili, as commander of the 10th Special Forces Group, Airborne. Since Shalikasivili was the commander of the group that carried out Operation Watchtower, he would surely be a the likely originator of it. In 1994, President Bill Clinton appointed him as Chairman of the Joint Chiefs of Staff.

THE HUB IN A CIA DRUG
TRAFFIC WHEEL

There is a single common thread in nearly all of the drug operations described in this chapter. That thread is George Bush, whose life is quite secret since most of his financial information and college records are sealed. We know that after returning from his stint in the Navy, George Bush, like father

Prescott Bush, son George W., and successor Bill Clinton, attended Yale University. Like his father, as a senior, George Bush was a member of the mysterious Skull and Bones Society, which seems rooted in opium smuggling and some pro-slavery advocates as explained by author Webster Tarpley. It has become a breeding ground for Bush's fellow CIA operatives and fellow CFR members.

Skull and Bones, the Russell Trust Association, was founded from the Yale graduating class of 1833, by William Huntington Russell of Middletown, Connecticut. His second cousin, Samuel, established Russell and Company, a huge opium syndicate that acquired opium from Turkey and smuggled it under the protection of the British Empire into China, where it was prohibited. The smuggling eventually led to the previously described wars between Britain and China.

Sometime after graduating from Yale in 1948, Bush helped form Zapata Corporation, a now fairly obvious Houston-based, CIA front company, which established oil drilling equipment in the Caribbean. Rodney Stich, in his book, *Drugging America*, states that investigators, CIA operatives and CIA cable analyst, Michael Maholy, revealed that Zapata Petroleum, Zapata Off Shore and Zapata Cattle Co. were heavily involved in drug trafficking.

The oil rigs were apparently used to carry out the drug operations. Drugs would be off-loaded from ships onto the drilling platforms and then taken into the nearby coastal areas in helicopters that were constantly carrying supplies and personnel. Maholy had learned about this both through cable traffic and his observations while on the rigs, which provided the perfect cover.

CIA AGENT BUSH

During that time period, as early as 1961, George Bush was almost assuredly a secret CIA agent. This was revealed by Joesph McBride, who found an FBI memorandum buried among 98,755 pages of FBI documents released to the public in 1977 and 1978, as a result of Freedom of Information lawsuits. The memo was dated November 29, 1963, and writtten from FBI Director J. Edgar Hoover to the Bureau of Intelligence and Research at the State Department. It summarized the briefings given by the FBI's W.T. Forsyth to Capt. William Edwards of the Defense Intelligence Agency and George Bush on

November 23, 1963, the day after the Kennedy assassination and just before Lee Harvey Oswald was killed.

The memo entitled "Assassination of President John F. Kennedy, November 22, 1963" explained the pro and anti-Castro Cuban sentiment in Miami communities regarding the assassination. It stated that "the substance of the foregoing information was orally furnished to Mr. George Bush of the Central Intelligence Agency."

The memo was significant because the CIA had repeatedly denied that George Bush was a CIA agent even though its policy is normally one of no comment on employees. In fact, the CIA tried to claim that the reference made by J. Edgar Hoover was to another George Bush in the CIA. When Joesph McBride contacted the other one, George William Bush, Bush told him that "it wasn't me" since he "knew neither one" of the other people involved in the briefing. George William Bush was a "lowly researcher and analyst", by his own description, who only worked at the CIA for six months during 1963-64. George William Bush eventually joined the Social Security Administration in January of 1968 after being employed as a social worker for the Alexandria Department of Public Works from 1965 until then.

The CIA continued to deny that George Bush was a CIA agent or operative even as President Gerald Ford appointed him to head the agency in 1975. Bush, who allegedly had no intelligence experience, was picked by Ford after he fired William Colby, who was cooperating with the Church Committee and the House Select Committee on Assassinations as they were investigating the JFK assassination for the second time.

Colby had already revealed CIA assassination plots against leaders of other countries, such as Fidel Castro of Cuba. Senator Frank Church, chairman of the Senate Select Committee on Intelligence, complained that the Bush appointment was a further attempt to cover up CIA assassination plots by President Ford, a former member of the flawed Warren Commission.

BUSH AND THE BAY OF PIGS

Bush's Zapata Corporation was also involved in another covert CIA operation that involved transportation of anti-

Castro Cubans to the infamous Bay of Pigs during their attempted overthrow of Fidel Castro. Fletcher Prouty stated that in his capacity as liaison between the CIA and Air Force at the Pentagon in 1961 he personally "sanitized" two freighters named "Barbara" and "Houston" for use in the Bay of Pigs operation which was code named "Zapata."

The Zapata operation was believed to be controlled from the CIA Miami office by the JM/WAVE group, which was also involved in the Castro assassination plots. Bush's connection to Operation Zapata is particularly intriguing since most serious Kennedy assassination researchers believe that the evidence clearly shows CIA elements from this Bay of Pigs operation were also involved in the assassination of John F. Kennedy, who refused to provide adequate air cover for the invasion. Specific units that have been implicated in the Kennedy assassination plots include the JM/WAVE group and ZRRIFLE assassination team.

The alleged Kennedy assassin, Lee Harvey Oswald, had several contacts with CIA and FBI personnel from the time he had been a Marine until he was killed by Jack Ruby, the day after the assassination. In his new video Daniel Hopsicker published pictures revealing that in the 1950s, Oswald and Barry Seal were in the same Civil Air Patrol unit commanded by David Ferrie, a CIA pilot. Ferrie also had contacts with the Carlos Marcello crime family in New Orleans and even flew Marcello back to America after he was deported, according to the person who picked up Ferrie at the airport.

While Oswald was in Dallas, his handler was George de Morenschildt, a CIA operative, who was shot to death just as he was about to be questioned by the House Select Committee on Assassination in 1976. Mark Lane and other authors reported that his personal telephone book was located after his death and found to contain the entry, "Bush George H.W. (Poppy) 1412 W. Ohio also Zapata Petroleum Midland".

Kennedy had agreed to one covert air strike against Cuban fighter planes on an airfield in Cuba to incapacitate them to the degree they could not stop the Bay of Pigs invaders. The CIA had made the strike from Guatemala using Cuban pilots in airplanes disguised to look like those of Cuba. They claimed to the United Nations that those pilots were defectors. However, the damage was not complete, and Kennedy refused a CIA request for another bombing run needed to ensure the safety of the landing party. Cuba had asked the U.S. and the U.N. to interview the pilot, and Kennedy was concerned about repercussions of finding direct U.S. involvement in the invasion.

The 1,500 invading anti-Castro Cubans were killed or captured by Castro forces who had been alerted and were waiting for them at the Bay of Pigs. The captured forces realized that they had been betrayed as soon as they were let out, and some even started firing back at the freighters. From that day on Kennedy was considered a traitor among those involved in Operation Zapata.

REAGAN ASSASSINATION ATTEMPT

In 1980, George Bush ran in the Republican primaries against Ronald Reagan where he uttered his famous quote that proposed Reagan financial policies were "voodoo economics". In spite of the quote, Reagan picked Bush as his Vice President after being coerced by his advisors, according to some authors. I was surprised to find out years later that Reagan and Bush were never that close.

George Bush gained unprecedented power as Vice President through control transfers of covert operations and national security matters from Ronald Reagan. The transfers were accomplished via Presidential Decision Directives and the signing of Executive Order 12333 in December of 1981. The power shift began after the March 30, 1981, assassination attempt on Ronald Reagan by John Hinckley. Like the Kennedy assassination, George Bush also had a direct connection to the Reagan assassination attempt as documented by Webster Tarpley in his book, *George Bush: The Unauthorized Biography.*

On Tuesday, March 31, the *Houston Post* published a copyrighted story under the headline: "Bush's son Was to Dine with Suspect's Brother". The lead paragraph read: "Scott Hinckley, the brother of John Hinckley, Jr., who is charged with shooting President Reagan and three others, was to have been a dinner guest Tuesday night at the home of Neil Bush, son of Vice President George Bush, the *Houston Post* has learned."

The article went on to state that Neil Bush admitted on Monday, March 30, that he had met Scott Hinckley once in the recent past and knew him. Neil Bush also stated that he knew the Hinckley family and referred to large monetary contributions made by the Hinckleys to the Bush 1980 Presidential campaign. Scott Hinckley, the Vice President of Vanderbilt Energy Corporation, lived in Denver as did Neil Bush. John Hinckley, Jr. lived on and off with his family in nearby Evergreen, Colorado.

Neil's wife, Sharon, stated that she knew the woman who was coming with Scott Hinckley to the dinner. She also confirmed that the Hinckleys "..have given a lot of money to the Bush campaign." Both Sharon and Neil stated that they did not know or recognize Scott's brother, John.

On April 1, 1981, the *Rocky Mountain News* carried Neil Bush's confirmation about the dinner party. The article also explained that Scott Hinckley had come to a surprise birthday party for Neil at the home of Neil and Sharon Bush on January 23, 1981. Scott had come to the surprise party with the same female friend of Sharon Bush. On the same day, the office of then Vice President Bush confirmed the dinner party, but both Neil Bush and the office stated that they had not received any campaign contributions from the Hinckleys.

The Bushes were never questioned or investigated in regards to the assassination attempt, the contributions or their connections with the Hinckleys, even though George Bush would have the most to gain from an assassination of Ronald Reagan. The national news media made the somewhat ludicrous claim that John Hinckley admired actress Jodi Foster and thought that shooting the President would somehow win her love.

There is no known evidence that would suggest anyone in the Hinckley family had knowledge of John Hinckley's intentions. Assume for a minute though, a four person family, each having close associations with 100 other families in a 280 million person population. I am not a mathematician, but it seems to me that the odds of the Vice President's family being that closely connected to the family of the man who attempted to assassinate the President are about 700,000 to one. Surely that justifies a serious investigation.

CONCLUSION

In regards to Nicaragua, three government investigations have confirmed, at a minimum, that:

- Nicaraguan Contras were supported by traffickers who transported drugs into America;
- The Contra supply line was used by traffickers who transported drugs into America;
- The CIA was aware of the drug trafficking operations but did nothing to stop or even hinder them.

These allegations can no longer be credibly denied. Two of the leaders of the Contra supply effort were Oliver North of the National Security Council and Felix Rodriguez of the CIA.

However, it is obvious that the CIA is far more than just a passive onlooker and that Contra related drug trafficking is only the tip of an iceberg in terms of CIA drug trafficking scope. Despite repeated denials by the CIA, the evidence presented by CIA operatives, Special Forces colonels, DEA agents, police officers and trial witnesses makes a clear case that:

- The CIA ran drug smuggling operations for the Contras from El Salvador through Felix Rodriguez;
- The CIA controlled operational aspects of Southeast Asian drug traffic originating in Burma;
- The CIA was ultimately in control of Operation Watchtower drug trafficking conducted by American military personnel between Panama and Colombia;
- The CIA was involved in Caribbean drug smuggling operations through the Zapata Corporation;
- The CIA was involved in Mena, Arkansas, based smuggling operations from various points in Central America through Barry Seal.

The evidence presented by CIA operatives, Special Forces colonels, DEA agents, police officers and trial witnesses illustrates that the scope of the corruption extends well beyond the CIA. The evidence establishes a clear, coordinated effort among elements in American government agencies and other foreign organizations to facilitate drug trafficking, money laundering, protection for those who are caught and elimination of those who get in the way. For example, this evidence indicates that:

- The Israeli Mossad was a partner with the United States in Central American drug trafficking operations and possibly others as well;
- American Defense Department and military personnel were used in Panama and Colombian drug trafficking operations for worldwide money laundering and as a link to organized crime figures for drug distribution in America;
- Elements of the CIA, DEA, Israeli Mossad and the American military were involved in other heinous crimes including multiple murders;
- Those government officials involved in drug trafficking and other heinous crimes were protected and promoted by the highest level of the American government, specifically United States Presidents, Bill Clinton and George Bush.

Even though all of the allegations of money laundering, drug trafficking, drug use and obstruction of justice made against Bill Clinton may well be true, the following evidence indicates that George Bush is the real cocaine kingpin of America:

- Bush oversaw Contra operations through his security advisor, Donald Gregg, who controlled both Oliver North and Felix Rodriguez;
- Bush oversaw the Burma drug trafficking operations through his CIA deputy, Ted Shackley;
- Bush protected Dick Armitage after he was confronted about his involvement in Southeast Asian money laundering and drug trafficking by Ross Perot;
- Bush attempted to prosecute Bo Gritz for using a fake passport while on a covert mission after Gritz had uncovered the Southeast Asian drug trafficking operation;
- Bush's Zapata oil rigs were found by investigators and a CIA cable analyst to be involved in smuggling drugs;

- Two attorneys verified that CIA operative and drug smuggler, Barry Seal, had Bush's phone number;
- Operation Watchtower began immediately upon the appointment of Bush as CIA Director;
- Bush is accused in the Tyree suit of ordering Albert Carone to obtain the Tyree diaries illegally to prevent Operation Watchtower from being exposed.

There are implications that we need profits from drug trafficking to fight communism. But if the billions of dollars collected from all of the government-sponsored drug trafficking operations were actually used to fight communism, it would have been eradicated worldwide by now. I believe that most of the profits are going to fund George Bush's New World Order and implement the global agenda of the Trilateral Commission and Council on Foreign Relations.

George Bush may have taken the Skull and Bones heritage to a new level. While cocaine has replaced opium and airplanes have replaced Clipper ships, the founding principle seems to be the same. Use government endorsed drug trafficking to gain wealth and power by feeding selected groups of people dope to enslave and control them.

REFERENCES

Drugs Law Enforcement and Foreign Policy Vol 1-2, Hearings Part 1-4, 5/2787, 7/15/87, 2/8-2/10/88, and 4/4-4/7/88, Subcommittee on Narcotics, Terrorism and International Operations for Senate Foreign Relations Committee.

Inspector General's Report of Investigation, Vol.1 The California Story, Central Intelligence Agency.

Inspector General's Report of Investigation, Vol.2 The Cortra Story, Central Intelligence Agency.

L.D. Brown, *Crossfire*, Black Forest Press.

Alexander Cockburn & Jeffrey St. Clair, *White Out*, Verso.

Celerino Castillo III & Dave Harmon, *Powderburns*, Mosaic Press.

Col. James "Bo" Gritz, *Called to Serve*, Lazarus Publishing.

Mark Lane, *Plausible Denial*, Thunder Mouth's Press.

Joesph McBride, *The Nation*, columns by July 16-23, 1988, August 13-20, 1988.

Terry Reed & John Cummings, *Compromised*, Shapolsky Publishers.

Rodney Stich, *Drugging America*, Diablo Western Press.

Webster Tarpley and Anton Chaiktin, *George Bush: The Unauthorized Biography*.

Gary Webb, *Dark Alliance*, Seven Stories Press.

Michael Ruppert, From the Wilderness newsletters, *From the Wilderness*.

Dan Hopsicker,*Barry and the Boys*, publisher to be announced

Dan Hopsicker, *In Search of the American Drug Lords* (video), Mad Cow Productions.

Michael Ruppert, *50 Years of CIA Drug Dealing* (video), Justice Vision.

Mena, Arkansas: Under Investigation (video), American Investigator, Free Congress Research and Education Foundation.

POW/MIA: You are Not Forgotten (video), Col. James "Bo" Gritz and Bobby Steward, Dandridge, Tennessee.

BUSH / CIA DRUG ALLEGATIONS

III
The Real America

CHAPTER ELEVEN
AMERICA IMPEACHED

THE REAL STATE OF THE UNION

On January 20, 1999, President Bill Clinton gave his State of the Union address after he was impeached for perjury and obstruction of justice. Two years earlier, Bill Clinton had given a State of the Union speech where he declared that "The era of big government is over" and then minutes later in the same speech, announced roughly 17 new government programs requiring unfunded mandates. He already had established a track record of lying without conscience and now the additional awkwardness of a perjurer giving a State of the Union speech left him little credibility. It was difficult for a listener to believe what, if anything, he said was actually true. Therefore, I began to consider the events of the past two years and reflect on the real "state of the union". I considered that:

- President Bill Clinton, an impeached perjurer, who almost assuredly committed multiple felonies, was in control of America;
- The President had set up a state of tyranny in America by using the FBI, IRS, INS and Treasury Department to persecute his political adversaries;
- The President and his political party, the Democrats, committed bribery by selling their souls to the Communist Chinese military through at least seven separate sources of illegal revenue;
- The President committed multiple acts of treason by being the first to export sophisticated military technologies to a Communist government over the objections of his own goverment agencies, including the DOD, NSA, Justice Department and State Department;

- The President planned the bombing of Sudan and Afghanistan without consulting his Joint Chiefs of Staff and bombed Iraq two weeks after it began complying with U.N. inspections, but just hours after finding that he could not stop his impeachment;
- The President established executive orders to rule America by a dictatorship that can legally take away property of any American citizen and subordinate his/her rights to the international agencies;
- The President had kidnapped the American justice system by dismissing the FBI director, firing every single U.S. attorney and installing Janet Reno as an Attorney General, to serve as his defense lawyer;
- The Attorney General turned the Justice Department into the "Injustice Department" by filing phony privilege claims for the Clintons and preventing the investigation of the Communist Chinese money flow into the President's campaigns and political party;
- America's alternate hope, the independent counsel law, was proven useless after two special counsels ruled that Chief White House Counsel, Vince Foster, committed suicide without getting his fingerprints on the gun that was used to kill him;
- Major media organizations had systematically protected the President by keeping the American public almost totally uninformed;
- Most amazing of all, the opposing Republican Party, which controlled Congress, did not think that any of this was an election issue in 1996 or 1998.

The American form of government had been almost totally destroyed, and it all happened on my watch.

THE PROBLEMS TO SOLVE

The major media organizations falsely portrayed the impeachment movement as consisting of people who hated Bill Clinton. I never hated Bill Clinton. I love America and want to help save it. America cannot survive as a free nation if we let a

President or any other elected official live above the law and desecrate the Constitution.

America has an intricate system of checks and balances to protect its citizens from corrupted individuals operating within the government. Therefore, the corruption of one individual, regardless of who it is, does not really bother me. What bothers me are the individuals and organizations who cover up the activity. These are the people who subvert the American system of justice and pose an equally as serious threat to our freedom as the offending individual. The mastery of Bill Clinton thrives because he appoints people who are willingly corrupted, he obtains compromising information on his adversaries, he takes orders from the globalists who drive his agenda and he maintains ongoing relationships to implement the agenda.

Bill Clinton developed a stream of organizations and individuals willing to protect him at almost all costs. These include: his fellow Democrat Party members, the major media organizations, the U.S. Attorney General who he appointed to head the Justice Department, two independent counsels and even key members portion of the opposing political party.

THE DEMOCRAT PARTY

During the 90s, the Democrat Party became morally bankrupt. Most Democrats are now perfectly willing to set up an unprecedented double standard of justice in America to protect a President just because he shares their political views. Based on the passed Articles of Impeachment, these separate standards of justice would absolve:

- A President vs. a judge who would be impeached;
- The commander in chief vs. a military officer or soldier who would be court-martialed;
- A government executive vs. a corporate executive who would be fired;
- An elected official vs. a private citizen who would be jailed.

The Declaration of Independence states "We hold these truths to be self-evident that all men are created equal." The Pledge of Allegiance states we are "one nation under God, indivisible, with liberty and justice for all." The Democrat Party has already destroyed these principles which most Americans hold dear.

Not only are the Democrats advocates of a double standard of justice, they are perfectly content to let the President set up a tyranny and engage in the fascist use of government agencies like the FBI, IRS and Treasury to persecute political adversaries. In fact, many Democrats now participate in the tyranny either directly or by helping to cover it up.

Worse yet, Democrats have even sold our souls to our enemies. The Clinton / Gore campaigns and the Democrat National Committee (DNC) had seven sources of revenue traceable through 11 streams to Communist Chinese government agencies and individuals connected with the People's Liberation Army. Even before receiving much of this money, the Clinton administration transferred export decisions to the Commerce Department by Executive Order and gave the Communists many dual use and military technologies, despite the objections of government agencies. Four separate transfers occurred over separate objections of the National Security Administration, Department of Defense, Department of State and Department of Justice. Never before in American history had any President given military technology to a Communist controlled military government over the objections of his own security and defense departments. This is as clear a case of treason as can be defined.

THE REPUBLICAN PARTY

When Republicans took control of Congress, they authorized roughly a dozen investigations into various aspects of the Clinton administration. These investigations uncovered astounding, irrefutable evidence of criminal activity in Arkansas, treason and bribery with the Communist Chinese military, abusive use of government agencies to persecute political adversaries and a whole host of obstructions of justice that even involve drug trafficking and organized crime.

All of this evidence, which would have easily established a national consensus for impeachment, was left out of the Articles of Impeachment by House Republican leaders, even though they have a majority in both the House and the Judiciary Committee. Instead, the Judiciary Committee and

House Republican leadership deliberately protected Bill Clinton by going forward with only evidence from the Starr report and throwing America into national sex soap opera.

When Articles of Impeachment based on the Starr report evidence passed the House, House managers tried to do the best they could with what they had been given. They requested only two weeks to present all of their evidence, including a brief presentation and cross examination of about 12 witnesses they felt were essential. (The Andrew Johnson impeachment trial had 25 witnesses in just over five days). But the Republicans in the Senate used their majority vote power to sabotage the case of the House managers.

The Senate Republicans eliminated all hostile witnesses that were to be called against President Clinton, eliminated much of the evidence that the House managers thought was essential to the case, prevented the public from hearing most of the actual testimony against Bill Clinton, prevented the Chief Justice from presiding over the depositions, instituted artificial time limits and implemented delaying tactics such as making motions, debating them and re-deposing all witnesses before they testified. It is clear that the founding forefathers, who thrived on balance of power, never intended for the Senate to redefine the Constitutional concept of a trial and usurp power from the prosecution, defense, presiding judge and American public.

Republicans could have gotten 12 Senate votes to convict Bill Clinton on a two-thirds majority at any time during the impeachment process simply by conducting a REAL trial and threatening to use Congressional investigation evidence of criminal activity, abuse of power, treason and bribery in additional Articles of Impeachment. Democrat Senators would then have been forced to convict Bill Clinton on perjury and obstruction or dismiss real crimes such as treason, which would not go over well with the American public. The Democrats stuck together without worrying about that because they knew there was no real opposition party.

After Bill Clinton gave his State of the Union speech on February 20, 1999, House members, Jennifer Dunn and former football player Steve Largent, gave the Republican response. Largent specifically mentioned that part of the Republican mission statement was to protect individual liberty. At the very same time, Republicans Senators were doing everything they could to destroy it by protecting the man who was threatening the liberty of every American citizen. The Republican Senators pandered to and assisted corrupt Democrats as they were destroying the republic. Republican leaders refused repeatedly to honor their mission statement to protect the individual liberty of citizens from tyranny, treason, fascism and communism. They clearly demonstrated that they are not a viable alternative to Democrats. I believe that the Republican Party has become a black hole that sucks up the legitimate Democrat opposition into a twilight zone of uselessness.

THE JUSTICE DEPARTMENT

The Justice Department is now totally unaccountable to the American citizens. Consider the following summary of actions by Attorney General Janet Reno to illustrate that point:

- She refused to support the conclusion of a Justice Department investigation that found an FBI sniper shot, which killed Vicki Weaver at Ruby Ridge, was unconstitutional;
- She approved the internationally banned CS military gas attack at Waco that led to the deaths of over 80 men, women and children who had never committed any crime;
- She stated that she "could not find anything wrong" with FBI actions in Waco, despite the fact that aerial videos show a tank destroying a Davidian building while people were still inside, and autopsy reports indicate that six bodies found in the rubble of that building were crushed to death;
- She fired all 93 U.S. attorneys for the first time in American history;
- She fired FBI Director, William Sessions, on trumped up travel misappropriation charges the day before Vince Foster was murdered;
- She hired Louis Freeh, who mishandled cases involving FBI files, FBI lab work, Waco, Ruby Ridge, Richard Jewell, Gary Aldrich, illegal immigration checks and the Oklahoma City bombing;

- She refused a 1993 FBI recommendation to prosecute the former Arkansas U.S. attorney who was to be tried for obstruction of justice for shutting down a federal drug investigation that would have exposed the Mena drug operation and likely solved the Ives / Henry murder case;
- She terminated the investigation of a union boss who raised nearly $17,000,000 for the DNC in 1995-96, despite a Justice Department complaint that he was "associated with, influenced from and controlled by" organized crime;

In addition, Janet Reno used the Justice Department as a defense team for Bill Clinton and essentially became his accomplice. Consider these actions:

- She stalled investigations by making repeated false privilege claims for both Bill and Hillary Clinton that were unanimously rejected by the Supreme Court;
- She appointed Robert Fiske as independent Whitewater counsel even though Fiske was a lawyer for the company that sold Clinton and McDougal Whitewater land;
- She barred expansion of the Mike Espy probe so that it would not include Don Tyson, a major Clinton campaign contributor and a possible suspect in the Smaltz investigation;
- She refused seven separate requests to appoint a special prosecutor to investigate different aspects of the Clinton / Gore and DNC Chinese fundraising scandal, despite clear evidence of treason and bribery.

We now have proof that any President can set up a tyranny in America simply by appointing a corrupt Attorney General who is willing to implement the Presidential agenda and ensure that he/she is above the law.

NON-INDEPENDENT COUNSELS

Independent counsels are supposed to resolve this problem, but in reality, the counsels that are appointed are frequently not independent. As previously mentioned, in 1993, Janet Reno appointed as Whitewater prosecutor, Robert Fiske, a lawyer for International Paper, the company that sold Clinton and

McDougal much of the Whitewater land. In 1994, when Fiske ruled Vince Foster's death a suicide and his background was exposed, he was replaced by Starr, who was appointed by a three-judge panel, despite being on the original Janet Reno short list.

As Chris Ruddy discovered, Starr's firm, Kirkland and Ellis, was hardly independent since it contributed 86 percent of its 1993-1994 PAC money to Democrat Party candidates. In addition, Starr was retained by Chinese Communist controlled Citisteel at the same time he confirmed the Vince Foster suicide ruling. Citisteel is controlled by China International Trust Investment Co.(CITIC) which also controls the China Ocean Shipping Company, that was caught shipping 2,000 illegal AK47s into the Oakland port after the CITIC chairman, Wang Jun, met with Bill Clinton in the White House.

Although Starr was portrayed as a biased Republican out to get the President, the history of his investigation tells another story. In 1994, Starr hired many liberals for his team such as Miguel Rodriguez, Sam Dash and Mark Tuohey, who had a party for Janet Reno in his house. In 1995, Rodriguez, who was sincerely trying to get the truth, complained to Starr that Touhey was interfering with the Foster investigation, and when Starr did nothing about it, he resigned, citing ethics problems.

In 1996, Starr confirmed the Fiske suicide ruling and attempted to resign under pressure for the obviously flawed decision. In his 1998 testimony before the House Judiciary Committee, he stated, "The controversy surrounding the death of Vince Foster has dissipated because of our thorough and accurate reporting."

Starr also testified that he could find no impeachable offenses in the FBI file scandal but never interviewed key witnesses, such as Director of Records Management, Terry Good, and Chief of Staff, Mack McLarty. When Congressman Barr asked Starr under oath whether or not his team had interviewed McLarty, Starr replied that he thought so.

Also in 1998, Starr withdrew his subpoena of Bill Clinton so that Clinton could find out what questions were to be asked before he would be forced to answer them during his grand jury testimony. The press also claimed that the Starr report would only have evidence regarding the Monica Lewinsky scandal, and it could have only found that out through a leak in Starr's office.

Replacement independent counsel, Robert Ray, a lifelong Democrat continued the trend set by Ken Starr. While rapping up the investigation into the illegal file acquisitions by the White House, Ray indicated that he had not spoken with Linda Tripp about her sworn testimony that she observed FBI files being loaded onto White House computers. Ray also admitted that he had not spoken to Betty Lambuth and Sheryl Hall, two White House whistleblowers who revealed that the White House had suppressed up to 1,000,000 Emails containing in-criminating evidence on the illegal file acquisitions and other scandals. He also stunningly confirmed that the files that were illegally obtained are still in a vault in the White House.

Independent counsels are appointed by the Attorney General or a panel of judges who have been given a pre-defined, carefully selected, narrow list of candidates to select from. In either case the independent counsel investigation is typically flawed because the selection process is corrupted.

Instead of fixing the independent counsel law to ensure that we have real independent counsels, the Republican-led Senate removed the law altogether by allowing it to expire in 1999. This eliminated one of the last threads that the citizens have to make government officials accountable to the same laws as citizens. It also illustrates once again the tyrannical nature of the Republican Party leadership.

MEDIA ORGANIZATIONS

Major media organizations stated repeatedly during the im-peachment process that America doesn't care. I say that America doesn't know. Media organizations covered up the Arkansas criminal activity of Bill Clinton to get him elected President of the United States. They covered up his abusive use of government agencies in Washington to get him re-elected. Then they covered up the Communist Chinese infiltration of the Clinton / Gore campaigns and the Democrat National Committee in an attempt to avoid his impeachment. Perhaps we should have impeached the media.

When knowledge of Clinton administration corruption became so great that media organizations could no longer cover it up, they were forced to adopt one of their standard back-up strategies, which is to attack the person that they are defending but use more trivial charges. In the case of Bill Clinton, the spotlight was shifted from Whitewater and government abuse to sexual related matters.

This accomplished three major objectives for them. First, it diverted attention from the real crimes and redefined the impeachment movement as a matter about sex. Second, it made the media appear more unbiased since it was finally attacking Clinton on one of his shortcomings after covering up all of the criminal, treasonous and tyrannical activity that he had undergone during his Presidency and governorship. Third, it fooled most Americans into thinking that Bill Clinton simply had a personal problem and was no threat to their freedom or the American form of government.

Like many others, I believe that the major media organizations are able to distort political information consistently because they are controlled by members of the Council on Foreign Relations (CFR). CFR members hold positions of power such as chairmen, presidents, managing editors, editorial page editors, network TV news anchors, magazine editors, political columnists and many other key positions in the media world. They control all of the political news at major networks, the AP and UPI political news wires and editorial pages of many major newspapers around the country. This allows them to distort political news consistently to fulfill their political agenda.

Congressman Oscar Callaway explained how all of this was implemented in the Congressional Record of 1917:

"In March, 1915, the J.P. Morgan interests, the steel, shipbuilding and powder interests, and their subsidiary organizations, got together 12 men high up in the newspaper world and employed them to select the most influential newspapers in the United States, and sufficient number of them to control generally the policy of the daily press...They found it was only necessary to purchase control of 25 of the greatest papers...An agreement was reached, the policy of the papers was bought, to be paid for by the month; an editor was furnished for each paper to properly supervise and edit information regarding the questions of preparedness, militarism, financial policies, and other things of national and international nature considered vital to the interest of the purchasers."

The dominance of their achievement with the media was shown shortly thereafter when the passenger ship *Lusitania* was being used to ship arms to the British. The Germans took out ads in major newspapers across the country to warn American travelers not to sail on the ship. The ads were rejected by all American newspapers but the *Des Moines Register*. The Germans then sank the *Lusitania* just after its naval escort had mysteriously deserted it, and World War I ensued. The *Lusitania* just happened to have been owned by a rival shipbuilder of J.P. Morgan.

Since 1915, CFR media dominance has expanded to include key network TV positions such as CNN news President, Tom Johnson, and ABC, NBC and CBS news anchors Peter Jennings, Tom Brokaw and Dan Rather. These media organizations allowed Bill Clinton to live above the law because he implemented their global socialist agenda for a one-world government. It is time that we realize we do not have American media. We have anti-American media.

THE ONE WORLD SOCIALIST GOVERNMENT

The not-so-hidden agenda of the CFR and its worldwide sister organization, the Tri-Lateral Commission, is to improve foreign relations by implementing a one-world government, which the members would essentially control. Their planned power comes at the expense of American sovereignty. Essentially, the members of a single organization dedicated to global socialism, currently establish American political agendas, control American monetary policy and manipulate public opinion to implement their agenda. This is what George Bush really meant when he talked about the "New World Order".

CFR members dominate many government agencies, educational institutions, public policy foundations such as the Rockefeller Foundation and monetary establishments such as the Federal Reserve, which is neither federal nor has adequate reserves. All presidents since Richard Nixon, with the exception of Ronald Reagan, were CFR members, and many of their cabinet members were as well. The CFR controls the Democrat Party agenda, has many Democrat Party members and includes key Republican members such as George Bush, Newt Gingrich, Henry Hyde and Jim Leach. All of these Republicans have protected Bill Clinton in various ways either before or during his Presidency. George Bush did not mention a word about Clinton corruption during the debates. All of the Congressmen were instrumental in preventing Congressional investigation evidence such as criminal activity, treason, bribery and abusive use of government agencies from finding its way into the Articles of Impeachment.

The CFR operates primarily in America, while the Tri-Lateral Commission, founded by former Chase Manhattan Bank chairman, David Rockefeller, consists of units representing Asia, Europe and the Americas. The power of these organizations should never be underestimated. A couple thousand strategically located CFR members dominate nearly all aspects of American policy without the knowledge of the American citizens. During the height of his problems just before his impeachment, Bill Clinton reportedly met with David Rockefeller on three separate occasions. Some of us believe that he was begging to keep his job.

Americans are kept uninformed about all of this through various media strategies that are discussed in the next chapter. One example is to keep America citizens divided on issues. The strategy pits one class of Americans against another so that Americans lose sight of the fact that their freedom is being stolen. This strategy is simply known as divide and conquer. The strategy divides America into rich vs. poor, black vs. white, Christian vs. Muslim vs. Jew, homosexual vs. heterosexual, conservative vs. liberal, left wing vs. right wing and so on. In reality, we are all Americans and want the same basic things. We believe in the American Constitution to protect our American freedom. The battle to be fought is not about conservatism vs. liberalism anymore. It is about Americanism vs. anti-Americanism.

THE COMMUNIST MANIFESTO

Although America was set up to be a free republic, its leaders have implemented many anti-American laws that facilitate the principles of Communism as defined in the *Communist Manifesto*, which was written by Karl Marx. The manifesto consists of ten basic planks. The planks with information on how they are being implemented in America are shown below:

Abolition of private property

The rights of private property are being attacked via environmental laws which have been used to take the property of citizens or render it unusable because of environmental considerations. There are numerous cases where environmental protection agencies have not allowed citizens to build houses or businesses on their property for esoteric environmental reasons. Executive Order 12986 also references a grant of immunity to international agencies which confiscate the property of American citizens for conservation purposes.

A heavy progressive or graduated income tax

This plank was implemented in 1913 when a one percent income tax was established and gradually increased to today's exorbitant rates, which exceed 50 percent total on federal, state and local taxes. When Ronald Reagan took office, the federal tax rate on income over $100,000 was 88 percent.

Abolition of all rights of inheritance

This plank is being implemented through inheritance tax. Many heirs have to sell the property that has been bequeathed to them so that they can pay the estete taxes on assets that were already taxed and paid by their ancestors.

Confiscation of the property of all emigrants and rebels

This plank is being achieved by asset forfeiture laws. Drug dealers have been used as the excuse to implement these laws.

However, several cases exist where private citizens have had cash confiscated and never returned, even though they were innocent of all wrongdoing.

Centralization of credit for the state through a central bank with an exclusive monopoly

This plank was implemented in 1913 with the establishment of the Federal Reserve, which is neither federal nor has adequate reserves. It is actually a private trust owned primarily by European families. The normal 10 percent reserves on deposits have gradually been reduced to under three percent today. American monetary supply is essentially controlled by foreigners, who do not necessarily share the interests of the American citizens.

Centralization of the means of communication and transport in the hands of the state

This is being achieved gradually by different organizations such as the Federal Aviation Administration and the Federal Communications Commission. You now must have an ID to board an airplane, and there has been a major attempt to standardize state drivers' licenses with fingerprints. Federally controlled organizations such as Amtrak, Pubic Broadcasting and National Public Radio have made inroads towards this goal, but automobiles and the Internet pose control problems for the Communist agenda.

Extension of factories and instruments of production owned by the state

Advances on this plan have been made through various government owned businesses throughout America, such as the Tennessee Valley Authority, which produces electricity.

Equal liability of all to labor

Advances on this plank have been made through the graduated income tax which attempts to equalize the income of all Americans. The minimum wage law is another smaller attempt to equalize income of Americans. Equalization of income facilitates equalization of labor.

Combination of industries and gradual abolition of town and country distinctions

Combining industries into larger, centralized ones can help facilitate nationalization of the industries by a central state. Abolishing territorial distinctions provides much greater emphasis on central government in lieu of state and local rights. American legislation decidedly favors big business and labor unions. Two examples that help large research-oriented businesses steal smaller business ideas are recent patent bills, HB-400, S507 and their successors, that contain clauses such as those requiring patent information to be published 18 months after an application is submitted, even if a patent has not yet been granted.

Free education for all children in public schools

This plank has already been implemented, and its purpose is to provide the children only what information the central government wants them to have. An excellent example is the Magruder's American Government textbook used in some high schools. Although the Second Amendment clearly states that "....the right of the people to keep and bear arms shall not be infringed," the text book claims that the amendment is "widely misinterpreted" and that it does not guarantee a right to keep and bear arms free from restriction by government. The textbook also states that the Constitution can be changed by "informal amendment" such as "the passage of basic legislation, actions taken by the President, decisions of the Supreme Court, activities of political parties and custom." Clearly, the founders of America never had any such intentions. I believe that these are rather blatant attempts to "dumb down" America's children to the point that they do not understand how they were able to be born free.

AMERICA'S FIRST STEPS TOWARD COMMUNISM

Dr. Edward Griffin, in his book entitled, *The Creature from Jekyll Island*, explains how many threads of Communism have been implemented in America. Several of the Communist planks were completely implemented during the Presidency of Woodrow Wilson, a Democrat elected in 1912 through a classic example of power politics. Wilson faced William Howard Taft, the Republican incumbent who had just opposed the Aldrich plan for a central bank, not because it was Communist in nature, but because it did not give the government enough power over the bankers who wanted to control the money supply. Taft had won the Republican nomination easily and was popular with the voters since he served during a time of prosperity. Wilson's dry personality and aloof mannerisms made Taft a clear favorite for the election.

However, two executives from J.P. Morgan and Company convinced former Republican President, Teddy Roosevelt, to run for the Presidency as the "Bull Moose" candidate of the Progressive Party, which was heavily funded by J.P. Morgan and Company interests. The third party entry of a former Republican successfully split the vote so that the chosen Democrat candidate, Woodrow Wilson, a champion of the central bank, was elected President.

Wilson was nominated by Colonel Edwin Mandell House, who had close contacts with J.P. Morgan and was a founder of the Council on Foreign Relations. House went on to become Woodrow Wilson's closest advisor and was the point of contact for the banking families who wanted to implement the federal reserve system to control privately the American money supply.

The system was conceived during a 1910 secret meeting at Jekyll Island, Georgia. Attendees included: Nelson Aldrich, Republican Senate Whip who was the father-in-law of John D. Rockefeller and chairman of the Monetary Commission; Henry Davison, Sr. Partner of J.P. Morgan and Co.; Paul Warburg, a Kuhn Loeb & Co. partner representing the Warburgs and Rothchilds in Europe; Frank Vanderlip, National City Bank of New York president representing William Rockefeller and

Benjamin Strong, the head of J.P. Morgan Bankers Trust who also became the first Federal Reserve head.

Carter Glass, the Democrat Chairman of the House Banking and Currency Committee, objected to the original plan in a 1913 House report because it lacked government control, concentrated power into the hands of the larger New York banks, established a banking monopoly, increased inflation and underestimated the taxpayer cost. However, in a textbook example of coordinated politics, he and Senator Robert Owen drafted a new federal reserve plan that was nearly identical to the plan he had opposed when originally presented by Nelson Aldrich. This plan became law in 1913.

During the Woodrow Wilson Presidency, the 17th Amendment to the Constitution was passed. It allowed the Senators to be elected by popular vote instead of by the state legislative bodies. While this appeared to give the people more power, it actually was a clever move to eliminate state representation in the federal government. Since most Senators have millions of constituents and massive fundraising machines, they have little accountability to the people they represent. This was clearly and recently illustrated when the Republican controlled Senate implemented sham trial procedures to protect Bill Clinton and sabotage the House managers' case. The amendment allowed the major socialist power brokers essentially to buy one half of the United States Congress.

Also in 1913, the burdensome federal income tax was implemented. This percentage began as an option applying only to one percent of foreign earned income and eventually grew to 88 percent of all domestic income over $100,000. Many Americans do not realize that the American government functioned superbly for 130 years with no personal income tax.

Woodrow Wilson ran for re-election in 1916 using the slogan, "He kept us out of war." Shortly after he was re-elected and began his second term in 1917, America entered World War I. Afterwards, Wilson tried but failed to form the League of Nations, the first attempt at global government and a precursor to the United Nations.

AMERICA'S DICTATORSHIP BEGINS

Franklin Delano Roosevelt (FDR) was the next President who moved America deeper into a Communist dictatorship. Immediately after being elected in 1932, he used the 1933 gold crisis to extract more power from the citizens. In March of 1933, Franklin Roosevelt issued Presidential Proclamations 2039 and 2040 to declare an ongoing national emergency that only another President could remove. He also got Congress to amend the Trading with the Enemies Act to give the President absolute war powers in a general state of emergency and automatic approval of all Executive Orders at all times. This was a major step in establishing unconstitutional dictatorial powers that could easily be implemented by a President during any perceived crisis.

Roosevelt also implemented a dramatic further extension of income tax by creating the Social Security system in 1935. Although it was unconstitutional in its forced savings, it was originally created as a legitimate retirement system. However, in 1939, Congress quietly transformed the system from a personal savings vehicle into another tax, when they began using the money to spend on other programs. This trend has continued through today where all social security revenue is included in the federal budget and the difference between revenue and expenses continues to be spent as soon as it is collected. Any announced budget surplus still includes the amount of social security revenue that exceeds expenses and, therefore, is not a surplus at all. Thus, our federal government robs from the citizens daily and then plans to rob our children to repay us.

Under Roosevelt, America entered World War II when Japan bombed Pearl Harbor. Reports have indicated that Roosevelt was forewarned of the bombing but sent a multi-day cable to warn the naval base at Pearl Harbor rather than using standard military intelligence communications. He also seemed to prolong the war until the second nuclear bomb was dropped on Japan while it was already prepared to surrender. Roosevelt was re-elected President three times, serving for 13 years until he died in 1945, the longest term in American history. After his death and the end of World War II, the United Nations was formed. Under the auspices of peacekeeping, it has become a vehicle to implement global government.

AMERICA MOVES TO TYRANNY
AND FASCISM

The first and perhaps, most important, sentence of the Constitution states that "... all legislative power granted herein is vested in Congress...". This clause was obviously given such prominence to prevent tyranny and fascism in America. However, during his presidency, Bill Clinton, implemented thousands of now automatic Executive Orders, many of which are unconstitutional because they exceed the authority of the executive branch and attempt to legislate to the American citizens.

Some of these orders have been described in this book, but perhaps, the most dangerous of all orders implemented by Bill Clinton is EO 12919. This order allows the federal government to take over our private property under any emergency that the President defines. Specifically mentioned are food, water, health resources, energy, transportation, materials and supplies. Therefore, if any emergency occurs, these orders could be selectively put into place. Given the track record of Bill Clinton for using government agencies like the FBI, IRS, INS and Treasury Dept. to persecute political adversaries, anytime could be a perfect opportunity for him, or a successor, to implement further tyranny.

Republican leaders are insincere in their attempts to resist these unconstitutional Executive Orders and offer half-hearted opposition while refusing to take them off the books. Although Republican leaders occasionally denounce Bill Clinton and Janet Reno, this book describes how the leaders have consistently protected them while they controlled Congress. The leaders have allowed Clinton, with protection from Janet Reno, to persecute political adversaries by constantly using government agencies. This is a dangerous form of fascism. During his presidency, Bill Clinton and the Republican leaders removed nearly all-remaining forms of accountability in government. Their actions have plunged America deeper into a hole of potential tyranny from which it may not be able to recover.

The tyranny was once again illustrated by the recent siege on the home of Elian Gonzalez. While the Communist Chinese infiltration of the American government impacts the freedom of all 280+ million Americans, the "American" news media successfully diverted attention for months to the freedom of this lone Cuban boy. The Cuban media also focused heavily on this story in what almost appears to be a coordinated multi-national effort. Cuban citizens were even pumped up with rallies by Fidel Castro, who seemed to know about the raid or the success of the custody battle well in advance.

Elian Gonzalez survived an escape from Cuba when his mother and the others in the boat, in which he was traveling, drowned after the boat capsized. He was rescued by fishermen and taken to a Florida hospital. After he recovered, the INS granted temporary custody of the boy to his uncle, Lazaro Gonzalez and his family. Juan Miguel Gonzalez, Elian's natural father who was divorced from his mother before the birth of Elian, was not allowed to travel from Cuba to the United States for months after Elian was rescued. Eventually Juan Miguel requested custody and the Clinton administration said they would let state courts decide the matter. About five months later in April of 2000, Juan Miguel entered America and the Clinton administration had the case transferred to a federal court that ruled in favor of the father. The Gonzalez family then made an asylum appeal and the 11th Circuit Court of Appeals at Atlanta agreed in April to hear the case on May 11.

Just days after the Atlanta appellate court ruling that also specifically denied a request by Janet Reno to transfer custody to the father, Reno took the law into her own hands. She ordered dozens of heavily armed agents to storm the house without presenting any search warrant or court order and without evidence of any crime being committed. Videos and family statements show they broke down the front door without knocking or identifying themselves, pointed their automatic weapons at everyone in the house, including two other children, cursed and threatened to shoot the people inside. A dramatic photo, by an AP photographer, who was invited to stay at the house captured the terror on Elian's face as the armed agent pointed his MP5 sub machine gun at Donato Dalrymple, the fisherman who rescued Elian and held him as they hid in a closet. A female agent took him from the house as he screamed "what's happening" and "help me". She rushed him to a white mini-van with a masked driver. When asked at her Saturday morning press conference about the incredible photos, Reno made the ludicrous excuse that the gun was not pointed directly at Elian and the agent did not have his finger on the trigger, as if that would make any difference to those inside. Reno stated that this level force was necessary "to uphold the rule of law".

To help resolve the custody dispute before the legal issues were settled during the next few weeks, the Gonzalez family asked to meet Juan Miguel and his family somewhere in the Miami area with "no pre-conditions, no government and no lawyers". Juan Miguel was apparently never allowed to do so by Castro and Reno did not agree to those terms of the meeting. Several community leaders who were helping in the negotiations sent Reno a signed fax at five PM on Good Friday, April 21 agreeing to the terms she outlined for the meeting. Family lawyer, Roger Bernstein, and others stated that between four and five AM just before the break-in, Reno changed the conditions and gave them 5 minutes to decide whether the new conditions were acceptable. Before they could respond Reno ordered the attack. Reno then claimed in her press conference that the Gonzalez family "moved the goalposts".

Reno had also told the Gonzalez family said she would not use marshals or come at midnight to take Elian away. Instead she used INS and border patrol agents who attacked at five AM. Reno stated in her press conference that eight INS agents participated in the raid even though videos clearly showed dozens of INS and border patrol agents were involved.

A day earlier, Greg Craig, a Clinton attorney who helped Juan Miguel, sent a two-page letter to TV network presidents requesting that they not cover this obvious breech of 4th amendment rights about to occur. Within hours, after the raid, Craig also produced photographs of a happy, well-rested Elian in the arms of his father while preventing the Gonzalez family or anyone other than propaganda specialists from seeing him. The photos caused Marisleysis Gonzalez to make a fascinating discovery that can be verified by most any American who has access to the photos of the raid, from inside the house, or the videos that were taken outside.

Marisleysis, the 21-year-old cousin who essentially became Elian's surrogate mother, during the five months he was in her care, discovered something only a mother would notice. She stated at the Gonzalez family press conference, on Easter morning, that photos of Elian with his father were doctored because she had just given Elian a haircut and the photos showed him with significantly longer hair than he had at the time of the raid. A simple examination of the photos confirms almost conclusively she is telling the truth. Elian is seen with a closely shaven head both in pictures taken in the house and the videos taken outside the house. The pictures allegedly taken when Elian was reunited with his father show he had several weeks of additional hair growth during the few hours of his incredible "hair raising" experience.

Immediately after the press conference CNN, in its classic style, repeated Marisleysis claim the photos were doctored but deliberately did not mention the hair discrepancy. They made the irrelevant point that his half brother, who was shown in some photographs, appeared to be the correct age and then asked the audience to make their own decision after failing to properly inform them. CNN was much more skillful and subtle than Fox News, who used a more blatant distortion later in the afternoon, when they said Marisleysis Gonzalez claimed it was not Elian in the photographs. Thus, once again when it came to real government corruption the national news media duped both sides of the political spectrum with fascist propaganda to cover up federal tyranny and deceit.

Janet Reno said in this case her interest was the child. She made the same claim about the children in Waco. While the Gonzalez family was fortunate to have independent photographers and news coverage, the federal agents were much more prepared at Waco. They confiscated and destroyed most film and kept photographers so far away they could not really see all of the details that forensic evidence, infrared film and debris have revealed. We are left with government-selected videos, pictures of charred bodies in autopsy reports and many provably false excuses for what happened there. The children at Waco were in a concrete bunker where there was a horrible fire that can be seen on the videos. Sources such as the video *Waco: A New Revelation* illustrate convincing forensic and debris evidence that some form of military explosives were placed on top of the bunker. Many of the women and children died from the explosion that created the horrific fire.

Regardless of whether you believe Elian should stay in America or return to Cuba with his natural father, I hope every

American citizen can see the severe threat posed by continual federal sieges against innocent American citizens in violation of the 4th amendment of the Constitution. Fascists selectively apply and break laws while using the power of government to achieve political tyranny and totalitarianism. I believe the Clinton / Reno Justice administration exemplifies a near true Fascist state that lacks only in total government control of commercial enterprises. Reno's actions at Waco, her extensive cover-up in the Communist Chinese military infiltration of the American government and a dozen other examples detailed earlier in this chapter must surely qualify her as the leading candidate for the most corrupt Attorney General in American history.

The threat posed to American citizens by the corruption of the American government is perhaps best illustrated by R.J. Rummel in his book, *Death by Government*. Rummel documents nearly 170 million murders that have occurred in the 20th century alone, all at the hands of the victims own "peace time" government. Most of these murders were conducted by Communist, Fascist or tyrannical governments who committed acts of genocide against their own people to fulfill their political motives. These figures do not include deaths of soldiers or other individuals in wars between countries. Thus, the most dangerous threat to any individual, exceeding any type of disease and all wars combined, is simply, government.

Politicians we have elected, primarily in the 20th century, have gradually shifted the American government to a similar type of pro-Communist, pro-Fascist tyranny as those governments who have committed these murderous atrocities against their own citizens. Those Americans who do not believe such atrocities can happen here need only to consider that, on one day, April 19, 1993, our government added more than 80 innocent men, women and children to this count when it attacked the Branch Davidian Church with military tanks, internationally banned CS tear gas and automatic weapons fire in violation of the Posse Comitatus act and their 4th amendment rights.

REFERENCES

G. Edward Griffin, *The Creature From Jekyll Island*,
    American Opinion Book Services.

Karl Marx, *The Communist Manifesto*, (reprinted by) The John
Birch Society.

John McManus,*The Insiders*, The John Birch Society.

Daniel New and Cliff Kincaid, *Michael New: Mercenary or
American Soldier*.

R. J. Rummel, *Death by Government*, Transactio.

Dr. Gene Schroder, *War and Emergency Powers*, American
Agriculture Movement.

The New American magazine, "Special report, Conspiracy for
Global Control."

Harry Browne,*Why Government Doesn't Work,* St. Martin's
Press.

Waco: a New Revelation (video), MGA Films.

CHAPTER TWELVE
SAVING AMERICA

REPUBLICAN FRAUDULENCE

Political parties and candidates can easily get people to vote for them, simply by telling Americans what they want to hear. The media makes it difficult for citizens to have any kind of detail knowledge about the legislation activity, voting records or backgrounds of most candidates. Therefore, there is no easy way for a citizen to verify whether or not candidates are fit for office or have kept their promises. The two major political parties are then free to operate fraudulently in regards to political issues.

This book has already mentioned several issues where the Republican Party has been fraudulent. This book also illustrates details of how during the impeachment process Republican leaders actually protected Bill Clinton while impeaching him. Although House Republicans voted to impeach Bill Clinton, House Republican leaders prevented the Articles of Impeachment from including any evidence of treason, bribery, Arkansas criminal activity and abuse of the FBI and IRS. Although Senate Republicans voted to convict Bill Clinton Senate Republican leaders sabotaged the House Managers' case by implementing unprecedented trial procedures to ensure that no damaging evidence or hostile witnesses would be presented to corroborate the charges against him. These tactics allowed both Democrats and Republicans to dupe their constituents into believing that there were real conflicts and differences between the two colluding parties.

One involved their subsequent efforts to pass a balanced budget amendment that failed to gain the required two-thirds majority by a single Senate vote in 1995. After the 1996 elections, when amendment supporters were elected to replace the lone Republican dissenter, Mark Hatfield of Oregon, and some Democrat Senators, Republican initiatives to pass the amendment suddenly ceased. Likewise, when Republicans launched and implemented the contract with America in 1994, it was so successful that it resulted in a complete change of power to Republican Congressional control for the first time in 40 years. But by 1996, Republican leaders abandoned the contract, did not even mention it and had no desire to duplicate its success. That should indicate the insincerity and fraudulent nature of Republican leaders.

One of the most fraudulent issues of all for the Republican Party is its advocacy of the phony drug war. Republican support for a law and order society has allowed its leaders to dramatically decrease the rights and freedoms of the American citizens under the guise of fighting drug distribution. If the Republican leaders were serious about fighting drugs they would have started by getting the CIA out of the drug business. But they cannot do that because of the involvement by George Bush in several worldwide operations previously described in this book. Even if some of the allegations raised against George Bush are proven false, it is inconceivable that he could be innocent on all counts. Thus, Republican leaders continue fighting the drug war and spending billions of taxpayer dollars to protect our children from drugs, all the while they knowingly run the drugs in through the back door of America for various profit motives. I cannot think of a bigger scam being played on the American people.

Another issue that illustrates the fraudulent nature of the Republican Party is the divisive issue of abortion. Many Republicans claim to want a constitutional ban against abortion. However, the party has never done anything to decrease abortion in America other than pass the partial birth abortion ban that they knew Bill Clinton would veto.

When Republicans took control of Congress in 1995 they could have quickly re-directed some Planned Parenthood funds into a nationwide "Just Say No" campaign against abortion and facilitated the development of an inexpensive web based adoption system. The adoption system that might also contain pro-life statements and articles could have been available in high schools, colleges, clinics or any home that has web access. Anyone could then go to the web site, enter a query and get pictures and background information on adoptive parent candidates. Therefore, almost any young girl unable to raise a child could choose prospective parents for her child as early as the first day that realized she was pregnant.

I am convinced if these approaches were correctly implemented, abortion in America would have been cut in half by now without passing a single law that infringes upon American freedom. Although Bill Clinton vetoed the ban on grotesque partial birth abortions, his support for a more sophisticated adoption system may actually do more to reduce abortion in America than anything Republicans have done in five years of controlling Congress.

The Republican actions on abortion perfectly implement the divide and conquer strategy of the media by giving it a divisive issue for the population. It appears that Republican leaders actually prefer to be viewed as divisive so they can return to minority status and not have to confront the media with the agenda of their constituents. Perhaps the most amazing aspect of the entire abortion issue is how the Republican Party continually gets support from Christian leaders without ever actually accomplishing anything significant for them. I know that God gave these Christian leaders a brain so I have to wonder whether some of them are sincere or whether they have their own agendas.

DEMOCRAT FRAUDULENCE

The Democrat party has the same type of stranglehold over the American Black community that Republicans have over the Christian community. Although Democrats convinced America's Black leaders that they represent their interests, history tell us a completely different story.

During the time of the civil war, pro-slavery Democrats were defeated by Republican President, Abraham Lincoln, who is credited by nearly everyone for his key role in abolishing slavery. During 1964, 100 years later, Democrats filibustered in the Senate to prevent passage of the Civil Rights Act, but the filibuster was broken by Republican Senate minority leader, Everett Dirksen. In 1968, although Blacks were accepted in Republican state parties, they were not allowed in the Mississippi Democrat party and were forced to form their own Freedom party in an attempt to be seated at the 1968 Democrat Party convention in Chicago.

It seems that Democrats have over emphasized racism and used a fraudulent commitment toward race issues to divert attention from the evidence of their anti-Black American history.

The American Black community continues to support them, in many cases at the request of Black leaders. The same question must be asked of these leaders as of some Christian leaders. Are they sincere or do they have their own agenda for personal power and wealth?

Another fraudulent issue for the Democrat Party is their concern for what seems like every cause under the sun. For example, environmentalism was the excuse when President Clinton repaid his illegal contributions conduit, as he helped Indonesia maintain a monopoly on clean burning coal by declaring 1.7 million acres around competing mines in Utah as a national monument. Likewise, curbing teen smokers was the excuse when the Democrat Party received a $400,000 contribution from the head of the Communist Chinese Pagoda Red Mountain Cigarette Company and initiated major anti-tobacco legislation against American companies.

These examples involve apparent pay-backs for illegal foreign contributions but others simply increase their power. If you analyze legislation and proposals by Democrat congress members and administrations, almost all of them involve better protection for the citizens by spending more federal money to increase the size and power of a central government. This theme is so consistent it cannot be an accident. I am convinced the Democrat Party is not truly concerned about these causes but support them only to implement their own agenda.

Both major political parties are anti-freedom. Democrats generally attack economic freedom while Republicans assault personal freedom. If you find this had to believe, try to remember when the last law was passed that gave Americans more freedom. For hundreds of years, both parties have consistently implemented new laws taking away freedoms by offering more security from a larger, more powerful, more centralized government. Their legislation strategy to obtain ultimate power has imposed increased risks of tyranny on American citizens.

THE ANTI-AMERICAN MEDIA

I believe that increasing government power over American citizens, while subordinating American law to international law, is actually the agenda of those who control the national news media. While individual media organization ownership changes hands from time to time, new owners always maintain Council on Foreign Relations control of the editorial process dating back to its inception as explained in the previous chapter.

Many Americans are easily susceptible to exchanging their freedoms for more security. The highest editorial levels of the national news media successfully program the American public by using a simple theme: Freedom for Security. Take some time to seriously consider the many news, political and trash talk programs conforming to the theme of having some form of government or law which protect Americans from dangerous, crazed, immoral or unethical individuals.

We are a trusting kind of people. We trust our elected officials to represent our interests. We trust the news media to keep us informed about what is happening. However, they have their own interests and power desires. Many federal elected officials use our trust to further their own power or the power of those who financially control them. In many cases, their controllers also control major media organizations.

Major media organizations are managed in a way so their political stories manipulate public opinion to support the agenda of their owners, associates and advertisers. Many of these same media organizations report non-political news fairly and therefore, are able to fool us into thinking they report political news fairly as well. Most conservative talk show hosts falsely claim that new media organizations are biased. As you can see from this book, the news media organizations are way beyond bias. They have established a tightly coordinated socialist propaganda machine that has driven an anti-American agenda for decades.

To discover the tight control of political news by the major media outlets get a copy of the *Washington Times* and *Washington Post*. Read the political news each day. After a few days you should be wondering whether or not these papers were produced in the same country, much less the same city. *Washington Post* reporting is relatively consistent with other major newspapers and networks. But during the impeachment, it was the *Washington Times* that broke one unreported story after another, which were proven factually correct by subsequent congressional investigations.

If you cannot get reasonably easy access to these newspapers, and have a satellite dish or expanded cable TV system, there is another test you can perform. Try watching politically oriented programs on the Fox News Channel during weekday evenings and compare them to the political content on CNN or the other network news programs. After a week or two you should find that you are being informed with significantly different information about the same events depending upon what channel you are watching. These experiments should produce a desire within you to seek the political truth. If so, you may be ready to subscribe to the Spotlight newspaper, for perhaps, the most unfiltered, yet disturbing political news in America.

In this chapter I identify techniques that media organizations use to misinform their audiences. To counter them, we must identify trusted news sources and become properly informed rather than depend on civic leaders to point the way. We must watch or listen to entire political events rather than rely on filtered news summaries. We must also be willing to communicate and distribute information as best as we can to all we know who show the slightest interest. Only then will Americans be able to judge politicians by what they do, not what they say.

I believe that media editors deliberately misinform their audiences so that the controllers of major media organizations can compromise both sides of the political spectrum and force conformance to their global new world order goals. They are attempting to convert America from a Republic based on the rule of law to a democracy based on public opinion derived from polls that they conduct. The conversion will allow them to control America by reporting news in a manner that manipulates public opinion to support their agenda.

REPUBLICAN AND DEMOCRAT COLLUSION

Libertarians, Reformers and Constitution (formerly U.S. Taxpayer) Party members have said for years that Democrats and Republicans are essentially two sides of the same party. I found this impossible to believe during the period when Republicans launched and implemented the contract with America. At that time, there appeared to be significant differences between the two parties over the strategic direction of our country. But in 1998 and 1999, the impeachment movement subtly illustrated massive collusion between the two major parties.

The key to understanding the extent of collusion is to acquire basic knowledge of the depth and breadth of Clinton administration corruption. Then it is possible realize the magnitude of cover-up that Republican leaders instituted during the impeachment movement to protect Bill Clinton.

Democrats had already performed the same favor for Republicans in the 1980s by focusing on the arms for hostage Iran-Contra minutia and covering up Bush related CIA drug trafficking operations. The idea that Republicans and Democrats may collude to protect each other could be foreign to some readers, but whenever there are only two controlling entities of any kind they can very easily achieve collusion.

Sometimes the collusion is very deceptive as demonstrated in a recent Email scandal example. The White House failed to record and search, under subpoena requests, more than 1 million e-mails and attached documents sent to at least 526 staff members during a period from August 1996 to May 1999. In addition, nearly all Email to and from Vice President Al Gore and at least 24 of his staff members has been omitted from archives. Most of the five Northrop Grumman computer contractors who testified in 2000 before Congress swore that high-level White House staff members threatened them in various ways including jail if they revealed the problem.

While Republicans have held few in the Clinton administration accountable for any serious wrongdoing including these threats, the House Government Reform and Oversight Committee was quick to refer perjury charges against White House computer specialist Daniel "Tony" Barry to the Justice Department. Barry had issued a sworn statement that said, "Since July 14, 1994, Email with the EOP (Executive Office of the President) system administered by the Office of Administration has been archived in the EOP Automated Records Management System (ARMS)." His statement cleverly omits the problems that resulted in the lost Email but is defensible as being technically true.

Although the House Committee appeared to be taking aggressive action against the culprit, WorldNetDaily investigative reporter, Paul Sperry, uncovered a completely different story. The former reporter for Investor's Business Daily found numerous White House internal memos and trouble reports, dated from August 13, 1998 to May 5, 1999, where Barry had alerted several of his superiors and associates to the problem as he attempted to seek corrective action. The memos are filled repeatedly with quotes expressing the frustration that Barry was having in attempting to get help to remedy the problem. Thus the "opposition" Republican Party, led by Chairman Dan Burton, actually became another Clinton "scorched earth" policy facilitator. Burton was also responsible for the firing of David Bossie, one of the most serious investigators on the committee.

Sometimes the collusion is not by agreement but by force. This book illustrates how only one hour after the House Judiciary Committee voted to begin the impeachment inquiry of Bill Clinton on October 8, 1998, the Clinton controlled CIA publicly released the Inspector General report Volume II on CIA drug trafficking. That report, while still essentially denying CIA involvement, confirmed many of the allegations against the CIA, particularly those regarding Contra related drug running managed by individuals under the control of George Bush.

We are programmed by the national news media to believe Democrats and Republicans are diametrically opposed to each other, and in less important instances, there are real differences. But when it comes to serious corruption, both parties help each other through compromise and cover-up to gain concessions. Before the impeachment, L.D. Brown, the former Clinton bodyguard, Arkansas State Police Association president and CIA recruit, summed up the collusion about Bill Clinton for me in three words: Mutually Assured Destruction.

OBSTRUCTION OF JUSTICE

Perhaps no better or more serious example of this Mutually Assured Destruction policy exists than the case of the "train deaths" murders of Kevin Ives, Don Henry and subsequently seven other individuals who had knowledge about the Ives / Henry murders. Linda Ives has undergone a 13-year struggle to seek justice for the murder of her son and his friend but has been met at every turn with another facet of the most massive corruption and cover-up by federal, state and local officials since the political assassinations of the 60s. I became motivated to fight for issues of honest government after seeing this story told in a riveting documentary, entitled *Obstruction of Justice*. The story has also been published in a book entitled *The Boys on the Tracks*. The video is something that every American should see. The following brief summary only begins to scratch the surface of the compelling drama shown on the video.

Early in the morning on August 23, 1987, a train ran over the bodies of Kevin Ives and Don Henry while they were lying across railroad tracks at Alexander in Saline County, Arkansas. Fahmy Malak, the Arkansas State medical examiner, ruled that the deaths were accidental because the boys were under the influence of drugs and had fallen asleep on the tracks. The parents did not believe the examiner and spent over a year trying to get a second opinion while Malak refused to comply with court orders for information. During a second autopsy, Atlantan Joe Burton and six forensic pathologists or homicide detectives determined that Don Henry had been stabbed in the back and Kevin Ives skull was crushed, before Malak mutilated it during the initial autopsy. A grand jury changed the official death ruling to murder. The L.A. Times documented nearly 20 suspicious or inaccurate death rulings by Malak, including ones that favored Clinton's mother, a nurse anesthetist. Other examples include a suicide ruling for Raymond Albright who was shot in the chest 5 times; also an ulcer as the cause for James Milam, who was decapitated. During the controversy, Bill Clinton introduced legislation to give an incredible 40 percent raise in pay to Malak, who reported directly to Jocelyn Elders. When citizens held protest demonstrations to force his resignation in 1992, Clinton created a new position in the state health department for Malak and told reporters that Malak was 'stressed out'. Elders stated, "Arkansas owes Dr. Malak a great debt and a real apology."

The video meticulously documents an incredible series of systematic cover-ups by local police, prosecutors, courts and federal agencies that did everything within their power to avoid solving the case. From 1988 to 1995, 7 people with knowledge of the Ives / Henry murders, including grand jury witnesses and people who were on the tracks that night, have also been murdered. Only one person has been convicted in any of the murders and only one other person has ever been charged with one murder.

Several drug traffic investigations revealed that Ives and Henry had likely stumbled across a drug drop point known as A12 by the pilots who had flown for Barry Seal. The drugs were dropped regularly out of planes flying from Columbia to Mena, Arkansas. Ground crews that picked up the drugs typically included local government officials and police. The investigations uncovered compromised local judges and prosecutors, drug operations at Mena, possible money laundering, suppression and distortion of information by the media and additional details about the murder of Kevin Ives and Don Henry, as well as the other subsequent deaths.

However, the federal drug investigation was shut down by then U.S. Attorney Chuck Banks, a Reagan / Bush appointee who dismissed a grand jury after the conclusions implicated a number of people within the state and local governments. Banks, was expected to be tried for obstruction of justice, as recommended by a 1993 FBI investigation, however, the FBI recommendation was ignored by the Clinton/Reno Justice Dept. Assistant U.S. Attorney Bob Govar, resigned as head of a federal drug task force in protest of the shutdown. He assembled a substantial amount of the federal information from Jean Duffey, head of a drug task force investigation that was shut down by Judge John Cole.

The persecution of Duffey, during her investigation, is astounding in itself. She was attacked with 200 false press articles, pressured to turn over evidence to the people she was investigating and threatened with imprisonment on an illegal warrant issued by the same judge who shut down her investigation. She was even forced to temporarily flee the state when her mother received a tip from a dispatcher that she would be killed if imprisoned. After nearly a decade of deceit, Dan Harmon, a prosecutor who she initially implicated, was tried and convicted in June of 1997 on 5 drug related felony counts. Harmon was one of the two prosecutors named in the video that was instrumental in creating public pressure for his arrest and trial.

THE $14,000,000 LAWSUIT TRIAL

Clinton apologists have attempted to discredit the video and write this story off as a fairy tale because of a recent verdict in a $14,000,000 defamation lawsuit brought by two officers. The video implicates the two officers among others, for further questioning in regards to the Ives / Henry murders. On August 9, 1999 a federal jury awarded them $598,000 in their suit against Pat Matrisciana and his related organizations. The award was made despite the fact that Linda Ives, and drug task force investigator, Jean Duffey, testified for the defense. Both stated emphatically that they are convinced the officers were the "hands-on killers" of the boys.

The trial was a classic textbook example of how a judge can make a single ruling to control the outcome of a case even if it requires a unanimous jury verdict. Before the trial, Judge Warren Urbom somewhat mysteriously replaced another judge who was already assigned to the case. Urbom had previously been selected to hear a complaint against independent counsel Kenneth Starr but withdrew citing conflicts of interest.

The plaintiff's defamation claim was based solely on a single word, "eyewitnesses" used once in a statement that asserted, "eyewitnesses had implicated several people in the murders and subsequent cover-up". Three police officers, a sheriff and two prosecutors were named. The plaintiffs challenged no other facts presented in the shocking, one-hour video.

One potential eyewitness named Ronnie, who may be the only one who has survived, was subpoenaed to testify by the plaintiffs and then released during a lunch break, on the second day of the trial, while the defense was not present. The witness fled the court as well as the state, and could not be relocated by the defense even though they hired a detective to find him.

Duffey explained to me that his eyewitness information was contained in a damaging police report as well as a police report that documented another witness. However, Judge Urbom ruled that information in many police reports and some corroborating affidavits were "prejudicial" so they were not admitted into evidence. Thus, without the police reports and corroborating affidavits the defense had no defense.

The "prejudicial" ruling was particularly unusual since the case of the plaintiffs was based almost exclusively on their own character witnesses. Over one-dozen of them testified for the plaintiffs, including some fellow police officers, two FBI agents and a sheriff. Their testimony was reminiscent of 1990 when a string of character witnesses including former Attorney General and U.S. Senatorial candidate, Winston Bryant, testified to have the license of prosecutor Dan Harmon reinstated after he was convicted on a tax evasion charge. Harmon was eventually fined $150,000 and convicted in 1997 on 5 drug related felony counts, each carrying a 20-year maximum jail sentence.

The defamation trial appears to have ushered in an incredible, complete, new round of cover-ups in the Ives / Henry murders involving still another policeman. Former Alexander Police Chief, John Brown, who appeared in the video, claimed during depositions, "...portions of the video containing statements from me were edited and spliced to give the appearance that I made a statement that was never made by me". This claim is particularly fascinating since Brown was satisfied, and even proud of, the video, until the lawsuit was filed. Brown had gone on radio across the country promoting the video, obtained 350 copies of his own, and displayed them proudly during his unsuccessful campaign for county sheriff.

After the lawsuit was filed, Brown claimed to disapprove of the statements about the officers and stated that he told Pat Matrisciana not to use their names. His testimony was contradicted by Ives, Duffey, Matrisciana and Pat's editor, who provided the jury with his notes and an unused film clip where Brown names the suspects himself. Brown also stated in the video that "we know who killed them" but claimed during the trial he was referring to Sharline Wilson, who was never mentioned in the video as a suspect.

In perhaps the most sensational testimony of the trial, Brown stated he had a signed confession to the stabbing of Don Henry from Sharline Wilson. Wilson was sentenced to 30 years in prison, on a minor drug possession charge, after being near the tracks the night that Ives and Henry were killed. Brown's testimony left the burning question as to why Brown, who had championed Wilson's release for years, would want to discharge someone from prison who he claimed to be a murderer.

Sharline Wilson has stated that, while in prison, Brown took her to another location for a polygraph regarding what she knew about the murders. Before the polygraph, there was an initial interrogation that included another sheriff. Afterwards, she stated that Brown interrogated her alone, roughed her up, "busted her lip", put her in a straight jacket and left her in a padded room for more than a day. When he returned, she agreed to sign a confession that he dictated to her. She also agreed to confess during the polygraph but she was found to be untruthful. When the polygraph administrator asked her why, she stated she was saying what they wanted to hear. The administrator then found those statements to be true. Later, John Brown returned, took her out to dinner and said he would help her, since the polygraph showed that she did not kill the boys. Brown, who was eventually found to be working closely with the FBI, had evidently gotten what he wanted: a polygraph is not admissible in a court of law while a signed confession is admissible.

But the cover-up didn't stop at the local level. The testimony of Bob Govar, was limited by an authorization letter that prevented him from discussing any details of the Ives / Henry murders. U.S. Attorney, Paula Casey, the Clinton appointee who replaced Chuck Banks, attended court during his testimony apparently to ensure that the letter was enforced. Likewise, FBI agent, Phyliss Cournan, testified under a similar authorization letter from the FBI and could not discuss any details of the murder case.

The jury reached its verdict after experiencing firsthand the lack of respect for the Constitution that has become commonplace in today's courtrooms, when they requested a copy of the First Amendment for deliberations and were denied access to it. After the trial, the defense filed a motion to strike the verdict as a matter of law, since a single questionable word, in an hour long video, should not qualify as "reckless disregard" for the truth. Judge Urbom denied the motion as expected, however, the content of his denial was stunning to most of us familiar with the trial facts. After less than a page of some related case analysis, the judge provided one paragraph about trial specific evidence to justify his ruling. It is loaded with so many statements I believe to be patently false that it requires the following sentence-by-sentence rebuttal:

"There is evidence in the record that the defendant Matrisciana had obvious reasons to doubt the truth of the statement before it was published, but he decided to do nothing."

Pat was aware of the police reports and still firmly believes, along with Linda Ives and Jean Duffey, that the statement about eyewitnesses was true.

"In particular, the defendant Matrisciana had been told by John Brown that there was no documentation that justified the statement. This is significant. Mr. Brown was a major source of information for the video that contained the statement. In fact, Mr. Brown had complete editorial control over one-third of the video. Mr. Brown was relied on by the defendant Matrisciana. His research was trusted for a major portion of the video."

Here the judge admits that John Brown had editorial control over his portion of the video while essentially supporting Brown's contradicting claim that the video was edited without his consent. The judge accepted John Brown's testimony over Pat's testimony even though Brown was contradicted by Linda Ives, Jean Duffey, Pat and Pat's editor, who even showed an unused video clip of John Brown naming both the officers as suspects.

"In addition, the defendant Matrisciana had knowledge of a signed confession from a Sharline Wilson, who claimed she was on the tracks with the boys that night and that she stabbed one of them. The confession did not mention (the plaintiffs) and thus it lends support to the doubts of Mr. Brown."

The Sharline Wilson confession was so coerced that most knowledgeable individuals believe it is phony. That is why she has never been charged with the crime. The fact the judge would even mention it as true is a very disturbing indicator that he may be a part of the corruption.

"This evidence demonstrates there was reason for the defendant Matrisciana to question the truth of the statement. Yet he did not interrogate his other sources or editors who had knowledge of the same facts."

Pat discussed the video content in detail with Linda, Jean, John Brown and his own editor.

"He avoided objective, independent sources such as the police file."

This is one of the most amazing and apparently false statements in the ruling since not only did Pat, Linda and Jean use the police files, but Judge Urbom specifically refused to allow information in important police files into trial evidence.

"He failed to follow-up with Ms. Wilson."

Pat was in frequent contact with Ms. Wilson and knew her confession was coerced.

"He made no effort to contact the alleged eyewitnesses."

Pat relied on Jean, Linda and John Brown to contact the eyewitnesses so there is no reason he would duplicate their efforts.

"In short, he made no attempt to confirm the truth of the statement. Instead he decided to turn the other cheek."

Pat confirmed the truth of the eyewitness statement through the police reports.

"He wanted to avoid the truth because he wanted to sell more videos. That is reckless disregard".

This appears to be the most blatant lie of the ruling since the word "eyewitness", buried one time in the film, certainly did not sell any more videos because buyers never even knew it was there.

I fail to see how the judge could find that a single word mentioned once in an hour long video could be construed as "reckless disregard" for the truth.

The defense has entered an appeal that is still pending so I have withheld the names of the officers in this book. Testimony indicated the officers were advised to sue, by FBI Agent, Mike Smith, who was also present in a meeting when Ives and Duffey asked the FBI to investigate the officers. Despite repeated pleas from Linda Ives to many law enforcement agencies, the officers have never been investigated for the murders and no other individuals have ever been charged. In short, Linda Ives has found that federal, state and local officials have deliberately impeded any serious effort to solve any of the murders.

MUTUALLY ASSURED DESTRUCTION

The Ives / Henry murder cover-up has persisted for so long because the related drug trail has compromised the highest levels on both sides of the political spectrum. In Mississippi, the federal government intervened to solve the 1964 slaying of three civil rights workers. However, that will not happen in this case, because members and agencies of local, state and federal governments would be implicated.

Former Arkansas Development Finance Authority (ADFA) director, Larry Nichols, explained that ADFA was established with Act 1072, which was originally drafted by Webster Hubbell. Former governor, Bill Clinton, totally controlled ADFA by appointing all members. Nichols statements indicate that Mena drug money was laundered through ADFA, which was also used to payoff Clinton campaign contributors. Mena drug trafficking was part of a longtime CIA operation. Many researchers discovered CIA involvement in American drug traffic sources from Burma, Laos, Columbia, Panama, Nicaragua, and El Salvador. Control of these operations has been traced back to various direct reports of former President George Bush, ever since he was appointed CIA director in 1976.

Thus, with both former opposing Presidents involved in one of America's darkest secrets, each side will do everything they can to protect drug sources and the public officials involved in local ground distribution crews. The Ives/Henry murders illustrate how powerful people in the federal government have instituted a criminal enterprise that is actually more authoritative and threatening to American citizens than organized crime.

ELECTION 2000: COMMUNISM vs. DRUG TRAFFICKING?

The Democrat and Republican front runners, who have been promoted by the national news media for President in the Year 2000, are Vice President Al Gore and Texas Governor George W. Bush, respectively. Both are handsome, attractive candidates who are perfectly positioned to continue the détente of existing corruption.

The main contenders to the Gore and Bush 2000 nominations were former Senator Bill Bradley, a member of the Council of Foreign Relations, and Senator John McCain, a member of the notorious Keating Five savings and loan scandal. All are insiders who have been anointed and were promoted by the national news media. McCain, a former POW who adamantly supported the NATO bombing of Yugoslavian citizens, still denies the U.S. left POW/MIA troops in Southeast Asia after the Vietnam War. Some POW / MIA families have expressed concern about the special treatment McCain received in prison, the warm hug he recently gave his former Communist prison commander and the possibility of psychological programming he may have received while he was removed from other prisoners. These concerns appear justified and may make John McCain the most dangerous presidential candidate in American history.

Only one picture is needed to understand why Vice President Al Gore should not become President. That picture shows Al Gore sitting at a table during an April 1996 fundraiser in the Hsi Lai temple in Southern California. It can be found In the book entitled, *Year of the Rat*, written by congressional investigators Bill Triplett and Ed Timperlake. Congressional investigation evidence indicated the temple laundered illegal foreign campaign contributions for the DNC and that it had a relationship with Al Gore dating to 1988. The picture shows Gore sitting with Maria Hsia, Ted Sioeng and a Buddhist monk, who is sworn to poverty.

Maria Hsia is a known Communist Chinese agent, who organized the fund raiser, supported three other fund raisers for Al Gore and formed the Pacific Leadership Council with John Huang to raise money for the DNC. Ted Sioeng is the head of the Chinese Communist controlled Pagoda Red Mountain Cigarette Co., which donated $400,000 to DNC. Immediately afterwards, the Democrats helped Sioeng get a foothold in the American market by introducing a significant amount of anti-tobacco legislation against American companies under the guise of concern about teen smoking.

Maria Hsia, who was convicted on all five counts of campaign finance violations brought against her, is apparently not the only Communist agent who has been supporting the Gore family. Other reports claim Al Gore has several Communist connections through his father, Al Gore Sr., Armand Hammer, and his son-in-law, Andrew Schiff, descendant of Jacob Schiff, who allegedly financed Trotski, and Lenin. The details of these claims are outside the scope of this book.

Meanwhile, the Republican alternative, George W. Bush, has been harassed repeatedly by the media to answer the question of whether or not he used cocaine. Republicans believe he has been harassed unfairly, considering the media suppression of cocaine use by Bill Clinton. But the media has actually protected Bush by suppressing a specific cocaine allegation that has been raised against him. The specific allegation is that in 1985, George W. and his brother, Jeb, were caught on video at the Tiamiami airport in a DEA sting operation picking up two kilos of cocaine for personal use from a plane owned by CIA operative Barry Seal. This book explains how the ownership of the plane was traced by serial number and FAA registration number from Seal through several individuals and organizations connected to various government officials and agencies. Its current owner is non other than the state of Texas, where it frequently was used by George W. Bush personally, as Governor.

The media has focused most of its attention on the cocaine allegation from the book entitled, *Fortunate Son*. The book states that George W. Bush was busted for cocaine around the same time frame as the drug drop and his father had to pull strings to turn a jail sentence into a year of community service for a project called Operation P.U.L.L.. The publisher, St. Martin's Press, eventually stopped distribution of the book, even though they reviewed it carefully before publishing. When questioned about the charges, Bush simply stated that the author, who still stands behind the charge, is a convicted felon. Bush refuses to talk about cocaine use or charges, during that time, has never offered an explanation as to why he would want to perform a year of community service in a ghetto during the prime of his party life when he was frequently intoxicated, according to his own family.

The most disturbing point, however, is that cocaine allegations are nothing new for the Bush family. This book describes three CIA run drug operations that have been traced to direct reports of former president George Bush since he was appointed director of the CIA, in 1976, by Gerald Ford. They include support of the Contras, operations in Southeast Asia during the Vietnam War, and control of special flights between Columbia and Panama that also involved Manuel Noriega.

Bill Clinton had knowledge of Bush involvement in CIA drug operations since evidence indicated that he and Web Hubbell set up the Arkansas Development Finance Authority, ADFA, which was used as a money laundering agency for the Mena, Arkansas drug operation, according to ADFA director, Larry Nichols. Bill Clinton attempted to spread some of this knowledge (exactly when his impeachment began) by releasing a CIA Inspector General drug trafficking report. I believe he successfully compromised the Republican party leadership, which was forced to protect the year 2000 candidacy of the former President's son, George W. Bush.

This makes the potential Bush / Gore election match-up in the Year 2000 one of compromise and corruption. If either is elected no one in the Clinton administration will ever be held accountable for their wrongdoing and America will continue to be desecrated by drug trafficking and closet communists determined to implement a new world order at the expense of American sovereignty. America is quickly running out of time to correct these problems. It is essential, for the citizens of America, to elect a third party Presidential candidate just to begin breaking the détente of mutually assured destruction that has strangled the integrity of our government.

MEDIA MISINFORMATION TECHNIQUES

In the future, Americans must not only develop trusted sources for news, but must also learn to distinguish and disregard false reporting. Many people are led to believe that misinformation reported by the media is a result of media bias. However, it should be clear to those who have read this book that media misinformation is not accidental but part of a carefully crafted plan to deceive the public and implement the agenda of those who control the media.

To help distinguish deceitful reporting, I have identified 25 misinformation techniques that are frequently used by many media organizations. To further illustrate these points, I have selected one chapter of a new book to use as an example. The book I have chosen is entitled, *The Hunting of the President* by Joe Conason and Gene Lyons. It describes "The ten-year campaign to destroy Bill and Hillary Clinton". I have chosen Chapter Nine, of this particular book, because I have some personal knowledge of the information it reports and have already written about that information in this book. Therefore, the readers should get a clear illustration of these misinformation techniques. Many of the examples could actually apply to multiple techniques even though they are listed under only one. The techniques and examples are:

Suppression of Major News

Media organizations frequently suppress entire stories or large segments of news they do not want audiences to hear because it might interfere with their agenda. For example, the sample book I selected purports to discuss the major Clinton related scandals in Arkansas but it completely avoids any details of the 13-year federal, state and local cover-up of the Ives / Henry murders and the direct connections that illustrate Bill Clinton participated in the cover-up.

Attacking Adversarial Motives

Media organizations frequently divert attention from allegations of corruption by attacking motives of those raising the allegations. On page 137 of the sample book, the authors refer to Citizens for Honest Government (CHG). They say, "In practice, the new organization had two main purposes; to propagate political and religious nostrums of the extreme religious right with which its founder and sole proprietor, Pat Matrisciana, was closely allied; and to promote and distribute videotapes produced by Jeremiah Films and Integrity Films, two 'for profit corporate entities' he owned".

First of all, the bulk of focus by CHG was on the murders of Kevin Ives and Don Henry, the murder of Vince Foster and drug trafficking through Mena, Arkansas. These have nothing to do with politics or religion since any sincere American citizen would be against murder and government sponsored drug trafficking. Periphery connections that involved Bill Clinton in money laundering and murder cover-up were not obvious until after the facts were investigated. Secondly, the film companies have not made any significant profit that has offset the cost of the videos. In fact, Jeremiah Films, which operated smoothly as a Christian film production company, was on the verge of bankruptcy after it produced the videos.

Selective Reporting

Media types frequently report only information supporting their agenda or a conclusion they want their audience to reach. On page 140 of the sample book, the authors report a few of the mysterious deaths that have various connections to the Clinton administration. However, all information about their suspicious circumstances and most of the connections to the Clinton administration were left out, even though this information was freely available to them on the web site that they researched.

Intentional Misleading

Media types frequently mislead their audiences by using a portion of the truth without explaining the entire subject matter. This is a particularly clever technique sure to fool most people. On page 143 of the sample book, the authors refer to information in The Clinton Chronicles video. They state: "One of the video's silliest charges was that the ADFA had laundered $100 million per month (or $1.2 billion per year) in illicit cash. In the agency's nine-year existence it made loans totaling only $1.7 billion". In the video, ADFA director Larry Nichols specifically states that funds he believed to be drug money went in and out during the month, were balanced before the end of the month, and not recorded on the books by month end. Therefore, no loans were ever made to launder the money. I believe the authors were fully aware of this and deliberately deceived their readers, but ultimately you can decide yourself.

Misquoting of Adversaries

Media types frequently misquote allegations made by adversaries and change the type of allegation so they can truthfully deny it. On page 146 of the sample book, the authors refer to the president's reaction to the videos. They state, " The president's complaints caused a flurry of front page stories in newspapers like the *Times* and *Philadelphia Inquirer* that inevitably focused on the more sensational accusations and observed that the videos offered no proof Clinton was a drug smuggling murderer". Many Clinton apologists have used the terms "drug smuggling" and "murderer" because they know there is no evidence to support those allegations. In fact, these exact terms were used directly by Hillary Clinton in an NBC interview. The videos have never accused the president of drug smuggling and murder. At the worst case, they have accused the president of involvement in money laundering and murder cover-up. The evidence to support these allegations is very precise and convincing.

False Implication

Media types will frequently report generic information essentially true in a manner to imply detail facts that are not true. On page 155 of the sample book, the authors refer to "an Arkansas lawyer named Jean Duffey who promoted a conspiratorial view of The Henry / Ives case". This is basically a true statement with a false implication that Jean Duffey is a little unbalanced. First of all, Duffey is not just a lawyer but was the head of the drug task force investigation that uncovered much of the corruption documented in this book. Secondly, she does believe there was a conspiracy to cover-up the murders of Kevin Ives and Don Henry, but that is not unusual since any truth seeking individual, who is familiar with the evidence, can clearly see there was without question, a government conspiracy to cover-up the murders. Third, I know Jean Duffey personally and she is an incredibly detailed and thorough investigator who is totally non-partisan and has detailed knowledge of drug corruption in Arkansas. This makes her a threat to corrupted government officials who hold positions of power in Arkansas.

False Insanity Implications

Media types typically attempt to portray adversaries as slightly crazy. To do this, they frequently use the word "conspiracy" as though anyone who believes in a conspiracy (such as organized crime) must be somewhat deranged. On page 145 of the sample book, the authors call Indiana Congressman Dan Burton "a Foster conspiracy buff." The implication is that anyone who does not believe Foster committed suicide is a nutty conspiracy advocate. The simple fact remains, Vince Foster's prints were not even on the gun that was used to kill him. This book only scrapes the surface of hundred of pieces of evidence confirming Vince Foster was murdered.

Inadequate Detail

Media types frequently leave out key details to keep their audiences uninformed about events where public opinion may conflict with media agenda. On page 142 of the sample book, the authors refer to allegations against Bill Clinton as made in The Clinton Chronicles. They state, "Had he, as the video alleged, issued a full pardon to a political supporter named Dan Lasater, who was convicted of giving cocaine to his acquaintances? Impossible because Lasater had pleaded guilty to a federal crime". First of all Lasater was charged with a federal crime but it was dropped when he pled guilty to a state crime. Bill Clinton then had full control of the case and got Lasater released after he served about five months of his sentence. The authors also did not mention that the acquaintances of Lasater were teenage girls.

Unsupported Conclusions

Many media types are notorious for making conclusions that have no basis in fact, in order to support their agenda. On pages 141 and 142 of the sample, book the authors refer to many other individuals such as reporters who have disproved various allegations made in CHG videos; however, they never explain precisely what evidence disproved a single allegation.

Attacking Adversarial Sources

When media types cannot factually refute adversarial sources, they frequently resort to attacking their perspectives. On page 155 of the sample book, the authors refer to Lt. Col. Tom McKenney as a " military intelligence figure with extreme right wing views". I know Tom McKenney personally. He is the kindest, gentlest, most sincere man I have ever met in my life. Honest individuals would never consider Tom to be "extreme" regardless of their political views.

Distortion of Facts

Media types frequently distort facts to the brink of falsehoods in order to support their agenda. On page 157 of the sample book, the authors refer to Kathy Ferguson: another mysterious death. They state, "Despondent over a failed love affair, she had called 911 and then turned a gun on herself". The authors mention that Chris Ruddy investigated her death and felt it was suspicious but they conveniently left out what Ruddy discovered.

Kathy was the ex-wife of Danny Ferguson, the trooper who brought Paula Jones to Bill Clinton at the hotel where he allegedly made improper advances. She was also a nurse who was found shot to death on May 11, 1994 after packing her bags to leave town. Her autopsy report that indicated suicide, was contradicted by six of her nurse friends and a doctor who stated she had a gunshot wound in the back of her head. Women rarely commit suicide with a gun and it is equally unusual for someone to shoot themselves in the BACK of the head.

The claim that she was "despondent over a failed love affair" is also unsupported and easily contradicted. Her fiance, Bill Shelton, was an Arkansas police officer highly critical of the suicide ruling. One month later, on June 12, 1994, he was found dead at her grave site. His death was also ruled a suicide and he, too, had a gunshot wound in the BACK of his head.

Credentialism

Many media types attempt to substitute credentials for facts they cannot refute. The implication is that large media organizations or famous media individuals cannot be wrong because of their established credentials. This helps media controllers implement their agenda. In many cases, media organizations idolize their own people by propagating awards and organizations to recognize them. On the jacket of the sample book, the author's awards are mentioned as an indication that they have the proper credentials to write the book regardless of how distorted its content may be.

Divisive Demonization

Media types frequently use divisive words such as "left wing" or "right wing" to demonize an adversary that they cannot factually dispute. The intent is to get the audience to classify the adversary negatively so they do not have to think about the actual facts being discussed. The audience is left with the assumption that the position of the adversary is not worth considering since he or she is of a different political persuasion. In the sample book, the authors use the term "right wing" several times in Chapter Nine to describe individuals such as Lt. Col. Tom McKenney.

Change of Subject

When faced with irrefutable facts contradicting their agenda, media types will frequently change the subject. All 400 pages of the sample book I selected, attempted to change the subject from the evidence of Clinton administration corruption to the background of the individuals who have presented the evidence.

Authoritative Cconfirmation

When media organizations want to impose their viewpoint upon their audiences, they frequently use experts who they know will provide a professional opinion to confirm the direction of the media agenda. For example, they may interview a general to confirm the need to bomb a country or tout a Congressman who is sponsoring a piece of legislation they are seeking to pass. For five pages of the sample book, beginning with page 153, the authors refer to former Saline County Sheriff John Brown as an authoritative source. As previously described, Brown's testimony in the defamation suit was refuted by four witnesses and Brown even went so far as to tout the coerced confession of Sharline Wilson during his testimony and make the ludicrous claim that she killed Don Henry.

Partial Quotation

Media types frequently pick selected words out of an adversarial quote to distort the original intent of the quote. This allows them to tell their audiences the adversary said something offensive or incorrect even though it never really happened. On page 372, in the Afterword of the sample book, the authors reference Congressman Barr. They state, "Barr did not serve his cause well when he characterized the effort to remove the president as a 'civil war' nor when he lectured a distinguished Black federal judge (testifying before the House Judiciary Committee) that 'real Americans' favored impeachment". The authors raise the classic racial implication so often used to divert attention from corruption.

First of all, although a Black federal judge did testify before the House Judiciary Committee, Barr made the remark during testimony by Alan Derschowitz, who appeared shortly thereafter and is neither black; nor a federal judge. The reference to "real Americans" refers to the citizens who are constituents of Congressmen and Congresswomen, not paid legal experts who frequently appear on talk shows to furnish propaganda in support of the media agenda.

Poll Manipulation

After adequately misinforming their audience, media organizations conduct polls intended to produce results supporting their agenda. The questions are frequently twisted so the answers yield the desired result. For example, during the height of the impeachment, one news organization actually conducted a poll that asked the question, "Should Bill Clinton NOT be impeached?" On page 370, in the Afterword of the sample book, the authors refer to Bill Clinton. They state, " A poll commissioned by CNN and the Wall Street Journal in early February 1998, recorded an astonishing 79 percent of respondents favoring him". I am by no means astonished that a CNN poll would claim a 79 percent favorable rating for Bill Clinton. However, I do not believe Bill Clinton, who never even gained 50% of a presidential election vote, has ever had a 79 percent favorable rating, particularly during a peak in one of his many scandals.

Corrupted Sources

Media types sometimes use corrupted sources to support their agenda when the facts do not support it. On pages 140 and 153 of the sample book, the authors reference CHG financial records and ledgers without explaining how they got them. The references state, "The authors also obtained CFHG internal documents, fund-raising letters and correspondence from confidential sources". The sources are not confidential to me or to Pat Matrisciana who told me about two employees I know who broke into the files. When the employees were terminated, they attempted to mis-appropriate computer equipment and take over the web site. After CHG filed legal action against them, Pat discovered they were under FBI protection from the Clinton / Reno Justice Department. Stolen copies of records, apparently including false information about a multi-million dollar bank account, was eventually leaked to the Salon web magazine, and picked up again by Geraldo on CNBC, immediately before the National Impeachment Town Hall and included in this sample book.

Mixing Lies w/ Truth

Media types will frequently mix a lie in with the truth to keep their audiences misinformed about facts that if known, could damage the media agenda. This technique makes it almost impossible for the audience to distinguish fact from fiction. On Page 154 of the sample book, the authors refer to the Ives / Henry murders. They correctly state the Obstruction of Justice video had claimed, "Eyewitnesses have implicated several people in the murders and subsequent cover-up". But the authors immediately state, "It then proceeded to list Prosecutor Dan Harmon and the two officers as the killers". The video never listed anyone as the killers. It only "implicated several people in the murders and subsequent cover-up". It suggested these people should be questioned and possibly investigated for their potential roles.

Blatant Lie

The final desperate attempt by media types, when they have completely failed to refute the facts is to blatantly lie. On page 153 and 154 of the sample book, the authors make their only significant reference to the Ives / Henry murders. They say, "The case first drew notice due to a foolish error by the state medical examiner." They continue with a run-on sentence. It states, "Whether the overworked medical examiner – deemed overly solicitous of law enforcement by some observers, incapable of admitting error by almost everybody – had simply misplaced a decimal point was hard to say". It is easy for almost anyone to understand an honest, competent medical examiner cannot mistake a stab wound and a crushed skull for marijuana intoxication. In addition, the medical examiner had many other bogus death rulings which were documented by the *L. A. Times*. To imply the medical examiner may have "simply misplaced a decimal point" is not only a terrible affront to Linda Ives, but one of the biggest insults to the intelligence of the American people I have ever seen.

I have illustrated 25 media misinformation techniques in a single chapter and Afterword of one sample book. In addition, the authors of the book attempt to discredit many people I know personally. A few them are Jean Duffey, Linda Ives, Pat Matrisciana and Lt. Col. Tom McKenney. I can truthfully say these people are my friends who I know well enough to trust them with my life. All of them have an uncompromising integrity that appears to be totally lacking in the authors of the sample book.

The back cover of the sample book references the sum of allegations against Bill Clinton. The cover states, "It is also the story of the most successful and long-running "dirty tricks" campaign in recent American history, fomented by a handful of professional Republican operatives and corporate lawyers and funded by a network of wealthy conservatives". This is the classic concept the Democrat Party uses to dupe their own members. When Republicans expose real Democrat corruption, Democrat apologists simply say they are up to their "dirty tricks".

I was deeply involved in the impeachment movement but I am not wealthy. I am not a lawyer but a computer consultant who has a typical analytical mind like many of those in my profession. I am not a professional Republican operative since the Republican Party disgusts me. I am not a conservative since conservatives would never talk about Bush drug trafficking allegations and the need to decriminalize drugs. I simply want honest government. I am convinced that most of the allegations against Bill Clinton are true and that is why I wanted him impeached.

GETTING INVOLVED

Because of the many corrupted media organizations who suppress critical information about inner government workings, most of us either do not realize our freedom is being threatened or do not realize the severity of the threat. We are caught up with our personal lives, our families, our friends and the overall fun of enjoying life in the world's most prosperous country. We have been successfully programmed into a state of complacency and lack of knowledge. Even many of us who realize the freedom of our children is in jeopardy, have been programmed to think we are helpless to do anything about it. Therefore, this is a fatal situation for America.

To counter this fatalistic complacency, we must get involved in our government. Voting is simply not enough. We must get to know our Senators and Representatives on a personal basis and should financially support those who we trust to do the right thing. Representatives still listen to their supporters, and can be effective in establishing an American agenda from the bottom up. We must avoid any financial contributions to national committees because they use the money in an attempt to get Congressmen to support a pre-established top down agenda that is invariably always corrupt.

During the impeachment, thousands of American citizens got involved in their government. They spent their personal time and money

- writing, calling, faxing and visiting their Congressmen,
- signing and collecting impeachment petitions,:
- participating in town halls and talk shows,
- explaining the facts to their friends, and
- pressuring the media organizations to tell the truth.

Protecting our freedom requires a commitment of some time and money. Freedom is not free. It was a key factor that cost me my marriage. If we want to preserve our freedom we must be willing to devote at least a small portion of our income and spare time to protecting it. We are in a battle for control of America being fought by two groups. One group is the citizens who simply want honest government. The other is the global socialist controlled media. They want to subordinate American sovereignty to a one-world government plan being implemented by compromised politicians who they control.

A PLATFORM FOR FREEDOM

To save America we must completely redirect our country away from the Communist mentality of our elected leaders and force them to implement a pro-American platform by systematically removing legislation that they have already adopted in support of *Communist Manifesto* planks. Ten points for a platform of freedom are:

1. Protect American sovereignty

All laws that subordinate American government regulations to global organizations should be eliminated. The Committee on anti-American activities should be restored and manned by independent citizens. Bills must pass Congress by a full majority of total members, not a majority of those present. Any bill submitted in either body of Congress should have at least three days of lead time to allow the members to review it before voting on it.

2. Stop unconstitutional executive orders

The first sentence of the U.S. Constitution says, "all power granted herein is vested in a Congress of the United States..." Therefore, Congress can stop executive orders at any time it chooses. The House Constitutional Subcommittee should review the books for all unconstitutional orders, list them and remove them in a single bill. All war powers acts currently in place should be terminated and the capabilities for automatic executive orders removed. Any rights given to the federal government, during the gold crisis in 1933, should also be reclaimed by the states.

3. Reform the election process

The book, *Votescam*, by the Collier brothers, illustrates voting improprieties that must be rectified. The election process must be reformed to ensure that :

- money does not play an overwhelming part in who is elected,
- only eligible voters are allowed to vote,
- the results of the voting can be certified for accuracy,
- existing election and finance laws are enforced, and
- no American taxpayer money should be used to fund any candidates whatsoever.

Taxpayer funding of political candidates should be terminated. Democrat and Republican presidential candidates currently get upwards of $60 million in taxpayer funds that give them an insurmountable advantage in the presidential elections.

The "soft" money donated to political parties should be eliminated since it helps to drive corrupted, top-down agendas. Only donations from individuals to candidates should be allowed. All corporate, union and non-local political action committee donations should be eliminated. Representatives should get their funds only from their respective districts, and Senators should get funds only from their respective states.

Any Presidential candidate on the ballot, in all 50 states, should be allowed to participate in debates. Debate questions should be asked not by media representatives, but only by American citizens who are selected randomly from the debate attendees.

The composition of the Federal Election Commission (FEC) should be changed to disallow political party members from serving. Political party independence could help achieve fairness for third parties since all current FEC members are either Democrat or Republican. The FEC must also be held accountable for proving to the American citizens that election results are valid.

Citizens must show some form of identification to cast their votes and prevent duplicate voting. Votes must be tallied and verified, at the precinct level, to prevent massive, centralized voter fraud. When procedures are violated at a precinct, an independent audit should be conducted to certify the results. If the results cannot be certified and the election hangs in the balance, then the voters at that precinct should be required to vote again. Manual vote counting should be filmed to ensure accuracy. Software must be impounded and readily available to verify there are no software irregularities that can be used to falsify election results. Election machine vendors unwilling to abide by the rules should be replaced with the new vendors.

4. Ensure Justice Department accountability

Justice Department agencies must be held accountable to the basic laws of the land and not serve as a defense agency for a President. The appointment of the Attorney General should be made by Congress, to help protect the citizens against a tyrannical dictatorship. All law enforcement should be consolidated under the Justice Department to ensure no rogue law enforcement outfits, such as previous IRS and ATF units, are allowed to operate outside the bounds of the law. ATF and IRS law enforcement agencies should be abolished in conjunction with eliminating the income tax. Each law enforcement agency must have public, Congressional accountability for its actions to ensure there will be no future events such as the FBI actions at Waco or CIA drug trafficking. A citizens' review panel must be established to ensure the Justice Department does not adopt a double standard of justice for government official vs. citizens. No individual or organization should be allowed to operate above the law for national security reasons.

5. Decriminalize drugs

The CIA has become so deeply involved in drug trafficking it is unwilling and unable to eliminate its entanglement with organized crime. The temptation of using the profits from drug running to fund covert operations, has made the CIA a willing partner to drug traffickers throughout the world for decades. Other military units have been involved as well. Congress is simply too intimidated by the CIA to make it accountable. The CIA essentially has a license to live above American law under the guise of national security. This concept is unconstitutional and a threat to every American citizen, regardless of what agency may happen to have such a privilege.

The phony drug war has been used as an illegal excuse to confiscate the property of honest Americans; destroy our Fourth Amendment rights to unreasonable search and seizure, and even kill innocent American citizens, such as those at Waco where the ATF used the false excuse of a non-existent drug lab to gain military training and equipment in violation of the Posse Comitatus laws.

The only viable solution is to decriminalize drugs to remove the profit in drug running. The illegality of drugs has caused prices to escalate to as much as 100 times their actual cost to manufacture. The removal of the profit motive will also spur a dramatic drop in crime and return America to a law and order society like we had during the 50s when drugs, such as cocaine, were legal but never used. Dramatic reductions would occur in drug-related crimes such as drive by shootings, gang-related murders and robberies to support drug habits. In addition, no pimps would find it worthwhile to hang around high schools and try to hook our children on drugs.

6. Eliminate asset forfeiture laws

There is no condition under which our government should be allowed to steal the property of its citizens against their will, even if they are suspected to have committed crimes. Federal, state and local governments should have no more rights over and above the victims of the crimes. Once an individual has been convicted of a crime where assets were acquired illegally, government should be allowed to file a grievance in the courts to recover incarceration costs, legal fees or other expenses incurred. Automatic forfeiture of property should not be allowed.

7. Balance the budget

Despite the claim of the politicians, the federal budget is not balanced. The difference between social security revenue and expenses must currently be added to the budget as income to balance it with the excessive spending that still exists. The budget must be balanced after social security funds are taken completely off line. All off budget projects must be eliminated or included in the normal federal budget. A balanced budget amendment must also be passed to force politicians into doing their duty.

8. Eliminate social security

Since the social security money we give our government is spent as soon as it is received, social security is simply another income tax that should be eliminated. Americans should be free to invest for their retirement wherever they choose, using their own personal accounts which would give them dramatically improved returns. Under no condition should money be taken from the citizens under false pretenses and spent against their will by legislators.

9. Eliminate the inheritance tax

Our government does not have a Constitutional right to seize property from citizens at the time of their death. Any taxes that apply to the transfer of assets to family heirs is an income tax that should be eliminated. This will help preserve the right of each American to a full inheritance undaunted by government interference at the time of their ancestor's death.

10. Eliminate income tax

The federal income tax must be removed, despite the complexity that may be involved. A flat tax would not resolve any of the IRS abuse cases where there were disagreements over the amount of income that was earned by the taxpayer. Therefore, if the government needs tax revenue, it should be collected at the time of consumption as a national sales tax. The advantages of a national sales tax over an income tax are:

PROMOTES FREEDOM
Citizens decide when and how much tax to pay through their purchases.

ABOLISHES COMPLEXITY
No personal time is required from citizens to pay taxes.

ELIMINATES INTRUSIONS
The IRS cannot be used to persecute citizens for political purposes.

REDUCES TAX BURDEN
The IRS cuts costs by dealing only with businesses and state agencies.

REDUCES LOBBYING
Tax breaks that account for about 65 percent of all lobbying would be eliminated.

TAXES UNDERGROUND
Criminals, drug dealers and illegal aliens must pay sales taxes just like honest folks.

IMPROVES TRADE DEFICIT
Reduced cost of producing goods with no employee income tax will increase exports.

STIMULATES ECONOMY
Potential for more personal savings will increase business investment and lower interest rates.

PROMOTES EQUALITY
No one receives arbitrary tax breaks or special privileges.

HELPS DISADVANTAGED
Lower income citizens benefit more from proposed-credit on social security tax up to poverty level.

If a sales tax is ever implemented in place of the income tax, Americans must ensure Congress does not quietly allocate part of the money to global causes such as the United Nations or international money fund. American sales tax collected from American citizens should not be used to fund the "New World Order."

SAVING AMERICA

These suggestions are just a starting point on the road back to true, honest government. We are running out of time. If we Americans do not act now, we will almost assuredly lose the gift we have been given in the next few years. Then what will we say to our children or grandchildren when they ask us what happened?

Although these platform planks would be desirable to most any American, neither Democrats nor Republicans are seriously trying to implement them, regardless of their rhetoric. That is why the battle today is not about conservative vs. liberal, left wing vs. right wing, rich vs. poor, Black vs. White or Christian vs. Muslim vs. Jews. The battle that must be fought in the new millennium is about Americanism vs. anti-Americanism. The majority of all Americans must unite in the new millennium to preserve the American freedoms to which we have grown accustom.

The time has come to get the closet Communists out of the American government, to get the government out of the drug trafficking business and to force our elected officials to implement a platform to restore the freedom of American citizens so that the government once again runs on the principles of the United States Constitution. It is my sincerest desire that every reader will join the battle by picking an issue and getting involved. Together, we can save America.

REFERENCES

Harry Browne, *Why Government Doesn't Work*, St. Martin's Press.
James and Kenneth Collier, *Votescam*, Victoria House Press.
Joe Conason and Gene Lyons, *The Hunting of the President*,
  St Martin's Press.
Paul Sperry, *Did House panel fry good guy?*, WorldNetDaily
Ed Timperlake & Bill Triplett, *Year of the Rat*, Regnery Publishing.

The New American magazine, "Al Gore's Red Connections,"
    3/31/97, American Opinion Book Services.
Michael Ruppert From the Wilderness newsletters, various issues.
Mara Leveritt,*The Boys on the Tracks*, St Martin's Press.
Obstruction of Justice (video), Integrity Films

ABBREVIATIONS

ACDA   Arms Control Disarmament Agency
ACEP   Advisory Committee on Export Policy
ACTION   Activate Congress to Improve Our Nation
ADFA   Arkansas Development Finance Authority
AP   Associated Press
ATF   "Bureau of Alcohol, Tobacco and Firearms"
BCCI   Bank of Credit and Commerce
CATIC   China Aero Technology Import/Export Corporation
CCP   Chinese Communist Party
CFR   Council on Foreign Relations
CHG   Citizens of Honest Government
CIA   Central Intelligence Agency
CIM   Chief of Implementation Mission
CITIC   China International Trust Investment Corporation
COCOM   Coordinating Committee on Multi-Lateral Exports Controls
COSCO   China Ocean Shipping Company
CS   Orthocholorbenzylidene Malonoitrile
DEA   Drug Enforcement Administration
DIA   Defense Intelligence Agency
DNC   Democrat National Committee
DOD   Department of Defense
DTSA   Defense Technology Security Administration
EDS   Electronic Data Systems
FAA   Federal Aviation Administration
FBI   Federal Bureau of Investigation
FDIC   Federal Deposit Insurance Corporation
FDR   Franklin Delano Roosevelt
FEC   Federal Elections Commission
FLIR   Forward Looking Infrared
FRY   Federal Republic of Yugoslavia
GAO   General Accounting Office
IBM   International Business Machines
ICBM   Intercontinental Ballistic Missile
IG   Inspector General

INS	Immigration and Naturalization Service
IPI	International Paper Incorporated
IRS	Internal Revenue Service
ISA	(Army) Intelligence Support Activity
KLA	Kosovo Liberation Army
LAPD	Los Angeles Police Department
MIA	Missing in Action
MIRV	Multiple Independent Re-entry Vehicle
MIT	Massachusetts Institute of Technology
MSNBC	Microsoft / National Broadcasting Company
MTOPS	Million Theoretical Operations Per Second
NATO	North Atlantic Treaty Organization
NET	National Empowerment Television
NRA	National Rifle Association
NSA	National Security Administration
NSC	National Security Council
NTSB	National Transportation and Safety Board
NYPD	New York Police Department
OSS	Office of Strategic Services
PBS	Public Broadcast Service
PLA	Peoples Liberation Army
POW	Prisoners of War
RTC	Resolution Trust Company
U.N.	United Nations
UPI	United Press International
VFR	Visual Flight Rules

Index

A
ABC, 53, 95, 131, 223.
Accuracy in Media, 21, 28, 116, 119.
Afghanistan, 60, 120, 125, 213.
Aldrich, Gary, 36, 64, 73, 94, 108, 218.
Anderson, Mari, 95, 97.
American Justice Federation, 32, 42, 116.
Atlanta Journal, 2-3, 33.
Atlanta Constitution, 53.
Arkansas Development Finance Authority, 17-18, 56, 92, 111, 187, 252, 254, 275.
Associated Press, (AP) 92, 122, 175-177,222,232, 275.
Armey, Dick,44-45.
Armitage, Richard, 125, 188-189, 191, 208.

B
Bank of Commerce and Credit, (BCCI), 93,111,275.
Banks, Chuck, 36, 110, 246, 249.
Barnes, Roy, 4.
Barr, Bob, 3, 29, 41, 45-47, 51-52, 64, 72-73, 76.
Barr, William, 187.
Becker, Brian, 129.
Begala, Paul, 55.
Bennett, John, 54.
Bentsen, Lloyd, 3.
Berger, Sandy, 137, 152.
Bermudez, Enrique, 175-178.
Bin Ladin, Osama, 120, 124-125.
Blair, Tony, 122.
Blandon, Danilo, 177-178.
Blumenthal, Sydney, 81.
Boortz, Neal, 44.
Bossie, David, 17, 244.
Brown, Floyd, 17.
Brown, John, 248-251, 261.
Brown, L.D., 91-92, 209, 244.
Brown, Ron, 23-24, 101, 113, 153, 163-165, 172.

McDonald, Larry, 2-3, 52.
McDonald, Cathy, 2, 52.
McDonnell, Douglas, 147-148, 150.
McDougal, James, 15, 46, 70, 89-91, 163.
McDougal, Susan, 91.
McHale, Paul, 69.
McLarty, Mack, 67, 96, 98, 169, 220.
McKenney, Tom, 18, 34, 259, 261, 264.
McManus, John, 52, 236.
McVeigh, Timothy, 22, 165.
Meneses, Norwin, (Cantero), 176.
Metcalf, Jack, 55.
Michael, Bob, 10.
Miller, Zell, 4.
Milosevic, Slobodan, 122-123, 130-131.
Missing in Action, (MIA), 187, 210, 253, 276.
Morgan, J.P., 39, 222-223, 228-229.
Mossad, 185, 198, 200, 208.
MSNBC, 55, 276.
Murphy, Tom, 3.
Mussolini, Benito, 123.

N

National Impeachment Town Hall, 263.
National Legal Foundation, 52.
National Rifle Association, 96, 276.
National Security Administration, 19, 68, 102, 115, 152, 199, 216, 276.
National Security Council, 179, 207, 276.
Newsweek, 43, 49.
Ng, Lap Seng, 100, 114, 156.
Nichols, Larry, 56, 92, 98, 111, 252, 254, 257.
Nir, Amiram, 184.
Noriega, Manuel, 175, 186-187, 198, 254.
North Atlantic Treaty Organization, (NATO), 118, 120-124, 126-134, 158, 190, 192, 252, 276.
Oliver North, 56-57, 176, 179, 182, 186-187, 193, 195, 201, 207-208.
Nussbaum, Bernard, 18, 41, 59, 66, 94, 109, 161.

O

O'Leary, Hazel, 150.
Oklahoma City, 21-23, 32, 36, 49, 108, 218.
Operation Pegasus, 186.